Non-Native Speaker

Non-Native Speaker
Selected and Sundry Essays

Charles Cantalupo

AFRICA WORLD PRESS
TRENTON | LONDON | CAPE TOWN | NAIROBI | ADDIS ABABA | ASMARA | IBADAN | NEW DELHI

AFRICA WORLD PRESS
541 West Ingham Avenue | Suite B
Trenton, New Jersey 08638

Book design: Dawid Kahts
Cover art: Painting by Yegizaw Michael from the Barbara and Charles
Cantalupo Collection
Cover design: Ashraful Haque

Library of Congress Cataloging-in-Publication Data

Names: Cantalupo, Charles, 1951- author.
Title: Non-native speaker : selected and sundry essays / Charles Cantalupo.
Description: Trenton : Africa World Press, 2017. | Includes bibliographical
    references and index.
Identifiers: LCCN 2017021716| ISBN 9781569025734 (hb : alk. paper) | ISBN
    9781569025741 (pb : alk. paper)
Subjects: LCSH: Ngũgĩ wa Thiong'o, 1938---Interviews. | African
    literature--20th century--History and criticism. | Eritrean poetry--20th
    century--History and criticism. | Eritrean
    literature--Translations--History and criticism. | Eritrean
    literature--20th century--History and criticism. | LCGFT: Essays.
Classification: LCC PL8010 .C26 2017 | DDC 809.896--dc23
LC record available at https://lccn.loc.gov/2017021716

Contents

Preface   vii

Acknowledgements   xvii

1. Introduction
    Non-Native Speaker   1

2. Reesom Haile, *getamay*   13

3. The Story on *Who Needs a Story*   31

4. Return to Rome   59

5. The Reluctant Translator   67

6. Literatures, Power, Translation, and Eritrea   83

7. Literature, Translation, and National
    Development in Eritrea   109

8. Africa Antetranslation   129

9. Two Moments in Kongo   149

10. *Three Interviews with Ngũgĩ wa Thiong'o*   157

    Moving the Center (1993)   159

    Penpoints, Gunpoints, and Dreams (1999)   181

    African Literature –Says Who?
    The Last Fifty Years with Ngũgĩ wa Thiong'o (2016)   199

11. Return to Kenya.   221

Index   227

Preface

The writing in *Non-Native Speaker – Selected and Sundry Essays* spans close to twenty-five years. Chronologically, it begins in 1993, with the first time I interviewed Ngũgĩ wa Thiong'o, and ends in 2016, with the third time I interviewed him. In between, I published eight books relating to African literature, including three books of translations of Eritrean-language poetry: additionally, three collections of poems, many of which relate to Africa, too. My memoir, *Joining Africa* (2012), recounts the personal experiences behind this work. *Non-Native Speaker* recounts it in the form of essays, in prose and verse. The eponymous opening, verse essay, "Non-Native Speaker," introduces most of what the essays cover in greater depth.

The word, "native," can denote a range of meanings, with positive, negative, and neutral connotations. For example, "native" in a positive sense refers to what Wole Soyinka in the "Author's Note" to *Death and the King's Horseman* (1975) calls "the indigenous" as opposed to "the alien culture...on the soil of the" former. Furthermore, there is no "potential equality" between them: "the alien culture" being a mere "incident" or catalyst while the "indigenous culture" is "the universe...the world of the living, the dead, and the unborn, and the numinous passage which links all."[1] "Native" in a positive sense also refers to what Ngũgĩ wa Thiong'o in the "Introduction" to *Decolonising the Mind* (1986) calls Africa's "resistance tradition" of "working people...students, intellectuals, soldiers and other progressive elements" as opposed to "[t]he imperialist tradition" of "international" and "multinational" colonialism that, Ngũgĩ adds, can clone itself in "neo-colonial," "native ruling classes."[2]

"Native" in a negative sense is

> Used as a…racialized pejorative by Europeans to describe the non-European races from the 18th century…. In colonial discourse it came to be associated with a position in the racial and civilizational hierarchy – that at the lower end. 'Native' came to signify 'primitive' and non-modern, evaluated in terms of European criteria of progress and modernity…. 'Native' was therefore coded as civilizationally backward…. 'Native' was also a term used to dismiss local (non-European) cultural practices, whether this was language, literature, arts or religion. Hence by the late 19th century one of the worst appellations a European could attract was that s/he had 'gone native'. Adopting local ways of dressing, eating or entertainment was also deemed to signify the loss of the European racial-cultural attributes, a dilution of the purity of the Western race – and thus attracted considerable opprobrium.[3]

In a neutral sense, the word, "native," usually connects with language and speaking. A "native speaker" refers to someone who speaks the language or languages of where he or she was born and raised. Related to this, the discipline of "Teaching English as a Foreign Language" (TEFL) employs "non-native speaker," which predates my use of the phrase as my title, simply as a term to designate someone who learns English subsequent to his or her first or native language. The TEFL term is so common that it has an acronym, NNS.

I base my title, "Non-Native Speaker," or "NNS," on Ngũgĩ and Soyinka's understanding of "native" and on the fact that I am writing or speaking about African literatures and languages as someone neither born nor raised nor living in Africa, that is, non-African. Whatever I know of them is subsequent to my first or native knowledge of English language and literature yet American literature, too, as well as European literature, mostly in translation.

From a more personal or specific perspective, my title, "Non-Native Speaker" derives from an invitation I received in 2007 to speak on a panel called "Enabling Practices: The Role of the Non-Native Speaker in Revival, Restoration, and Visibility." This would take place at a conference called Global Conversations: A Festival of Marginalized Languages at the University of California, Irvine. I was invited to speak from experience and personally about my work on contemporary Eritrean poetry and on African language literature in general, which derived from working with Ngũgĩ on several projects.

My statement became the poem, "Non-Native Speaker." It recounts my involvement in African language literature and translation as an unlikely story. The same applied to my memoir, *Joining Africa*. Thus, how could *Non-Native Speaker* be any different? Nevertheless, my inclusion on the panel implied that my work was "Enabling...[the[Revival, Restoration, and Visibility" of African languages.

"Enabling" the "Revival, Restoration, and Visibility" of African languages and literature, frankly, sounded heroic, but my role felt more modest. I was the "non" and not the "native," which I also wanted to express. Therefore, I applied a caveat to the poem in the form of a refrain: "White man and non-native speaker, could I ever understand?" My "enabling" African literatures and languages, as my unlikely story presented, yet as the history of colonialism in Africa absolutely demanded, had to be ironic, at least in part.

More longstanding than my Africa-related "enabling practice" was my writing, my practice of poetry for over fifty years. Writing poetry for me was the expression of conflict, usually unresolved. Moreover, the irony of my "enabling practice" as a "non-native speaker" represented a conflict, too. Therefore, to write a poem to express and to try to resolve it, a practice that I had been following for so long, felt like a natural, even a native thing to do. It could be an essay, but in verse, too.[4] Moreover, a verse essay, "On Metamorphosis," was one of the first poems I ever published.[5] Returning to the form after twenty years felt a like a homecoming.

The verse essay's near disappearance from most contemporary poetic practice in English is proportionally opposite to the poetic form's widespread employment in English and European literature before the 20th century, reaching back to Roman and Greek literature, citations of examples from which recur in the essays of *Non-Native Speaker*.

A verse essay like a prose essay tries to be expository, analytic, and persuasive, whatever the subject. Like the verse essay, "Non-Native Speaker," the three additional verse essays in the book similarly address their own conflicts. So do the six essays in prose and the three interviews as well. The difference is in form but not in intent or purpose, although the subjects can overlap. One of the essays, "Africa Antetranslation," exists as a verse essay, too, although it is not included in this collection.[6]

The irony I recognize in my "Enabling" the "Revival, Restoration, and Visibility" of African languages and literature is not only reinforced by the use one of the oldest Western poetic forms. The verse essays of *Non-Native Speaker* are also written in a modified version of dactylic heroic hexameter, the standard epic meter in classical Greek and Latin literature, Homer's *Iliad* as well as Virgil's *Aeneid*. Of course, this meter is standard in neither English nor American literature, my native tradition, although the dactylic hexameter might be considered my pre-native tradition since my European ancestors, at least half of them, worshipped in, spoke, and wrote in Latin. With notable exceptions, however, examples of English poetry in dactylic hexameter are uncommon.[7] Therefore, my employing the classical poetic form of the verse essay as well as the epic poetic metrics of classical Greek and Latin in lines of English to claim that a non-native speaker can enable African literatures and languages doubly reinforces the irony of any enabling by me – offering a kind of *caveat emptor* or *lector* as well as reinforcing my sense of playing a supporting or minor role.

The second essay in *Non-Native Speaker*, "Reesom Haile, *getamay*," recounts my introduction to the contemporary Eritrean poet, and the first whose work I would translate. As this essay and subsequent essays in *Non-Native Speaker* relate, playing the supporting role of Reesom's translator developed into a productive and engaging relationship. Together, we published two collections of his poetry, *We Have Our Voice* (1998) and *We Invented the Wheel* (2002), before his unexpected death in 2003.

"The Story on *Who Needs a Story*," the third essay in the book, narrates the development and publication of the first anthology of contemporary Eritrean poetry ever published, which I co-edited and co-translated. The compilation of an anthology might be expected to be a fairly straightforward process, with the greatest difficulty, perhaps, being the editor's securing of permissions. "The Story" of this anthology was anything but the expected, at least for me. In a world where literary anthologies of contemporary American poetry, Irish poetry, French poetry, Italian poetry, British poetry, and the poetry of most developed nations are abundant, an anthology of Eritrea's contemporary poetry in Tigrinya, Tigre, and Arabic (only three of its nine languages) presented a variety of unique and telling, critical challenges, with literary and life concerns frequently inseparable.

Non-Native Speaker's fourth essay, "Return to Rome," returns to the form of the verse essay. It also returns to the years 1970-1985, before "I saw Jericho's twenty ancient cities reduced to / Derelict refugee camps and dust" and first visited "Cairo's state museum," that is, before I began writing about Africa, as noted in "Non-Native Speaker." Moreover, returning to Rome thirty-five years after my first visit and many returns to Rome after that before 1985, I recall my "Euro-American, Casaubon"-like frame of mind back then in conjunction with seeing the city and other parts of Italy anew, twenty years since I last visited yet after many trips to Eritrea. In the interim, Italy's colony had all but taken over my vision Rome and Italy itself. "Return to Rome" connects the two pictures.

Extending the discussion from previous essays of the translation of Eritrean poetry, the fifth essay in *Non-Native Speaker*, "The Reluctant Translator," again engages the question of prose or verse. Comparing the critical reception of translations of Eritrean war poetry and a short story with the same focus, I ask why the publication of the latter achieves a sudden popularity while the former is more coolly received. Questions of genre, aspirations, national and/or international understanding, audience, popularity, literary history, African languages, and contemporary literary practice can, at least in part, explain such a quandary. Yet a limited personal experience and literary disposition can also make the translator "reluctant."

Non-Native Speaker's sixth essay, "Literature, Power, Translation, and Eritrea," focuses on the nation's millennia-long history of literature and how this reinforced the establishment and development of the international conference, Against All Odds: African Languages and Literatures in the 21st century, which took place in Asmara in January 2001. This history and the conference also provide an added context for the longstanding African language advocacy of Ngũgĩ wa Thiong'o. Yet the essay highlights the centrality of literature in Eritrean culture and national identity. Contemporary examples of this include the first publication of two Eritrean novels never before translated from Tigrinya into English, in 2012 and 2013, respectively: *The Conscript* (1950) by Ghebreyesus Hailu (1906-1993) and *Mezghebe: Would You Say He Was Mad* (1958) by Beyene Haile (1941-2012). Both require a rewriting of African literary history. Their translation, furthermore, in conjunction with similarly recent efforts to translate traditional and contemporary Eritrean-language poetry, should provoke a reappraisal of the state of African-language literary translation in general, particularly when African literature exists primarily in African languages, which require translation. What nation can ever be known without its literature being known? Yet what nation can be known without its greatest literature being translated, too? Monuments of world literature in their original languages and in translation have for the most part yet to be joined by their African language counterparts.

The next essay in *Non-Native Speaker*, "Literature, Translation, and National Development in Eritrea," attempts to answer the question of what is the role of literature in the way forward for Eritrea, particularly in education. Should encouraging and investing in literature be among Eritrea's development aspirations? Yet to question what is the role of Eritrean literature in the development of Eritrea is also to ask what is the role of Eritrea in the development of Eritrean literature. To go forward, they go together, because they have always gone together – be this recorded on an ancient stele in southern Eritrea's countryside, in 19th-century traditional poetry, in its vital continuation into the 20th and 21st century and in its accompaniment by new contemporary poetry – yet resounding in the presence of many African language poetries that rung out at the Against All

Odds conference. Eritrean literature's responsibility to Eritrea has been and continues to be inseparable from Eritrea's responsibility to Eritrean literature.

"Africa Antetranslation," the eighth essay in *Non-Native Speaker*, concentrates on African language translation itself. The publication of African language literature is more firmly established in the 21st century than ever before. Yet as African language literature forges ahead, its translation lags behind. The greatness of African literature in European languages is inestimable, but how could African language literature, both in its original languages and in translation, be any less and not much more? Still, African language literature remains in a state of antetranslation—a small and not the main part, as it naturally could be, of African literature. Achebe's "An Image of Africa: Racism in Conrad's *Heart of Darkness*" (1977) relates the incalculably adverse legacy of colonialism and racism, but the essay's near universal assent might also reinforce the antetranslation status quo. Achebe scorns the "African woman who has obviously been some kind of mistress to Mr. Kurtz," but what if she were invoked as a patron saint or *nkisi n'kondi* to move beyond antetranslation?

The ninth essay yet the third verse essay in *Non-Native Speaker*, "Two Moments in Kongo," focuses on the same region where *Heart of Darkness* takes place but juxtaposes a precolonial and colonial vision in a postcolonial perspective. They connect, if only for two moments, which are happy. The first moment of initial encounter between European and Kongo cultures late in the 15th century is auspicious and creative, spurring a partnership of equals, albeit only momentary. The second moment arrives roughly four hundred years later, in beholding the fruits, the arts of this momentary peace, revealed at the outset of an exhibition that also includes the artistic legacy of the next four hundred years of colonial exploitation and genocide.[8] The second moment is the attempted recovery of the first after such horror. This might raise a question, although in a different context, like T. S. Eliot's "Gerontion" (1920): "After such knowledge, what forgiveness?"[9] "Two Moments in Kongo" doesn't ask for forgiveness but offers a meditation on the tragic expression of the conflict in the *nkisi n'kondi*, or power figure, a form of wood sculpture in Central Africa, particularly southern Congo and northern Angola, during the 19th and early 20th centuries.

I designate the essays in *Non-Native Speaker* as "sundry," that is, of various kinds, not only because it contains verse essays. It also includes three interviews, each with Ngũgĩ wa Thiong'o, in 1993, 1999, and 2015. The book's introductory verse essay states, "let an obvious point be made: a non-native speaker / First is empowered by native speakers, never the reverse." Admittedly, an interview is not usually considered an essay but, for this non-native speaker, these encounters over the years, in addition to the many more that never resulted in the publication of a formal interview, have provided a concentrated exposure to as much new knowledge in a brief, dynamic, and persuasive way as any great essay should. The dialogic form of the interview is an essay – an attempt, an effort – to understand African literature according to one of its greatest exemplars. Independent of the book, these essays provide in themselves occasions to hear, enjoy, and learn from Ngũgĩ, and there can never be too many such occasions. Spanning the chronological composition of all of my essays in this book, these interviews, for the most part, guide them, too. Where they lead, I have tried to follow.

The last essay in *Non-Native Speaker*, a verse essay, "Return to Kenya," connects my first going there, which changed my life and what I wanted to write – before meeting Ngũgĩ and not even knowing who he was – to returning there almost thirty years later. Considering "...stereotypes of my colonialism? / Neo or post? Neo-post? Post-neo?," I try to "move on,"

>...back here again, having added what I'm not sure of
>To what I'm also not sure of, since it, however silly,
>Innocent, guilty or telling led me farther than I could
>Ever expect or imagine....

The non-native speaker, I conclude, "Not knowing Africa always has been Africa to me. / Not only in the beginning, it continues to answer...."

1   Wole Soyinka, "Author's Note," *Death and the King's Horseman* (1975), *Modern African Drama*, ed, Biodun Jeyifo (New York: W. W. Norton, 2002), 548.

2   Ngũgĩ wa Thiong'o, *Decolonising the Mind: The Politics of Language in African Literature* (Oxford, Nairobi, Portsmouth: James Currey, East African Educational Publishers, Heinemann: 1986), 2. Further references to this source are noted parenthetically in the text as *Decolonising.*

3   Pramod K. Nayar, *Postcolonial Studies Dictionary* (Oxford: John Wiley & Sons, 2015), 112.

4   See Paula R. Backscheider, "The Verse Essay, John Locke, and Defoe's *Jure Divino,*" *ELH* 55, no. 1 (1988), 100-103. Backscheider discusses the verse essay in English from the 16th to the 18th centuries. She notes that the form was considered "heroic" or "greater poetry," similar to the epic and panegyric." Employed by John Davies, Fulke Greville, Samuel Daniel, John Dryden, and Alexander Pope, among others, the verse essay was also represented in classical poets like Persius, Juvenal and, most of all, Lucretius.

5   Charles Cantalupo, "On Metamorphosis" (1984), *Studia Mystica* 4:2, 50-63.

6   Cf. Charles Cantalupo, "Africa Antetranslation," *Minor Heroics* (unpublished manuscript).

7   The most notable exception is "Evangeline" (1847) by Henry Wadsworth Longfellow. Other poets in English who have employed dactylic hexameter in their work include Philip Sidney during the Renaissance and Robert Southey, Samuel Taylor Coleridge, and Arthur Clough in the 19th century.

8   "Kongo, Power and Majesty," The Metropolitan Museum of Art, New York, 18 September 2015 through 03 January 2016, Alisa LaGamma, Curator in Charge.

9   T. S. Eliot, "Gerontion" (1920), *T. S. Eliot: The Complete Poems and Plays* (New York: Harcourt, Brace & World, 1952), 22.

Acknowledgements

If *Joining Africa* (2012) recounts the personal experiences behind *Non-Native Speaker*, these acknowledgements should first mention the people who made the experiences possible. Following the order of the essays, "Non-Native Speaker" again makes the

> ...obvious point...: a non-native speaker
> First is empowered by native speakers, never the reverse.
> Otherwise, I wouldn't be here, frankly; Kassahun, Reesom
> Zemhret, and Ngũgĩ revealed a way I couldn't find alone.

In the late afternoon of a snow-encrusted day in January 1993, Ngũgĩ welcomed me into his home and into the subject of African literature. In a sense, he has let me stay there ever since. The former, ironically, was five minutes from where I was born in Orange, New Jersey, yet from the beginning Ngũgĩ made me feel that the latter could be just as close.

Kassahun Checole provided a similarly warm welcome to Africa World and Red Sea Press in 1995, providing a home for five of my books since then, and now a sixth, with a constant stream of intellectual challenges, help, and unflagging friendship. Little did I know that in 1995, when he heard that I was planning to attend an African languages and literatures conference in Tel Aviv, and he told me that I should visit his home country, Eritrea, "while I was in the neighborhood," that I would find another kind of home there, too.

Reesom Haile allowed me the absolute privilege of translating into English, joining, and sharing his meteoric, all too brief five-year life as a major lyrical voice in post-war Eritrea and its first poet to put the nation on the map of the world of international letters. The almost daily frequency with which he published his poems to widespread national and diasporal acclaim on the most popular Eritrean website at the time, *Dehai*, prompted the comparison of his work to daily bread for his readers. To have him deliver it personally to my email inbox and almost as often to translate it with him through an exchange of drafts throughout the day, and to repeat this process day after day, was as nourishing and life sustaining an experience as any poet could imagine.

Yet all my work and writing in connection with Eritrea has depended on the support and camaraderie of Zemhret Yohannes. I would have been lost there – not even there – without his constant, insightful, wise, and practical guidance. An intellectual leader, dynamic thinker, revolutionary, patriot, publisher, bedrock supporter of Eritrean letters and arts and of Eritrea itself, dear and trusted friend, he has allowed me to join his efforts as well as the means to try to be worthy of such an honor. For me, Zemhret stands for Eritrea.

My work as organizing co-chair on the conference that I write about, Against All Odds: African Languages and Literatures into the 21st Century, and on The "Asmara Declaration on African Languages and Literatures" – in addition to working with Ngũgĩ wa Thiong'o, Kassahun Checole, and Zemhret Yohannes – also included Nawal El Saadawi and Mbulelo Mzamane. Respectively, from the top and the bottom of the African continent, these two literary colossi bestrode it, and I benefited greatly by laboring in their shadows.

Still going back to that cold January day in 1993 when I went to meet Ngũgĩ for the first time, I must record that I didn't go alone. I went with the photographer, graphic artist, and professor, Lawrence F. Sykes. In a way, I have been traveling with him ever since, at times in person, yet always with as much of his vision and of his voice as I could retain in my mind. An artist with a fondness for maps and cutting them up, he always lent me his compass to find the direction I should follow. Orange, NJ to Asmara, Malawi to Massawa, Boston to Bethlehem, PA – my journey in this book begins by walking with Larry Sykes, and subsequently I have tried to make sure that somehow I am always walking with Larry Sykes.

The recurring and generous support of Eritrea's Cultural Affairs Bureau has been vital to my work there. My writing projects and seminars in Eritrea over the years have depended on the openness and facilitation of Cultural Affairs' Director General, Ibraham Ali; Managing Director, Tewelde Keleta Kahsay; and their many able and collegial associates and assistants. In addition, I have benefited from the knowledge and friendship of Solomon Tsehaye, one of Eritrea's greatest contemporary poets and its greatest scholar of Eritrean traditional, oral poetry.

In Eritrea, my thanks also go to the support of its Research and Documentation Centre (RDC), whose inspiring archives are one of its nation's greatest resources. Similarly, I thank Eritrea's Ministry of Education.

In addition, I am indebted to Eritrea's greatest historian yet also one of its greatest writers regardless of discipline and genre, Alemseged Tesfai, whose knowledge and friendship are consistently inspiring and resourceful, yet to such a personable, elegant, and totalizing degree that any attempt really to know Eritrea requires knowing Alemseged.

I could not have written in connection with Eritrea without many others' support, for which I am also grateful: my co-editor and co-translator, Ghirmai Negash, in *Who Needs a Story? Contemporary Eritrean Poetry in Tigrinya, Tigre, and Arabic*; Hdri Publishers with Isaak Yosief; the poets who appear in *Who Needs a Story*; many other Eritrean writers and students with whom I have worked in various seminars, mostly in Asmara, but also in Keren, Dekemhare, and Massawa; Tsigye Hailemichael, Ruth Mesun, Yegizaw Michael, and Solomon Abraha. I also thank Ali Jimale Ahmed, Michael Bronner, Alexandra Dugdale, Bob Holman, Miriam Kotzin, Noam Scheindlin, and Bhakti Shringarpure for their previous support of earlier versions of essays that appear in this book.

My thanks also go to Walter Bgoya, Managing Director of Mkuki na Nyota Publishers Ltd, which has published my books, *War and Peace in Contemporary Eritrean Poetry* (2009) and *Where War Was* (2016), in which material from *Non-Native Speaker* has previously appeared. I am also indebted to Justin Cox, CEO of African Books Collective and these books' distributor.

Longstanding and generous support from the Pennsylvania State University has also enabled my work, and for this, in the words of the alma mater, I "raise the song." My academic home has "many mansions," including the Schuylkill Campus, University College, College of Liberal Arts, Global Programs, and the Department of English.

Without the constant support and love of my family – my wife, Barbara, and my children: Elizabeth, Christopher, Alicia, Alexandra – I would have gone nowhere. How can my thanks be more than a token, like a grace before an unending feast?

Earlier versions of essays in *Non-Native Speaker* have been previously published as follows, for which I am deeply appreciative.

"Non-Native Speaker, " *Warscapes*, 03 December 2013, http://warscapes.com/poetry/non-native-speaker. Accessed 02 February 2017. Also published in *War and Peace in Contemporary Eritrean Poetry* (Dar es Salaam: Mkuki na Nyota, 2009), 134-138.

"Reesom Haile, *getamay*," *The Road Less Traveled: Reflections on the Literature of the Horn of Africa*, ed. Ali Jimale Ahmed and Tadesse Adera (Trenton & Asmara: Red Sea Press, 2008), 135-150.

"The Story on Who Needs a Story," *War and Peace in Contemporary Eritrean Poetry* (Dar es Salaam: Mkuki na Nyota, 2009), 1-20.

"Return to Rome," *Where War Was* (Dar es Salaam: Mkuki na Nyota, 2016), 42-46.

"The Reluctant Translator" *Warscapes*, 03 August, 2014, http://www.warscapes.com/opinion/reluctant-translator. Accessed 02 February 2017.

"Literature, Power, Translation, and Eritrea" (2013), *Journal of Eritrean Studies*, 6:2, 1-39.

"Literature, Translation, and National Development in Eritrea" (2016), Proceedings for International Conference on Eritrean Studies: *The Way Forward* (Asmara: Hdri Publishers, 2017).

"Africa Antetranslation" (2016), *Research in African Literatures*, 47.3, 1-17.

"Moving The Center: An Interview with Ngũgĩ wa Thiong'o" (1995), *Paintbrush: A Journal of Poetry, Translations, and Letters* XX: 39 & 40, 207-28. Also published in *The World of Ngũgĩ wa Thiong'o* (Lawrenceville, NJ: Africa World Press, 1995), 207-228 and *Ngũgĩ wa Thiong'o Speaks: Interviews with the Kenyan Writer*, ed. Bernth Lindfors and Reinhard Sander (Trenton: Africa World Press, 2008), 333-52.

"Penpoints, Gunpoints, and Dreams: An Interview with Ngũgĩ wa Thiong'o" (1999), *Left Curve* 23, 30-35. Also published in *Ngũgĩ wa Thiong'o Speaks: Interviews with the Kenyan Writer*, ed. Bernth Lindfors and Reinhard Sander (Trenton: Africa World Press, 2008), 385-98.

"African Literature – Says Who? An Interview with Ngũgĩ wa Thiong'o" (2016), *Transition*, 120, 4-21.

My gratitude extends to the following conferences, universities, and venues where earlier versions of the essays in *Non-Native Speaker* took the form of scholarly talks, lectures, and readings: Across Languages and Cultures (West Chester University), Africa Centre (London), African Creative Expressions: Mother Tongue and Other Tongues (University of Florida), African Languages in ICT for Development in Africa (The World Bank), African Languages Teachers Association, African Literature Association, African Studies Association, Against All Odds: African Languages and Literatures into the 21st Century (Asmara, Eritrea), Alliance Française (Asmara, Eritrea), Alwan for the Arts (New York City), American Center (Asmara, Eritrea), American Literary Translators Association, Associated Writers Programs Conference, Biblios (New York City), Biennial Conference for Contemporary Literary Translation (Stephens College), Breaking Boundaries: Beyond the Land of Cush – New Critical Encounters with Languages and Literatures of Sub-Saharan Africa (University of Tel Aviv), BUWA: African Languages and Literatures into the 21st Century (Pretoria, South Africa), Bowery Poetry Club (New York City), Case Western Reserve University, Cultural Affairs

Bureau (Asmara, Eritrea), Donbosco Technical School (Dekemhare, Eritrea), Ecole des Haute Etudes en Sciences Sociales, Expo Festival (Asmara, Eritrea), From Asmara 2000 to Nairobi 2014: New Horizons and Trends in Africa Languages and Literatures (Kenyatta University), Gallery Z (Providence, Rhode Island), Global Conversations: A Festival of Marginalized Languages (University of California, Irvine), International Conference on Eritrean Studies: The Way Forward (Asmara, Eritrea), Keren Municipality Hall (Keren, Eritrea), Kimako's Blues People (Newark, New Jersey). Majoritizing Minority Literatures Through Translation (Penn State University), Malawi Literary Festival (Blantyre, Malawi), Massawa Library (Massawa, Eritrea), Michigan State University, National Union of Eritrean Youth and Students (Asmara, Eritrea), Modern Language Association, New Federal Theater (New York City), Ngũgĩ wa Thiong'o: Texts and Contexts (Penn State University), Northeast African Literature: Exploratory Seminar (Princeton University), Northwestern University, Ohio University, Penn State Berks, Penn State Lehigh Valley, Penn State Schuylkill, People's Front for Democracy and Justice (Asmara, Eritrea), People's Poetry Gathering (New York City), Revolution Books (New York City), Robin's Book Store (Philadelphia, Pennsylvania), Tufts University, University of Asmara, University of Delaware, University of Michigan, United States Speakers Program, Warscapes Readings Series (New York City), Weequahic Park Association Cultural Series (Newark, New Jersey), Yale University, Youth Conference of the People's Front for Democracy and Justice (Washington D.C.).

1

Non-Native Speaker

White man and non-native speaker, could I ever understand?
Africa witnessed enough of my kind – as in the scene from
Lee's life of Malcolm: the white girl asks him, "What can I do?
    What
Can I do?" "Nothing," he answers coldly. "You can do nothing."[1]
And didn't Biko believe the same?[2] Black consciousness needed
No one like me to enable it and think I could do more.
Words like "revive" and "restore" can be intimidating, too.[3]
Someone like me making women, men and language they wrote in –
Language a decade ago I wasn't even aware of –
Visible where they had been unknown, invisible before?
It seems unlikely, I know, and here I am to tell you how?

Ignorance first was my teacher, yet I knew I didn't know.
In 1970 I swore I should know my own culture
Rather than – at least before – my learning anyone else's.
Euro-American, Casaubon for nearly fifteen years,[4]
When I saw Jericho's twenty ancient cities reduced to
Derelict refugee camps and dust, I felt my existence
Was an illusion and, one week later, I could have been on
Mars as I looked around Cairo's state museum and didn't
Understand anything[5] – most of all I didn't understand
I was in Africa, and the bottom (literally, if

1

You think of it geographically) had dropped out from under
My oath to only know what I thought essentially was me.

Making a long story short – or six long, dense poems later,
Based on my going to Africa, and no more to Europe –
Africa seemed to take over my ideas and my English.
White man and non-native speaker, couldn't I still understand?
African writers – of course, in English – finished the picture,
Ngũgĩ included, until I met him and saw it missing
African languages, as he gently but firmly told me.[6]
Still as important as hearing him make this point, at least then,
Which was an interview for a journal, my friend took pictures –
Only of Ngũgĩ I thought, but two weeks later when Larry
Sykes sent me contact sheets, I was shocked by what he included:[7]
Photos of Ngũgĩ and me exchanging questions and answers;
Sharply contrasting and black and white: a dialogue, "cultures…
[L]anguages…translat[ing]…into their own languages," one of
Ngũgĩ's most often repeated absolutes,[8] and which seemed to
Situate me in the picture, too, but not as I first thought.

As I continued to listen, Ngũgĩ's African language
arguments let me return to just how Renaissance Europe
Scared off the "Ghost of the…Romane Language," if I may quote
   Hobbes,[9]
When writers started to use their native tongues and not Latin.
Why not in Africa but with English, French and whatever
Languages colonization ordered? Ngũgĩ convinced me.
White man and non-native speaker, even I could understand.

But then I went to Eritrea and witnessed a nation
Using its languages – all nine[10] – just as Ngũgĩ envisioned,
And as it had for four thousand years, although "against all
   odds."[11]
I thought the phrase to describe the bloody, thirty-year struggle
For independence the country suffered basically alone
Could be applied to the way that writers had to survive in
African languages, making Ngũgĩ, Kassahun Checole,

Red Sea and Africa World Press founding publisher,[12] me, and
Zemhret Yohannes in Eritrea,[13] formerly fighter,
Now a political leader and devoted to culture,
Set up a conference in Asmara called Against All Odds.

Featuring African writers who used African native
Languages, funded by many NGOs and foundations,
And most of all with the people of Eritrea's support,
Hundreds of writers and scholars at the end of the meeting
Ratified African language independence, declaring,
"African languages must take on…etc." – you can
Google the rest because here I must get back to my story:[14]
Non-native speaker who practices enabling, more simply,
Translating, getting it into print, and noticed by the world.

Traveling frequently to Asmara, planning AAO,
I met a poet whose readings in Tigrinya amazed me,
Even though I couldn't understand exactly what he said,
Rousing his crowds like a rock star by performing his language.
How could I not think he had to be translated…I could try!
"Translating poetry in Tigrinya? No one can. Too much.
Too many levels of meaning, rhyme, allusions and word play,"
Kassahun answered when I shared my objective, hoping that
He would be willing to publish our book, first in Asmara,
Then in New Jersey, since he had staff and offices in both.
Hearing him say "I would love to," was enough for this speaker
With no Tigrinya to go to Reesom Haile, the poet.[15]
"No," he said matter of factly. "It's too difficult. I've tried.
Our tongue has too much to get across. Our poetry has not
Lived in a book for a very long time.[16] But I can email
Something if you really want to try," and half a year later,
"*Alewuna*" showed up in my mailbox – Reesom's best poem,[17]
Or his most popular and, therefore, a difficult double
Challenge of poetry too great for translation and language
Also uniquely beyond translation (or so it was claimed).
"*Alewuna*" seemed to fit Charles Olson's "field" theory of verse,[18]
Or so I thought as the poem in translation "projected"

Energy onto the page – a first draft Reesom rejected.

But we got better and better, settling into a style half
Beat poet,[19] half *Greek Anthology*,[20] at least that's what I heard,
Not knowing oral traditions of Tigrinya performance.
Reesom addressed me as "Joiner" – "Mighty Joiner," I'd call him.
"Poetry" had no Tigrinya word but "joining" for the art.[21]

Now let an obvious point be made: a non-native speaker
First is empowered by native speakers, never the reverse.
Otherwise, I wouldn't be here, frankly; Kassahun, Reesom
Zemhret, and Ngũgĩ revealed a way I couldn't find alone.
They controlled any reviving visibility – not me.

Happily I played along and handled matters in English.
Reesom and I finished one book, then another but always
Printing the poems on facing pages, even in journals.
Finding an idiom and poetics both of us could share,
My job as translator also meant I had to appeal to
My target audience – English speaking; what the Tigrinya
Actually sounded like or exactly meant could come second,
On the condition that first the English had to be measured
Next to the rhythm of the Tigrinya's comprehensive sense.

Making a poem sound good in English was my first calling,
Still only half of the bargain. I knew, but Reesom didn't,
How to get published in journals, garner invites to readings,
Festivals, rich U.S. colleges, and line up reviewers:
In brief, I handled the cultural production and its means,
Other than publishing our text – maybe call this enabling?

White man and non-native speaker, in a country still lacking
Such opportunities, I could understand at least how to
Get Reesom's poetry known worldwide, and he became the first
Poet who wrote in Tigrinya, and who was Eritrean,
Famous outside of his country: poet laureate, some said,
Of Eritrea, although there really wasn't one, of course.

Claiming this bothered a lot of poets from Eritrea
Good in their own right and speakers of Tigrinya, yet other
Speakers of languages also widely used there, like Tigre,
Arabic, Bilen – remember, there are nine – and when Zemhret
Told me the problem had bothered him, too, I was persuaded
That it was real and not merely ego, jealousy, or worse,
Politics stemming from Reesom's recent change of heart, joining
Parties opposed to the PFDJ government,[22] which had
Formerly held him in high esteem, especially Zemhret.

Now he invited me back to Eritrea to translate,
Edit and publish a new book: an anthology; poets
Writing in Arabic, Tigre and Tigrinya...for a start.
Three if not nine would be possible and bold enough. My co-
Editor, Ghirmai Negash,[23] a very good Eritrean
Scholar, and I took the tough and still debatable option
Not to include any oral poets – they deserved a book
Unto themselves, we agreed and planned on doing it someday.
Who Needs a Story, the present project, would be the first book
Of Eritrean contemporary poets in local
Languages and in translation: published locally, too, by
Hdri ,which Zemhret directed in Asmara yet, I hoped,
Marketed globally and not only in Eritrea.
I wanted readers to enter bookstores, find the shelves labeled
Poetry, go to anthologies, and there – with the standard
German, American, French, Italian, English, Chinese or
Whatever else has been there for ages – reach out for the book
That should have been there before but never was until today.
"*Who Needs a Story*? What's that?" she says in some Barnes &
    Noble.
"I never heard of this. Let me buy it. I kind of like it."

Back to reality, or what led to this dream coming true.
"You'll be a symbol – just used for propaganda and seen as
Evidence freedom of speech is guaranteed by the regime."
Growling at me through the phone from Brussels, Reesom said
    "Fuck you,"
Ending our partnership. Others also told me not to go,

5

Except for Larry who said, "The door is open, so go in."
Post 9/11 and Eritrean politics aside,
I went and worked with great poets who knew beauty and said so.
Anyway I couldn't translate propaganda if I tried.
Poetry yes, yet the way things worked with Reesom – producing
Cultural means for the work's dissemination? – came up, too.
This time the challenge was even greater: with which I'll conclude.

Doing the book in Asmara was a story in itself.
Seemingly half of Asmara's university taking
Part in the translating process with Tigrinya and Tigre –
Ghirmai Negash was in charge of getting good first drafts to me.
Arabic poems were first sent to a translation center
Set up in Lebanon – Zemhret handled this – and instead of
Feeling as usual like an author writing a book in
Private, I seemed like one person in a Renaissance workshop
Doing my part on a massive painting titled, perhaps, "War,
Peace and the Word in the Eritrean Struggle to Survive,"
Pictured in two local and two global languages worked on
Over and over by many people's hands into poems.

Many got published in journals, good ones, too, and the map of
Poets worldwide now includes the poets from Eritrea,
Heard and made visible outside Eritrea in their own
Languages and in translation. OK. But let me tell you,
Getting the Arabic and Ge'ez scripts right where they belonged,
Recto from Latin, drove Ghirmai crazy. Hdri had problems
Figuring out how to use its new technology shipped from
I don't know where and with God knows what directions. But
    even
Stranger, at least so it seemed to me, were some other issues.
White man and non-native speaker, would I ever understand?
Copyright in Eritrea was discouraged since the war –
Smacking of ego and counter-revolutionary, too.
Ghirmai insisted, and Zemhret made sure that we would have it.
Globalization meant our book needed its ISBN.
No Eritrean book ever had it, with one exception:

Kassahun's. When I was certain Hdri got us our number
I thought our problems were solved, but Zemhret also assigned me
To find distributors, of which I knew nothing but learned fast,
Getting rejected by mega firms like Bowker, who didn't
Recognize "999," Eritrea's national number,
First or its ISBN, since no book came from there before.
"I never heard of it. Where? The Horn? In Africa? Really?"
Said the nice customer service rep who didn't believe me,
Numerological paranoia darkening the mood.
Then there's the time when I went to pick up proofs in Asmara.
Crossing a field to the building of the printer, Sabur, led
Also to peacekeeping UN soldiers camped right next door. Barbed
Wire and six satellite dishes made them happy – I didn't.
Two of them cocked their machine guns, aimed, and Sabur's gate
    opened.
"*Entra qui*," and an old veteran smiling welcomed me inside.

In *Joining Africa,*[24] my prose memoir, many more stories
Like what I've already noted reinforce what I've said here.
Call it enabling, but it must go two ways *and* back and forth.

Postscript: remember Hobbes's phrase, "the Ghost of the…
    Romane Language?"
I chose dactylic hexameter, the epic line –Virgil's
In the *Aeneid* and Homer's in his epics, too[25] – for my
Poem ironically: using Greek and Latin poetics –
But not too slavishly, which would make no sense and not sound
    good –
In my vernacular English, claiming African language
Poetry can be enabled by a non-native speaker.
Politics might say I contradict my argument, using
Some other language's forms of beauty not really my own;
Arguing African language poets should be more widely
Heard in their languages, meaning their unique poetics, too.
But here I have to confess my doubts political power
Comes from whatever enabling I do – it's about beauty.

1 Alex Haley, *The Autobiography of Malcolm X* (New York: Ballantine Books, 1965), 292. Cf. *Malcolm X*, dir. Spike Lee (Burbank: Warner Brothers, 1992), access 11 November 2016, https://www.youtube.com/watch?v=ArHhMabjWwg.

2 Steve Biko (1946-1977) was a South African activist, theorist, and leader in the Black Consciousness Movement. Founder of the South African Student Organization (SASO), he was killed in South African police custody.

3 "Non-Native Speaker" was originally conceived as a presentation for a panel on "Enabling Practices: The Role of the Non-Native Speaker" at the conference, Global Conversations: A Festival of Marginalized Languages, at the International Center for Writing and Translation, University of California, Irvine October 24-26, 2007. Another panel at the same conference focused on "Technology: Revival, Restoration, and Visibility."

4 Edward Casaubon is a fictional character in the novel, *Middlemarch* (1874), by George Eliot. He aspires to an all-encompassing and universal knowledge in writing a book called *Key to all Mythologies* that he fails to complete.

5 The Museum of Egyptian Antiquities, also known as the Egyptian Museum or Museum of Cairo.

6 Ngũgĩ wa Thiong'o (1938 -): "I began writing novels, short stories, plays, and essays in 1960, when I was a student of English at Makerere University in Uganda, then an affiliate of London University. So...I have been writing for the last forty years.... From 1960 to 1977, I wrote in English, even though all the books were mostly about Kenya and Kenyan people. But from 1977 up to the present I have written my novels, short stories, plays, and books for children in Gĩkũyũ language, one of more than thirty languages in Kenya. So half of my 40-year writing life was taken up with English and the other half by Gĩkũyũ language.... Since the 60s...of the last century, when African countries started getting their independence, European languages have become the ones setting the terms of the debate on the literature of the continent. In schools and the colleges in Africa and abroad, the literature that is taught and labeled African literature is still the one mostly written in European languages. We can do more for our languages in our languages. I've said it before, and I say it again that we must do for our languages what all other intellectuals in history have done for theirs: by producing the best that

can be written and thought in the world." *Against All Odds: African Languages and Literatures into the 21ˢᵗ Century*, dir. Charles Cantalupo (Asmara: Audio Visual Institute of Eritrea, 2007; distributed by African Books Collective).

7   Lawrence F. Sykes (1941-) is a photographer and graphic artist, formerly Professor of Art at Rhode Island College. His photographs and collages appear in *The World of Ngũgĩ wa Thiong'o*, ed. Charles Cantalupo (Trenton: Red Sea Press, 1995).

8   Ngũgĩ wa Thiong'o, *Penpoints, Gunpoints, and Dreams: Towards a Critical Theory of the Arts and the State in Africa* (Oxford: Clarendon Press, 1998), 100. Further references to this source are noted parenthetically in the text as *Penpoints*.

9   Thomas Hobbes, *Leviathan* (1651) ed. C. B. Macpherson (Hammondsworth: Penguin Books, 1968), 712. "The Language also, which they use, both in the Churches, and in their Publique Arts, being Latine, which is not commonly used by any Nation now in the world, what is it but the Ghost of the Old Roman Language?" Further references to this source are noted parenthetically in the text as *Leviathan.*

10   Eritrea has at least nine languages and no one official language. The most widely used languages are Tigrinya, Arabic, and Tigre. Minority languages include Kunama, Bilen, Saho, Afar, Hadareb, and Nera. Tigrinya, Arabic, and English predominate in business and government. Cf. Tekie M. Woldemichael, "Language, Education and Public Policy in Eritrea," *African Studies Review,* 46:1 (April 2003), 117-34. "The outcome that Eritrea expects from its language policy is that every person will be well versed in her or his mother tongue and also will have the ability to communicate in the working languages of Eritrea – Arabic and Tigrinya – and in the international language of English."

11   Cf. Dan Connell, *Against All Odds: A Chronicle of the Eritrean Revolution* (Trenton: Red Sea Press, 1997). The popular application of the phrase "against all odds" to Eritrea's efforts originates with Connell's book.

12   Launched in 1983 by Kassahun Checole with the publication of *Barrel of a Pen: Resistance to Repression in Neo-Colonial Kenya,* Ngũgĩ wa Thiong'o's first book of essays, Africa World Press is devoted to the publication of books on the history, culture, and politics of Africa and the African diaspora, including Eritrea. Two years

later, Kassahun founded the Red Sea Press. Subsequently, he has published over 2000 titles.

13   Zemhret Yohannes has directed the Research and Documentation Center (RDC) and Hdri Publishers in Asmara, Eritrea.

14   For more on the conference in Asmara, see Charles Cantalupo, *Joining Africa – From Anthills to Asmara* (East Lansing: Michigan State University Press, 2012), chapters 8-12. Cf. Charles Cantalupo, "The Words from Asmara," http://www.samizdateditions. com/issue6/and-wordasmara.html. Cf. https://www.youtube.com/ watch?v=a2FM4-nkPLw; http://poetry.about.com/library/weekly/ aa000201.htm; http://www.africanbookscollective.com/books/.-all-odds; http://www.samizdateditions.com/issue6/and-wordasmara. html. Accessed 30 November 2016.

15   Reesom Haile (1946-2003) was Eritrea's first internationally known poet. He wrote in Tigrinya, one of Eritrea's nine major languages. In exile during Eritrea's war for independence from Ethiopia, he served, with a PhD in Media, Culture, and Communication from New York University, for over two decades as a development communications consultant, working with UN Agencies, governments and NGOs around the world before returning to Eritrea in 1994. His first collection of Tigrinya poetry, *Waza ms Qum Neger nTensae Hager* (1997), won the Raimok prize, Eritrea's highest award for literature. He published two other books of poetry, translated by Charles Cantalupo and published by Red Sea Press – *We Have Our Voice* (2000) and *We Invented the Wheel* (2002). Cf. "Reesom Haile, *getamay*" below.

16   Cf. Reesom Haile, *We Have Our Voice*, trans. Charles Cantalupo (Lawrenceville and Asmara: The Red Sea Press, 2000), ix. Further references to this source are noted parenthetically in the text as *Voice*.

17   A kind of Eritrean anthem, "*Alewuna, Alewana*," "We Have, We Have," made Reesom Haile at the beginning of his poetic career so widely beloved throughout his young nation that the eponymous refrain practically became interchangeable with his name. To walk with Reesom Haile anywhere in Eritrea, through the busy streets or the lonely fields of the countryside, was to hear people call him not by his name but "*Alewuna, Alewana*."

18   Charles Olson (1910-1970), an American, second generation 20th-century modernist poet and innovator, argued in *Projective Verse* (1950) for the disavowal of any traditional poetic meter and

form to invigorate poetic syntax and logic. Furthermore, a poem should "project" a form of spontaneous energy into a field, that is, onto a page, revealing at the same time a unique aural and visual quality.

19 The Beats were "[a] national group of poets who emerged from San Francisco's literary counterculture in the 1950s. Its ranks included Allen Ginsberg, Lawrence Ferlinghetti, Gregory Corso, and Gary Snyder. Poet and essayist Kenneth Rexroth influenced the development of the "Beat" aesthetic, which rejected academic formalism and the materialism and conformity of the American middle class. Beat poetry is largely free verse, often surrealistic, and influenced by the cadences of jazz, as well by Zen and Native American spirituality." Poetry Foundation: https://www.poetryfoundation.org/resources/learning/glossary-terms/detail/beat-poets. Accessed 24 November 2016.

20 A collection of poems comprised mostly of epigrams from the classical to the Byzantine periods in Greek literature, *The Greek Anthology* has a long history, stemming from ancient times through medieval, leading to its translation into modern European languages and widespread popularity. Including a diverse range of inscriptions, erotica, anecdotes, satire, and more, the dominant style of its poetry and its translation is concise, clever, coherent, and clear.

21 The Tigrinya word for "to join," referring to poetry, is "*gtmi*." A male poet is a *getamay* (pl. *getamo*). A female poet is a *getamit*. The plural, *getemti*, refers to men and women. Cf. page 21-22 below.

22 The PFDJ, the People's Front for Democracy and Justice, is the ruling party of the State of Eritrea. In 1994, the PFDJ succeeded the EPLF, the Eritrean People's Liberation Front, which had become Eritrea's dominant political organization during its 30-year revolution. Triumphing in 1991, the EPLF declared Eritrea independent in 1993 after an UN-supervised, popular referendum.

23 Ghirmai Negash is the author of *A History of Tigrinya Literature in Eritrea: The oral and the written* (Leiden: CNWS Publications, 1999; Trenton: Africa World Press, 2010) and *The Freedom of the Writer & Other Selected Literary and Cultural Essays* (Trenton: The Red Sea Press, 2006). He is the translator of *The Conscript* (1927) by Ghebreyesus Hailu from Tigrinya into English (Athens: Ohio University Press, 2013) and, with Charles Cantalupo, co-translator and co-editor of *Who Needs a Story? Contemporary Eritrean*

Poetry in Tigrinya, Tigre, and Arabic (Asmara: Hdri Publishers, 2005).

24 Charles Cantalupo, *Joining Africa – from Anthills to Asmara* (East Lansing: Michigan State University Press, 2012). Further references to this source are noted parenthetically in the text as *Joining.*

25 Cf. Lawrence S. Cunningham, John J. Reich, Lois Fichner-Rathus, *Culture and Values: A Survey of the Western Humanities*, Volume 1 (Cengage Learning, 8th ed, Boston: Cengage Learning, 2014), 52. "The *Iliad* and the *Odyssey* are written in heroic verse, which is generally associated with the meter, or rhythm, of epic poetry in Greek and Latin. In Greek and Latin the meter is dactylic hexameter. *Hexa* – means six and derives from the same root as the six-sided geometric figure we call a hexagon.... [A] line of dactylic hexameter consists of six [feet].... A dactyl is a unit or foot of poetry containing three syllables; the first is long or stressed, and the following two are shorter or unstressed.... [T]here are very few examples in English."

2

Reesom Haile, *getamay*

I first encountered Reesom Haile in Asmara in August, 1998: one evening during Eritrea's annual, outdoor, 8-day cultural festival; a popular event, thronged with people from Asmara and from throughout Eritrea, and featuring all of the arts – agricultural, domestic, industrial, language, performing, technological, visual. Taking place in the extensive fairgrounds called "Expo," the festival's theme was "Inheritance." It encouraged Eritreans from all walks of life to taste and see their new nation through the many forms of its longstanding and highly valued multicultural and multimedia expression. Be it a poem, a computer program, a painting, an ancient manuscript, a display of tools, a dance, desert housing, a popular song, a camel, a coffee, a textile or a pile of particular wood to make a fire, people could look all around them at a wealth of highly varied examples of their culture, including each other, and marvel, in Reesom Haile's words from his most famous poem, "*Alewuna, Alewana,*" "We have…we have…" (*Voice*, 44-45).

I was following the crowd to a poetry reading. The area where it took place seemed to be shaped like a basin, with children – whom I didn't expect to see at such an event – seated in the middle, the poet and the audience at opposite edges. Actually, the arrangement was a mere platform with a podium and the audience gathered in a flat place in front of it – but my initial misimpression was telling. To speak of the transcendent power of poetry is a commonplace but, in this this case, the poet's performing his work seemed physically

13

to raise up the audience and the reading space to his eye level. The children in the middle were joining Reesom Haile in his lines, anticipating and echoing them, with great pleasure, too, especially when he spoke, "*Alewuna, Alewana*." It swept through the crowd and was sweeping the entire nation and its diaspora with the verbal music of Tigrinya affirmation:

> We have men and women...
> We have women and men....
> Without end in the struggle
> To grow, study and persist.
> Who think and think again
> To teach, learn and know...
> Without the lust for power.
> Who stand up or down
> With our consent.
> We have God and a future.
> We have men and women
> Who belong in our nation
> And we belong with them....
> We have women and men.
> Rejoice.
>
> *Voice*, 44

"Rejoice." I say it again when poetry can become a kind of daily bread or currency for all kinds of people – writers, children, artists, young professionals, working people, the elderly, government people – and create a rapport and a give and take among all, including the poet. This is a work of high value.

Reesom Haile was from a family of traditional farmers in Eritrea, where he was born, raised, and educated through high school. After working as a radio and television journalist in Ethiopia, he continued his education in the United States. Obtaining a doctorate in Media, Culture, and Communication in 1987 from New York University, he served for twenty years as a development communications consultant, working with UN Agencies, governments, and NGOs around the world, He returned to Eritrea in 1994. From then until his death in 2003, he wrote, at least, a thousand poems in Tigrinya. His first collection, *Waza Ms Qumneger Ntnsae Hager* won the 1998 Raimok prize, Eritrea's highest award for literature. His first collection in English was *We Have Our Voice*.

Widely published and recognized for his revolutionary modernization of the traditional art of poetry in Tigrinya, one of Eritrea's main languages, Reesom Haile attracted scholarly and critical attention and extensive media coverage, including the *BBC* (UK*)*, *CNN* (USA*)*, *Deutche Welle* (Germany*)*, *RAI* (Italy), *Dmtsi Hafash* (Eritrea) *Radio Vatican* (The Vatican), *NPR* (USA), *SABC* (South Africa), *SBS* (Australia), and *VOA* (USA). His performances in Tigrinya and English inspired audiences throughout Africa, Europe, and America. The enormous popular appeal of his poetry – in print and on the internet – was evident from the streets of Asmara to the far fields of the Eritrean countryside, where to stroll with Reesom Haile at any hour was to be approached by the young and old and all kinds of people who delighted to quote his lines back to him. Reesom Haile explained the phenomenon of his popularity this way:

> Our poetry is not something that has left our tongue and lived in the books for a very long time. Our poetry is participatory. When I recite my poetry at home, the people listening to me will say, "add this to that, add this to that." It is participatory. It's not something that we put on the wall and say, "Oh, this is pretty." Our traditional poetry form is *ad hoc*. Someone will just get up and say something to try to capture the spirit of that particular time. And people will add, "why don't you say so, why don't you add this, why don't you extend it." It is very much part of the tradition. I am putting it on paper because I think it is about time we start storing it for the next generation.
>
> *Voice*, ix

For Reesom Haile, his poetry revealed a joining of words and worlds from the perspective of the collective, the community, and the society of which he was a part. In oral if not in written form, according to Reesom Haile,

> Poetry is not a special activity of poets, for everyone is a potential a poet. Only that some people are more gifted than

15

others in the art and their words and words more memorable. The poem is not an object separate and apart from its function: to ease the pain and to celebrate the pleasure of life. Women and men alike express themselves in music and poetry while at work or at play.[1]

Reesom Haile considered his writing in Tigrinya

> A going back to what God has given you and saying "I'm not going to give it up." It's your freedom, your speech, your self-definition, and your self-expression. You cannot give it up. If you lose your language, it isn't just the language you lose. It's the cultural codes imbedded in that language. It's the values, the sense of community, and the sense that I am responsible for my brother, my sister, my mother, and they are equally responsible to me. This is what I do not want my people to lose.
>
> *Wheel*, 225

Reesom Haile also wrote in a spirit that was inseparable from Eritrea's century-long struggle for independence. In his own words, "The Eritrean struggle for independence is the primary motive force for my art.... We Eritreans have taken on all comers for our right to self-determination, and my art is but a continuation and an expansion of that struggle aimed at self-definition" (*Wheel*, 236).

Eritrea's war for independence was simultaneously a war for its culture: its ancient traditions as well as its modern manifestations and transformations. Again in Reesom Haile's words,

> Successive enemies of Eritrean independence over the years have tried defining Eritrea in ways that would justify the outrageous measures they would take to deny Eritrea its place in the sun. They have tried to diminish Eritrea politically, economically, militarily, and culturally into non-existence except as an appendage of the builders of colonial and neo-colonial empires. But Eritrea has proved a survivor....
>
> *Wheel*, 237

War as a cultural education towards making peace requires not only the barrel of a gun but also the barrel of a pen, as in Ngũgĩ wa Thiong'o's formulation.[2] In his words, "[T]he biggest weapon wielded and actually daily unleashed…against…collective defiance is the cultural bomb. The effect of a cultural bomb is to annihilate a people's believe in their names, in their languages, in their environment, in their heritage of struggle, in their unity, in their capacities, and ultimately in themselves" (*Decolonising*, 3). The cultural bomb is as deadly as bombs falling from the sky. What is in the mind of the person holding the gun and pulling the trigger? The fighter and the writer not only need each other. They are often the same person and, perhaps, even more often the same person in spirit.

As Reesom Haile also recalled:

> I returned to Eritrea in 1994 after twenty years of life in exile. I came back to find our languages and our poetry a bit battered, but well, considering they too had been targeted for extinction.… But we carried our languages and our art in our memories and our voices, and we used them as effectively as we used our weapons to defend ourselves throughout the struggle.
>
> *Wheel*, 237

Vitally linked, Reesom Haile's language of self-determination and political self-determination produced a supreme poetry of resistance with the confidence to ask, in "The Transit of Tigrinya,"

> But what did you assume
> About Tigrinya?
>
> Eritrea's daughter,
> She wants respect,
> The same as you.
> Dare her,
> She'll dare you, too.
>
> She knows the way
> To overcome
> The invading tongues:

> Her words, her names
> Cut them off.
> *Wheel,* 216

A local language and its poetry became the means of survival, an historical imperative for Eritrea if there ever was one, as "Believe It or Not" made all too clear:

> Remember the Italians
> Who invaded and said
> *Eat but don't speak?*
>
> Remember the English
> Who invaded and said
> *Speak but don't eat?*
>
> Remember the Amharas
> Who invaded and said
> *Don't speak and don't eat?*
> ...
> Believe it or not,
> They want to kill us...
> *Wheel,* 154

Reesom Haile's poetry of resistance was inseparable from the life of the poet and his country, as the poem, "*esh!*" concluded with a casual yet deadly aplomb:

> The Dergue
> Behaved better
> Than the latest
> Swarm of invaders,
>
> Haile Selassie
> Better than the Dergue,
> And Menelik
> Better than Selassie.
> ...

But my country says
Forward,
And *esh* the Turkish,
esh Egyptians,
esh Italians,
esh the English,
esh Amharas,
esh Tigreans,
esh the locusts.
esh!
Like a flywhisk.[3]

Wheel, 158

While focusing on and from Eritrean culture, Reesom Haile's poetry of resistance also had a global dimension as a part of, again in his words, "the indomitable struggle of humanity" (*Wheel,* 229). He had a self-stated "mission...to create links between my country and the world." Celebrating a "genuine," "Eritrean culture" that expressed "the essence of human struggle," his poetry simultaneously partook of a literary impulse that was universal, making a literary truism breathe new life. His "imagination" with his "poet's pen," in Shakespeare's words, could "bod[y]... forth / The forms of things unknown" to "[t]urn... them to shapes, and give... to aery nothing / A local habitation and a name."[4]

But if the habitation was African, for Reesom Haile the name should be African, in his case, Tigrinya. Yet from a pan African perspective, he called out for and exemplified that the word itself and the word "language" in African languages should ring out all over Africa: *Mutauro, Ulwimi, Edi, Okasa, Asusu, Lolemu, Ulimi, Lakk, Ruthiomi, Lugha, Harsha, Luqha, Qwanqwa.* They were the medium *and* they were the message, summed up, perhaps, in the Zulu's resounding word for "power" and, inevitably, freedom: *Amandla!* The resounding African word could be universally understood – as if the story of Babel and the confusion of tongues were not true – by people of all walks of life, all ages, and in many languages, local and international, from under the giant Sycamore trees of arid Eritrea to the elegant arts venues of downtown New York City; from the poor, local communities of Johannesburg, South Africa, or Newark, New Jersey to the halls of the world's most distinguished universities.

No one cultivated in poetry the freedom in Tigrinya and the "local habitation" in Eritrea like Reesom Haile. His two bilingual – Tigrinya / English – collections of poems, *We Have Our Voice* and *We Invented the Wheel*, presented a myriad of subjects, including: gender equality, colonialism, foreign aid, the use of knowledge, bureaucracy, history, crime, priests, travel, daughters and sons, sisters and brothers, camels, books, education, homecomings, exile, money, computers, braggarts, religion, political leadership, hopes, delusions, bravery, civic responsibility, stars, God, illiteracy, ambition, divisiveness, survival, Satan, democracy, old friends, mothers and fathers, cities, small towns, cruelty, soccer, intolerance, impulsiveness, love, language, nightlife, freedom, writing, indecision, non-governmental agencies, learning, sex, super powers, bread, marital responsibility, competition, snails, American foreign policy, democracy, women's rights, global politics, casualties of war, love, the young, elders, the nature of advice, spousal abuse, cooking, cannibalism, coffee, self-image, sleeping together, proverbs, ethnic conflict, carousing, biblical stories, tourism, national identity, aging, values, the future, the pen, words, exile, shoes, masculinity, teaching babies to walk, videos of weddings, religious hypocrisy, history, body parts, suicide, funerals, taboos, freedom, independence, infidelity, flywhisks, community, temptation, unspeakable evil, spirits, old and new housing, frankness, circles, labor, ancestors, mothers, prayers, parenting, toys, food, starvation, war, donkeys, the millennium, Jews, Muslims, Christians, punctuation, political evil, weather, onomatopoeia, loss, wisdom, literature, peace, jokes, teachers, culture, hierarchy, individualism, letters, pastry, paper, poverty, hope, surnames, God, George Bush II, sacrifice, survival, African leaders, dictators, devils, language, relationships, regrets, dependable people, dissent, angels, and home – and often humorously. If ever there was a poetry with something for everyone, this was it: which also accounted for the great popularity of Reesom Haile's poetry in Eritrea and became a major factor in his international acclaim.

Tigrinya is a Semitic language and, like the languages of Tigre and Amharic, derives from the ancient language of Ge'ez. It derives, like Hebrew and Arabic, from Aramaic, which is often thought to have been a language – along with Greek and Hebrew – of the original composition of much of the Old and New Testament and of Jesus. The translation of Reesom Haile's poetry raised the question of the degree to which translations into English could match the style and music of the original. Addressing the literal, oral and aural, literary and poetic sense of the original, and more, impossibilities of translation arose. Not all of the levels of meaning and association that a Reesom Haile poem offered to anyone who heard or read it in the Tigrinya original could be offered in English, though of what language and its translation could this not also be said? For example, in the original Tigrinya there was an absolutely daunting abundance of rhyme that would be impossible in English of any period or any serious style except, perhaps, in rap or hip hop. Nevertheless, while speakers of Tigrinya and English knew what any merely English version continued to miss, what if great poetry could contain, in its original language or translation, a universal music?

In addition to the challenge of translating the style and music of Reesom Hailes's poetry, there were its forms and genre. He would claim that they derived from a unique and continuing connection with Tigrinya and oral culture. In his words,

> The form of the poem is derived from its function. There are forms for work, for praise, for prayer, for bragging, for battle, for joining, weddings, funerals, criticism. My poetry makes use of all these forms, sometimes separately and sometimes in combination. And I have developed new forms for the challenges of building a modern, democratic nation.
>
> *Wheel*, 236-37

An Eritrean conception of the role of the poet can be relevant to the difficulties and limitations of African language or, frankly, any language's poetry translation. Consider the European derived formulation of the role of the poet as "maker," *faber* or *makir*, or as *vates*, "a prophet," with connections to the spiritual, the underworld, the irrational, and the marginal that these terms can connote. Derived from the Tigrinya infinitive *mgtam*, literally *to join*, the Tigrinya word for poetry – *gtmi* that is, "joining," – and the poet – *getamay*, that is, "joiner" – are comparatively humbler. The Tigrinya terms deflect the more sublime sense of an individual who creates and even speaks for the gods or God. The poet as "joiner" is like a carpenter or a tinker. Similarly, classical Greek words for "artists" have associations with manufacturing. The word *demiourgos* can be defined as a worker for the people, and the *techne* or art involved can include cooking as well as poetry. *gtmi, demiourgos* or *poietes*, the poet can be a kind of blacksmith: a sense that echoes the role in ancient Greek mythology of Hephaestus making – or *joining*, with gold, silver, and less precious metals – the shield of Achilles in book XVIII of Homer's *Iliad*. Fundamental to poetry, the same process applies to translation, particularly to translation of an African language. Like the common assumption that translating African languages is quixotic because there are so many is mistaken, the impression that Tigrinya is a uniquely difficult African language whose poetry is essentially untranslatable is similarly common, even among many speakers of Tigrinya itself. Guided by the humble conception of *gtmi* or "joining," however, rather than loftier conceptions of making, creating, and speaking like a prophet, the translator's work can seem more, practical, everyday, and honest. The well-known formulation in Italian – *traduttore, traditore*: translator, traitor – can be justified, but seeing a translator in the role of a trader offers some redemption.

Reesom Haile's poetry also offered a special perspective on two other universal impulses: the political and the religious.

A big reason for the popularity of Reesom Haile's poetry was its political and sometimes impolitic content. He patriotically rallied his nation any number of times – and there were many – most famously with his poem "*Alewuna, Alewana,*" "We Have, We Have." Nevertheless, his political role turned just as readily to that of the poet, in Lawrence Ferlinghetti's phrase, as the "gadfly of the state."[5] Moreover, near the end of his life he wrote a poem called "Intifada," aiming to criticize the Eritrean government for its treatment of journalists and interpreted as a call for an uprising against the state.

Eritreans,
Bowing our heads

To no man,
Let the child be born –

Like David
With a challenging song
And a stone
Flying from his sling.

Eritreans,
Bowing our heads
To no man,
Let the child be born![6]

Politically, Reesom Haile valued his individual liberty and conscience more than the authority of the state. Contention between the writer's liberty and the state's authority is an age-old conflict. At the outset of *Leviathan* (1651), for example, Thomas Hobbes characterizes his own writing as wounded "between the points of those that contend on one side for too great Liberty, and on the other side for too much Authority" (*Leviathan*,75).[7] Yet Reesom Haile's poetry ranged freely yet artfully from international to national to local targets: from the politics of bedrooms to the politics of presidential offices. Because he frequently used allegory, thick and thin, the local could be readily seen as universal and the national as a redemptive paradigm for the international. He wrote according to a timeless criterion that the use and abuse of power were ubiquitous. Similarly, the stakes in such writing were always to be high and hotly contested, justifiably so, since the prize was nothing less than individual, national, and spiritual survival, as in the poem "Freedom of Speech."

Like animals
People can agree.
But to argue
Seriously or for fun
We have speech.

If we fail
To keep it free,

> Not giving everyone,
> A say, remember
> Babel – it fell.
>
> *Wheel*, 94

His strong and prevailing sense of political struggle and ideals might be considered romantic if they were not so realistic and rooted in the unassailable Eritrean political experience of standing alone and winning a 30-year war for independence. Thus, joining ancient symbol and the modern Eritrean war for independence, as in "The Leader," he could directly and easily address him and, by extension, any national leader who needs to know the ultimate source of his or her power:

> You wear our crown of leaves
> As long as we're free
> To say "yes" without force.
> As in the beginning,
> This covenant sways
> With each other's words,
> Leading to the good
> And holding us together
> Not apart in the storm
> To a stranger's delight.
> This way ? That?
> Around? Between?
> With this crown of leaves
> We meet heart to heart:
> With much to learn, but smart
> Enough to know what hurts.
> We choose you
> To wear our crown of leaves.
> It possesses no magic
> But our history and your name.
>
> *Voice*, 40

As if breathing the poetic air of Rome when it was a republic, Reesom Haile swept even further back in time to Rome's Rome, evoking a Greco-African model.

Greek seedling,
Dear democracy,
Please come with me to Africa.
I have water for the heat
And fire for the cold.
My medicine of local holy water
Will control the termites
And keep you rooted.
Forget your fear.
Come live with me.
I need your shade to rule
When the representatives meet,
With only an acacia
To prick me with its thorns.
Voice, 52

The scholars may debate her origins,[8] but a black Athena was alive and well in Eritrea.

Peace
Eritrea's daughter
Says what is
God her witness

Peace
She knows the worst
Goes hungry
Feeds her children first

Peace
Eritrea's daughter
Makes a home
For young and old

Peace
Eritrea's daughter
Drips her honey
Greater than Eritrea's gold

Eritrea's daughter
Also knows war
Forgets fear
Wears a bandoleer

Peace
Eritrea's daughter
Love her in all you do
And she drips honey on you[9]

A closing word about the center justification of Reesom Haile's poetry: in their original forms, in Ge'ez or in Latin script, he always center-justified them. Eritrean poetry, regardless, has no more a tendency to center-justify than most other languages. Moreover, Reesom Haile stands all but alone among Eritrean poets who do and do it well. He has imitators, but they are, for the most part, amateurish and fail to come close to the quality of his work. And why did he center-justify? Frankly, I never asked him before he died. While I have no special desire to see center-justified poetry in Tigrinya, which Reesom wrote in, or in other languages, including English, I simply took Reesom's center-justifying as a given. His choice – his way, his right – for his translator to follow. Thinking more about it now, I see his center-justifying, if a pun may be excused, as central to his poetry in print. More than simply his preference might support this. Contemporary poets in Eritrea who are widely recognized as the most accomplished – whether they write in Tigrinya, Tigre, Arabic, or other Eritrean languages – were more attracted to and praiseworthy of his reading or performance style than his poems themselves. It electrified his local audiences, drew large crowds, and filled stadiums, as I have never seen any other poet do before. On one level, therefore, center-justifying his lines signifies his unique voice in the history of Eritrean poetry. Center-justifying is like a trace element of his inimitable performative power.

Reesom Haile's life of writing poetry in Tigrinya spanned a little more than half a decade, when he died in 2003. Before returning to Eritrea in 1994, he wrote poetry in English but never published it. His life as a poet, moreover, derived from his reconnection with Tigrinya, in which the language, the poetry, as well as the poet thrived. Living in Asmara, Eritrea's capital, he was constantly high-spirited. His poems consistently exhibited a playful tone or, in his more serious lyrics, a playful edge. They also provided a window to see Eritrea as it had never been seen before. He believed deeply that Eritrea was best known through its languages – in his case, Tigrinya – and specifically through Eritrea's literature. From that moment I heard him performing his poetry at the Expo cultural festival in Asmara to an audience of thousands in August 1998, I knew he was right. I have known it ever since. Yet to know Eritrea is to read – to witness – the poetry Reesom Haile wrote like a once-appearing comet across the Eritrean skies.

He published *"Teshewano"* or "To My Graceful People" several times: in 1996, 1998, and 2002. Yet the internal and intense Eritrean politics it highlights – "We can cultivate the art to unite, / Or fight each other and fall apart"[10] – could be as much an issue now as when the nation was in its romantic infancy.

Another poem, "Shakespear Bejaka" or "Shakespeare, Enough" implored Eritreans to move beyond such polarization to peaceful resolution and "A new kind of love…. / A love of Eritreans / For green Eritrea"[11] – no less timely a dispatch. Reesom emailed it to me in February 2002, roughly a year after he sent me *"Teshewano."* He often wrote a gloss for any poem he sent, but all he said about this one is "Shakespear did it. A little conceit." England; Eritrea. Reesom Haile "joined" Eritrean poetry for both…and for the world.

---

1   Reesom Haile, *We Invented the Wheel*, trans. Charles Cantalupo (Lawrenceville & Asmara: The Red Sea Press, 2002), 237. Further references to this source are noted parenthetically in the text as *Wheel*.

2   Ngũgĩ wa Thiong'o, *Barrel of a Pen: Resistance to Oppression in Neo-colonial Kenya* (Trenton: Africa World Press, 1983).

3   The land of Eritrea has a long history of colonization, including Turkey from the 16th century, Egypt in the 19th, Italy from the end of the 19th century into World War II, the British after World War II, and Ethiopia after the British until Eritrean independence in 1991. In the case of Ethiopia, its king, Haile Selassie, a member of the Amharic

ethnic group, ruled from 1962 until 1975, when a Marxist revolutionary government, the Dergue, who originated from the Tigrean ethnic group, took over the government. As emperor of Ethiopia from 1889-1913, Menelik defeated the Italians at the battle of Adwa in 1896 and expanded Ethiopian rule in the Horn.

4   William Shakespeare, *A Midsummer Night's Dream* (1595), in *The Riverside Shakespeare*, ed. G. Blakemore Evans (Boston: Houghton Mifflin Company, 1974), V.1. 14-17, page 242. Further references to this source are noted parenthetically in the text as *Riverside Shakespeare*.

5   Lawrence Ferlinghetti, "What is Poetry?; A Non-Lecture" (2003), Poetry Society of America, https://www.poetrysociety.org/psa/awards/frost_and_shelley/frost_medal_lectures/lawrence_ferlinghetti/. Accessed 30 November 2016.

6   Trans. by Charles Cantalupo, unpublished manuscript, transcribed from email to author (10 April 2002).

intifada

eirtrawyan
nab seb aytsgedu!

wledu wledu
Hade kem dawit
wenCf ab idu

wledu wledu
Hade kem dawit
getamay nAdu

eirtrawyan
nab seb aytsgedu!

7   As J. G. A. Pocock notes, "By 1651, when *Leviathan* appeared…the collision between private inspiration and the authority of the civil magistrate has become a staple of political debate. See J. G. A. Pocock, *Politics, Language and Time* (New York: Atheneum, 1971), 171.

8   Cf. Martin Bernal, *Black Athena: The Afroasiatic Roots of Classical*

*Civiliz*ation (New Brunswick: Rutgers University Press, 1987). Extending over three volumes, Bernal's controversial work advocated for the culture of ancient Greece having its origins in Egypt and Mesopotamia. Furthermore, he contended that Western European culture was premised on the distortion and concealment of this legacy.

9   Reesom Haile, "Eritrea's Daughter," trans. Charles Cantalupo, *Modern Poetry in Translation* 2013: 2, 28.

10   Reesom Haile, "To My Graceful People," trans. Charles Cantalupo, *Modern Poetry in Translation*, 2016: 2, 91. Further references to this source are noted parenthetically in the text as *Modern Poetry*.

11   Reesom Haile, "Shakespeare, Enough," trans. Charles Cantalupo, *Modern Poetry in Translation*, 2016: 2, 92.

3

The Story on
Who Needs a Story

In 2002, I was invited to Eritrea to explore the possibility of translating and editing an anthology of contemporary Eritrean poetry. A new nation, it was an ancient country with a tradition of writing going back at least four thousand years in many languages.

On behalf of Eritrea's Hdri publishers, Zemhret Yohannes invited me. He felt that many more Eritrean poets deserved the kind of attention I had given Reesom Haile in *We Have Our Voice* (2000) and *We Invented the Wheel* (2002). After meeting with many of the poets, the chair and founder of the University of Asmara's Department of Eritrean Languages and Literatures, Ghirmai Negash, and other experts in Eritrean literature, I knew Zemhret Yohannes was right.

With very few exceptions Eritrean poetry had been unheard of in the modern world of letters until poems by contemporary Eritrean poets began appearing in the first decade of the 21st century in distinguished literary journals like *Exquisite Corpse*; *Left Curve*; *Drunken Boat; Words Without Borders; Two Lines*; *War, Literature and the Art; Modern Poetry in Translation*; *Rattapallax*, and more – even in the *New York Times* and on *CNN*, not the usual venues that might feature the poetry of a small, new African nation.[1]

With these publications and my previous two books of translations serving as a kind of prelude, in 2005 Hdri Publishers took the bold step of tapping its scant resources, and issuing *Who Needs a Story? Contemporary Eritrean Poetry in Tigrinya, Tigre and Arabic* (ISBN: 99948-0-008-6) – the first anthology of contemporary Eritrean poetry ever published.

Who Needs a Story was unique – a first in a world where literary anthologies of contemporary American poetry, Irish poetry, French poetry, Italian poetry, British poetry, and the poetry of most developed nations are abundant. Like many poets who write in African languages, Eritrean poets writing in their own languages or in translation could not be found on the shelves of the world's bookstores and libraries. But now contemporary Eritrean poets were well on their way to being known and enjoyed throughout Africa and the world, much as poets of other countries had achieved, however belatedly, worldwide recognition: for example, the way that contemporary Eastern European poets were first read widely in the 1970s or South American poets in the 1960s, and without whose influence most contemporary poetry in English and most languages was unimaginable since these poets expressed and explored a sensibility not widely recognized before them.

Yet the publication of *Who Needs a Story* was a story in itself. How did the first anthology of contemporary Eritrean poetry in translation ever published come into being?

By 2003 over sixty Tigrinya, Tigre, and Arabic poems had been translated and evaluated in Asmara for their quality and accessibility to determine the actual feasibility of the project. The poets represented a wide cross section of Eritrean society, including men and women from their 20s to their 80s as well as scholars, professional writers, journalists, social scientists, cultural activists, teachers, actors, theater directors, and performers. Furthermore, most of the poets participated in the Eritrean struggle for independence (1961-1991) as freedom fighters and/or as supporters in the Eritrean diaspora.

Rahel Asgedom and Nazreth Amlessom, both lecturers in the English department at the University of Asmara, made the first translations of about half of forty Tigrinya poems which would be short-listed for inclusion in the book. Adem Saleh, an Eritrean television journalist, and Dessale Berekhet, a columnist for the newspaper, *Haddas Eritrea*, and a senior student in English at the University of Asmara made the first drafts of poems in Tigre. Ghirmai Negash coordinated and supervised this first phase of the translations in Tigrinya and Tigre, translated the second half of the Tigrinya poems, read all of the translations, and made changes for accuracy and readability. Negash would be the books co-editor and co-translator with me.

The widely respected and senior journalist, Said Abdulhay, with whom I also met in 2002 to discuss the prospect of the book, accepted the responsibility of coordinating the translation of poems in Arabic. Since the Arabic poems' inclusion in the book was considered essential from the start, they were sent for translation to *Mekki for Translating & Printing*, an international translation office in Beirut, Lebanon, which provided translations of the Arabic poems' first drafts in English.

Receiving the first drafts in English of all of the translations by the end of 2003, I began working on their second drafts. Checking for linguistic accuracy and reading and rewriting the work as an English-speaking poet, literary critic, and scholar, I produced a complete book manuscript, which I then returned to Ghirmai Negash, who read and commented upon it.

At the end of the summer of 2004, Ghirmai Negash and I met in Asmara for the final stage of the project. Basing our discussion of the poems on Ghirmai Negash's comments, we began an engaging, at times intense yet always pleasurable, dialogue about the poems in Tigrinya. In addition, we consulted with Said Abdulhay and Musa Aron, whose knowledgeable and insightful comments on the Arabic and Tigre poems respectively, along with their English translations, resulted in a similarly happy, challenging, and productive process of literary collaboration. With the guidance and the critical corrections of the text provided by Ghirmai Negash, I then wrote the final version of the book.

One difficult decision Ghirmai Negash and I had to make, anything but unique to anthologists, concerned whom to include. The book's final version required that the number of poems and poets whom we had originally translated and planned to include had to be cut. We wanted to include more poets and more poems by them than we had space for. Of course, we desired to present only the best and the most representative of contemporary Eritrean poets. Moreover, many of the poems we cut were too similar to these poets' work. We also cut poems that seemed too cryptic or opaque in their translation, although they could be wonderful in the original.

An even more difficult decision had to be made about whether to include only written poetry and not Eritrean oral poetry, which had a long and rich tradition and which was still very important and pervasive in Eritrea. An objection to this critical decision would surely be just. We argued about it ourselves and could still be arguing about it.

The importance of our decision on whether to include Eritrean oral poetry in the anthology spurs me to this day to recall the exact spot in Asmara, rounding the corner of Tegedelti Street, and the blinding sunshine when we finally settled on only written poetry. Yet at the same time we firmly resolved that the depth, breadth, and high quality of Eritrean oral poetry warranted a translation project and an edition of its own. Ultimately, we foresaw a mapping of the Eritrean poetic genome to include all of Eritrea's languages as well as their performative and literary dimensions, with *Who Needs a Story* making only several steps in such an ambitious endeavor.

The story of how *Who Needs a Story* came into being also stretched back to the literary festival held in Asmara, Eritrea, in January 2000: Against All Odds: African Languages and Literatures into the 21st Century. Countries, universities, corporations, publishers, writers, scholars, artists, students, and children would converge for a weeklong conference and festival at a crossroads of centuries and a crossroads of cultures to make a historic intervention in Africa and the world, embracing people everywhere who would use languages and literatures to embody their dreams for a better world. From this gathering emerged the "Asmara Declaration on African Languages and Literatures," which was translated into a wide range of African languages and other languages worldwide. *Who Needs a Story* was the fruit of many of the historic "Asmara Declaration"'s most important points. For example, *Who Needs a Story* celebrated "the vitality of African languages and literatures," specifically the languages of Tigrinya, Tigre, and Arabic in the contemporary poetry of Eritrea, "and affirm...[ed]...their potential."[2] Furthermore, *Who Needs a Story* "note[d]...with pride that despite all the odds against them," the African languages of Eritrea – and Tigrinya, Tigre and Arabic were only three of them – "as vehicles of communication and knowledge survive[d] and ha...[d] a written continuity of thousands of years." Corresponding again to the mandates of the "Asmara Declaration," the Tigre, Tigrinya and Arabic poems of *Who Needs a Story* "t...[ook] on the duty, the responsibility and the challenge of speaking for" Eritrea and more, embracing people everywhere who use languages and literatures. Also in line with the language of the "Asmara Declaration," "the vitality and equality" of Eritrea's languages and their poetry had to "be recognized as a basis for the future empowerment" of the Eritrean people. Also, "[t]he diversity of" Eritrea's "languages reflect...[ed] the rich cultural heritage of" Eritrea and was "an instrument of" Eritrean "unity." In the words of the declaration, "[d]ialogue among" Eritrean "languages [wa]...s essential," and Eritrean "languages must use the instrument of translation to advance communication." Yet again following the Declaration, *Who Needs a Story* promoted "research on" Eritrean "languages" as "vital for their development." The poetry of *Who Needs a Story* was written in the spirit of reinforcing "what [wa]...s essential for...the African Renaissance." As a direct outcome of the "Asmara Declaration", the book was a prototype for books of African language poetry to be published in other parts of Africa and the world.

In short, the "Asmara Declaration" was the theory, and *Who Needs a Story* was the practice.

My own experience in Eritrea went back five years before the Against All Odds festival. When I first visited Asmara, the capital of Eritrea, early in the summer of 1995, I saw a new nation at peace and in action – with women fighters serving in the government, children learning in their mother tongues, a grass roots constitution process coming to fruition and so much more – developing itself with confidence, joy and incredibly hard work. This was four years after Eritrea's victory "against all odds"[3] – including overcoming the opposition of both the United States and the Soviet Union – in the brutal 30-year war for independence from Ethiopia. Yet in 1995 Eritrea embodied an enlightened political and social vision intimated in the texts of many of Africa's greatest writers – like Chinua Achebe, Ngũgĩ wa Thiong'o, Tsegaye Gabre-Medhin, and Nawal El Saadawi – whose own countries had lapsed into unenlightened and visionless neocolonialism. The achievement of Eritrea was, truly, "against all odds," yet considering the political and social problems of 20th-century Africa, the same phrase – *against all odds* – also characterized the struggle of these writers and many more of their African contemporaries in literature and its study.

Yet the story of *Who Needs a Story* would be incomplete without also considering the practical means of cultural production behind such a book. Little did I know when I began working on *Who Needs a Story* that the experience would sometimes feel like its own little "against all odds," or echo the title of my second book of translations with Reesom Haile: we invented the wheel.

Publishing books anywhere presents problems in editing, scheduling, printing, frustrating delays, and more. For example, I could complain that publishing the book in Asmara took too long, longer than I have had to endure in publishing my books in the United States. Then again a book by so great world-renowned an African author as Ngũgĩ wa Thiong'o remained unpublished at a major American publisher after over four years![4] Nevertheless, as far as I know, "the wheel" needed to publish a high quality book of poetry in four languages – two local, two international – and three fonts requiring different programs and new technology had never been invented before *Who Needs a Story* finally rolled off the presses in Asmara.

Writing a book is often a private, at times lonely, methodical process. Producing *Who Needs a Story* employed a huge cast of performers. At times each had his or her script as well as literally their own font, which brought together on a single page could wreak editing havoc. Or, *ut pictura poesis*[5] – as is painting so is poetry – they came together as in a Renaissance artist's huge workshop. It produced a kind of massive public painting or altarpiece of the Eritrean struggle in war and peace expressed in poetry, attributed to two co-authors yet the work of so many more, including faculty and students at the University of Asmara, Eritrean journalists and linguists in three languages, an international translation center, Eritrea's People's Front for Democracy and Justice, staff at Eritrea's Research and Documentation Center (RDC) and, of course, the poets themselves. Reinforcing my sense of the communal process that produced *Who Needs a Story*, in my walks around Asmara during the time when I was in working on the book I observed many large murals painted on buildings and city walls of the collective efforts that went into winning the Eritrean war of independence.

Many of poets in the book gathered for a group reading one night just before Eritrean New Year's, the feast of *Meskerem*, in September 2004, at Asmara's most famous traditional restaurant, Giday's. Each poet performed his or her work in the original to the group seated at long tables, eating dinner and drinking *sewa*, Eritrea's traditional barley beer, out of large porcelain plated metal goblets, in the traditional style of Eritrea's oral poets, the *getemti*, the *getamay* and the *getamit*. After each reading, Ghirmai Negash and I alternated, reading our translations. This means of literary production, though powerfully performative and memorable, did not seem necessarily unique, until one of the poets who wrote in Tigrinya approached me. He said that our translations into English, a language he knew, made him feel for the first time that he understood his fellow freedom fighters, with whom he had marched and bled, who wrote in Arabic, which he didn't know very well.

Also notable about the event, it included a reading of "Naqra" by Fessahazion Michael. The poem was controversial, based on an allegation that its author, a fighter, had died in the field under suspicious circumstances in 1976. Furthermore, rumors currently circulated in Asmara that "Naqra," the infamous island prison in the Red Sea to which many Eritrean fighters were condemned during the revolution, which the poem memorably described, had been reopened to house current Eritrean dissidents. Would reading the poem that evening enflame such rumors and/or arouse official displeasure and censorship and even endanger the evening's performers? But why should it, I thought, since the poem was included in the anthology in the first place? Moreover, any fears about what reading the poem might provoke reminded me of the initial fears and objections about my going to Eritrea in 2003 to begin work on the anthology, which are also a part of the story of the book. Thus, Ghirmai and I discussed the issue and decided that the poem should be read. Nor were there any repercussions. On the contrary, the poem resonated in the room and beyond as one of Eritrea's finest poems of war.

Another poet performing his work that evening, Solomon Tse-haye, the author of Eritrea's national anthem, revealed another strange aspect of Eritrea's literary production on a reading tour in 2005 when I was in Asmara to put the finishing touches on the manuscript. We had stopped in the city of Keren near its famous camel market and wanted to buy some of the region's equally famous mangoes to take back to Asmara. I bought some green chilies and tomatoes for lunch. As I held the bag on my lap in the car, Solomon suddenly remarked, "That's my poem!" When I asked "Where," he said, "On the bag." Three stanzas in Ge'ez script decorated the bag, although not without an error in one line, which Solomon corrected with the pen I had given to him with a request that he autograph the bag. In the second decade of the 1800s, might Francis Scott Key have found stanzas of his national anthem for the United States, "The Star Spangled Banner," printed on the wrapping paper of some vegetables or crabs that he bought in a Baltimore farmer's market? Roughly a hundred years earlier in England, Jonathan Swift satirized poets who had pages from their discarded books end up as the lining of pie and muffin tins. Writing his own "Verses on the Death of Dr. Swift" (1731) fourteen years before he died, the poet imagines when "Some Country Squire to Lintot goes" and "Enquires for Swift in Verse and Prose." He's told, "Sir, you may find them in Duck-lane: / I sent them with a Load of Books, / Last Monday to the Pastry-cooks."[6]

With a caveat about the critical limitations of applying Western or any paradigms to unique African circumstances to make comparisons between them, I still bring up these historical instances to contextualize at least in part this moment with Solomon Tsehaye in the Keren market and, more generally, literary production in Eritrea as I have experienced it.

Literary production in contemporary Eritrea offers additional points of comparison with publishing history in the United States and England. For example, for American poets and writers from the 17th to at least the middle of the 18th century – the time of Anne Bradstreet, Edward Taylor, Mary Hutchinson, Philip Freneau, Thomas Paine, and Joel Barlowe – American publishers, newspapers, broadsides, chapbooks, magazines, and general support for writers were almost nonexistent, except on a few streets in Philadelphia just before the revolution, in comparison with London at the time.[7] Yet going back in English history roughly a hundred years more, a comparison between Elizabethan England and contemporary Eritrea reveals that the transmission of poetry in both cultures, with similar literacy rates between fifty and sixty percent, is identified more closely with oral performance than with written text.[8]

Low literacy rates and both the lack of recognition and of opportunity in publishing combined to make the concept of an author as we know it inconceivable in England until the Restoration in 1660 and the literary career of John Dryden. Yet in Eritrea the concept of an author in Eritrea was similarly blurred. Furthermore, for a writer to claim the copyright – nowadays a kind of absolute acknowledgement of an author for his or her work – was often there viewed as unnecessary. A new development in Eritrean publishing, in some quarters an author's claiming his or her copyright was even considered unwelcome, smacking of ego and a kind of individualism which Eritrea's 30-year armed struggle for independence simply could not afford.

Securing the equally essential, bottom line kind of identification for a book, an ISBN number, presented an even bigger challenge than copyright in the case of *Who Needs a Story*. Hdri had never published a book with an ISBN number, and few books in Eritrea ever were, with the exception of several titles from Africa World / Red Sea Press, which had an American as well as an Eritrean base. Most books published in Eritrea stayed in Eritrea, which made ISBN numbers for the most part superfluous and/or irrelevant. The standard Western practice of obtaining an ISBN designation so that a book would be entered into electronic databases and other records of "books in print," leading to its recognition and sales through the internet yet also through bookstores nationally and internationally did not apply. If *Who Needs a Story* were only to be published for Eritrean circulation, an ISBN number would not be required. However, precisely because the book was seeking an international as well as a national audience, such a designation had to appear on the anthology, and happily it did, although not without much hand wringing and persuasion. Thus, with an ISBN of 99948-0-008-6 *Who Needs a Story* added still another historic dimension – besides its being the first anthology of contemporary Eritrean poetry in the original and in translation, in two local and two international languages – to the history of publishing in Eritrea and worldwide.

As I have suggested, nevertheless, these historical comparisons between the means of literary production in contemporary Eritrea and in the past in Europe and the United States are limited and can only go so far. For example, if we are talking about the history in Eritrea of written literature, as Ngũgĩ wa Thiong'o has said about *Who Needs a Story*, "For at least four thousand years – from the ancient stele in Belew Kelew to the 20th-century battlefields of Eritrea's heroic struggle for independence – into the 21st-century, Eritrean poets have never given up writing in their own languages, which is why their poetry thrives."[9] Standing among the longest and most continuous traditions of the art of the word in the world, Eritrean literature and the means of its cultural production flow from the stele, outward to include Arabic and Orthodox Christian writing, through colonial Italian newspapers published in Asmara at the turn of the century, to the mimeograph machines that pumped out translations into Tigrinya of Gorki, Dickens, Shaw, and Tolstoy – secreted in caves and away from the enemy MIGs trying to destroy them in the battlefields during Eritrea's 30-year war for independence – to *Who Needs a Story*. Who needs a story?! Eritrea's incredibly long history of written literature provokes this question and it can only be rhetorical. Ironically, such a long historical perspective can still produce a book of historical firsts.

This long history led me to a day late in July 2005 in Asmara, one of the rainiest summers most Eritreans can remember. *Who Needs a Story* was supposed to have been published nine months earlier when it was delivered to the printer. However, I needed a print out for a presentation I was making later that day. I called Sabur, the printing firm, and reached the printer. He said I could come over and he would print out a copy. Sabur stood in a kind of sparsely populated industrial park behind my hotel. I had to walk a zigzag pattern across a vast, red mud field to avoid the deep puddles. Sabur also stood contiguous to a UNICEF outpost wrapped in barbed wire, enclosing six huge satellite dishes and three towering communication towers. The path leading to Sabur's gate also led to the UNICEF encampment. As I approached, I saw three UN guards – they looked Indian – get up and start walking towards the heavily barricaded gate. One turned around and spoke, although I couldn't hear him, and two more guards followed. They looked Irish. All five wore blue helmets. At the time I did not make the connection that the guards might be walking towards me. I thought they were only checking the gate, which the puddles all around compelled me to walk straight towards. Around ten yards away, I saw the two Irish guards raise their guns and heard the safety caches – click, click – removed from their triggers. Turning around to see if anyone was behind me, seeing that there was not, and continuing to walk, I realized the guards were pointing their guns at me. At the same time, a deep puddle cutting off the path forced me to make a sharp turn to the left around five yards from the UNICEF entrance to the Sabur gate. Two old men attended it. They immediately swung it open and welcomed me in Italian: "*entra qui.*"

This moment of personal danger took place in a time marked by political danger, too. For example, my first visit to Eritrea in 2002 to research the possibility of publishing the poetry anthology that became *Who Needs a Story* came directly after the fateful fall of 2001, in which the United States suffered the Al Qaeda attack of 9/11, destroying the World Trade Center and leading the United States to go to war. At nearly the same time, Eritrea suffered a political crackdown by its government, which resulted in the jailing of a host of political leaders and the shut down of eight of its privately owned newspapers along with the detention of their editors and reporters. The situation was further complicated by the renewed outbreak of fighting between Eritrean and Ethiopia year and a half before, in May 2000, in which Ethiopia invaded and seized significant amounts of Eritrean territory, and which left tens of thousands of dead on both sides.

Amidst such dire circumstances, *Who Needs a Story* struggled to be born. The glory days of the Against All Odds conference had faded and its international financial support had dried up. By 2002, the governments of Eritrea and Ethiopia had agreed to a demilitarized zone between the two countries, but it would be on Eritrean soil. UN peacekeeping troops would be in charge. Danish soldiers filled most of the seats my plane coming into Asmara. Italian troops stayed in my hotel, with racks of dry cleaned uniforms lined up outside of their rooms every afternoon. I had never seen so many white Toyota Land Cruisers in one place except on the docks of Port Newark, New Jersey, from where the vehicles made their ways to American suburbs and shopping malls. Zemhret Yohannes referred to the troops as "crusaders." Did they and did the countries they came from think they would save Eritrea? If so, from whom? In the past, Eritrea had already saved itself from Ethiopia, repeatedly. In the past, Eritrea had also saved itself – repeatedly – from the colonial aspirations of many of the same countries whose troops came once more, only now labeled as peacekeepers.

Yet the presence of the troops also suggested that Eritrea needed to be saved from itself. Their clean boots, pressed uniforms without a spot of dirt, and ascots represented a political order for the most part without political detentions, students allegedly killed for demonstrating, the banning of a free press, the imprisonment of journalists, the postponement of elections and a constitution put on hold. If major international news outlets that once featured stories on Against All Odds and interviews with Reesom Haile reported now on Eritrea at all, they either focused on the political stalemate over its disputed border with Ethiopia or Eritrea's internal political repression.

Even more discouraging, when I asked friends and professional colleagues what they thought about my going back to Asmara to work on the poetry anthology under such circumstances, all but one questioned whether amidst such a political crisis a book like *Who Needs a Story* would be advisable or even possible. None questioned it more vehemently than my greatest mentor, dearest friend and collaborator in Eritrean poetry, Reesom Haile.

"They'll use you as a symbol," he growled over the phone from Belgium, where he now lived in self-imposed exile from Eritrea again, a mere two years after *Against All Odds*. "They'll parade you around as evidence that the country is still open and encouraging freedom of expression. They'll use you for propaganda."

I had called from my home in Bethlehem, Pennsylvania to ask his advice about accepting the invitation to come to Eritrea to produce the anthology. "But Reesom," I replied, "if I read a poem that sounds like propaganda, it cannot be a good poem. And I am not going to translate bad poems."

Our conversation ended abruptly, and it was our last. The days when we would address each other as "Joiner / Joiner / Mighty Joiner," *getamay* to *getamay*, joiner to joiner, poet to poet, had ended. Our near daily emails – his sending me a poem in the morning, with my returning a translation by the end of the day, including many emails of rough drafts in between – dried up worse than an Eritrean river, and a rainy season to make it flood would never come again.

Reesom also believed that the anthology would not include him due to his falling out with Eritrea's ruling party and his writing poems that opposed it, despite my repeated assurances that, Eritrean politics notwithstanding, I would not allow this to happen. But as with the initial opposition to the anthology that I encountered from friends and colleagues other than Reesom, yet similar to the alleged threat of political and personal repercussions if the poem, "Naqra," were read at the celebratory gathering of the anthology's poets, no one and nothing stood in the way of the anthology's going forward as its editors saw fit. Moreover, it included two of Reesom's best and most famous poems, "We Have" and "Voice," simply because it had to include them as two of Eritrea's best contemporary poems

One night at the *Against All Odds* conference in Asmara in January 2000, I saw Reesom hotly arguing with Zemhret Yohannes about a comment Reesom had made from the podium in his reading a few minutes before. The situation ominously foreshadowed his eventual estrangement from the Eritrean government and his exile, but when I asked him about the incident a few days later, he responded as if to reassure me that he had promised himself "not to be distracted by politics over poetry." I believed him, but it was a promise he would not – or could – not keep.

I will leave to others any further explanation of the politics surrounding *Who Needs a Story* and how they relate to Eritrea, Africa, and the world. Nevertheless, I do confess uncertainty about the extent of any political power that derives from or depends on the book or any book of poetry.

An Eritrean colleague once urged me to believe that the book, in his words, is "helping people to know the other face of Eritrea because the world has never seen or heard Eritrea's voice except through the gun."[10] For me, nevertheless, the book was about beauty: in particular about the beauty of the moment when a nation as well as a person might begin to realize that he or she needed a story yet already had a story waiting to be told. Such a realization led me to Africa in the first place, twenty years before *Who Needs a Story* was published.[11] Furthermore, such a realization is the basis of a poem by Ghirmai Yohannes, which is included in the book and gave it the name: "Who Needs a Story?"

> I needed a story
> And asked myself all day –
> What can I write?
> It kept me awake all night –
> What do I have to say?
>
> I emptied so many words
> And ideas out of my brain
> It would have floated away
> If not tied to my heart.
> Now I needed art.
>
> Paper and pen in hand,
> Tomorrow I would start . . .
> But wait.
> What is this all about?
> Do I really need a story?
>
> All this time and hard work –
> For what?
> I hate myself for thinking this.
> I already have a story

That nobody knows and it's great –
I am the story.

Story, 79

Reesom Haile used to say when we would read together, and I would go first with my English translation, "the original in Tigrinya is much better."[12] However true this might be about its sound and its sense, like Reesom's poems as well as the poems throughout *Who Needs a Story*, Ghirmai Yohannes' poem ponders a problem that is not original but common to Eritrean writers, African writers, and writers worldwide.

The subject of the poem "Who Needs a Story?" is not unique but conventional: "I needed a story / And asked myself all day – / What can I write?" The poet confronts his desire to write a poem without knowing what to write: a rhetorical or poetical occasion marked many times and in many languages. In English, for example, the first line of the first sonnet in the famous sonnet cycle, *Astrophil and Stella* (1591) by the 16th-century poet, Philip Sidney (1554-1586) begins, "Loving in truth, and fain in verse my love to show...."[13] As in the poem by Ghirmai Yohannes, Sidney proceeds to count the ways that prevent him from writing his "verse." Unexpectedly, perhaps, both poets had battlefield experience in common — one in 20th-century Eritrea, the other in 16th-century Holland – but the fact that they both struggle with the same literary convention in trying to write poetry might not be as surprising.

In the 20th century, the Anglo Irish poet, William Butler Yeats, provides another famous example of the same problem, as in the first line of a poem he wrote late in his career, "The Circus Animals' Desertion": "I sought a theme and sought for it in vain."[14] Yeats explores the theme by flipping through a variety of poetic subjects – from Irish mythology to contemporary Irish politics – that have obsessed him over his long career, before he concludes, "Maybe at last being but a broken man, / I must be satisfied with my heart...." Writing this kind of poem leads Yeats through intensely personal, poetic introspection finally to discover, "I must lie down where all the ladders start, / In the foul rag and bone shop of the heart" (*Yeats*, 348). Similarly, Ghirmai Yohannes in "Who Needs a Story?" engages in an intense, form of personal, poetic and sometimes painful self-scrutiny extensive – "It kept me awake all night" – to find out "What do I have to say?"

Struggling to find his "story," the poet confesses that he has

Emptied so many words
And ideas out of my brain
It would have floated away
If not tied to my heart.

Uniquely identified not only with feeling or emotion but also with thinking, the Tigrinya word for "heart," *lebi,* introduces a distinctly Eritrean quality to Ghirmai Yohannes' quest. As Alemseged Tesfai, Eritrea's premier historian has observed in the documentary, *Against All Odds: African Languages and Literatures into the 21st Century:*

In most of our Eritrean languages, the heart is not just a life-giving organ. In Tigrinya, a wise man or wise woman is called *lebam*, and wisdom is *lebona*.... Like all humanity we think with our heads, but we say we think with our hearts. The heart is the creator. The pen is the creation of the heart. When I speak of the pen, I speak of the heart....Performance also is the performance of the heart....As a writer I...speak from the heart.[15]

Then again, Ghirmai Yohannes invoking his own heart as a resolution for the dilemma of his poem also recalls Philip Sidney, who finally resolves his problem of not being able to write a poem by hearing from his muse, who counsels, "Fool...look in thy heart, and write!"

Still, the problem in "Who Needs a Story?" of the poet finding a story for himself remains unsolved despite the heart's undeniable strength because, as he immediately adds, "Now I need...art." Furthermore, the art must be his own, since he holds the "Paper and pen" in his "hand," implying that the contemporary poet who writes also confronts a different problem in finding a story for him or herself than does the oral poet who can, for one thing, at least rely on a long and continuous tradition upon which to base his or her story. The poet suggests that his "heart" may be as strong and dependable, but it cannot begin to compare its powers of articulation since such a "heart['s]" self assertion cannot measure up in terms of "art" with the oral tradition's powers of poetic performance. Nearly overwhelmed with this realization, the poet wants to escape his dilemma, or at least put it off, by saying "Tomorrow I w[ill] start." However, a more self-defeating problem exists for him than mere procrastination in another question: start what? It provokes him to pause for a moment in his self-dramatization of the poetic process with "But wait."

At this point in the poem, Ghirmai Yohannes asks,

> What is this all about?
> Do I really need a story?
>
> All this time and hard work –
> For what?

A poet or a writer is not a given or *a priori* assumption without a story, since he or she cannot even exist without it, notwithstanding the inevitable "time and hard work" that realizing a story involves. Poets and writers must recognize their own, individual stories before anyone else does in order to write them: to be determined enough to take "Paper and pen in hand" or computer keyboard and screen, expend the "time and hard work" and then offer it to someone else.

At this point, the poet's dramatized self-examination of his writing process becomes most unrelenting. His disgust over his work – signaled by the abrupt question, "For what?" – at seemingly wasting his time thinking about what to write but producing nothing – except his excellent poem, ironically – turns to self disgust: "I hate myself for thinking this." He hates himself either for thinking that he has no "story" or for thinking that "words," "ideas" and "art" will be the source of his story. He hates himself in fact for hating himself so much that thus far in the poem he hasn't thought that he is worthy of writing a poem or telling the story he knows best. He suffers not so much from a lack of imagination or information or writer's block as he does from low self-respect and a lack of confidence, until the most basic kind of self-realization dawns on him: he exists, and his reaching the end of his poem is the clearest evidence of his existence and his story, so that he can matter of factly state, "I already have a story / That nobody knows and its great – / I am the story."

As Ghirmai Yohannes realizes he has a story, contemporary Eritrean poetry – in fact the entire long tradition of Eritrean poetry – has a story, too. The poems in *Who Needs a Story* account for, at least, part of it. Little did I know when I began working on the book, *Who Needs a Story*, that it would have its own story to tell, too.

1   Interviewed on CNN's "Inside Africa" by Sally Graham in 2001, Reesom Haile recited excerpts from several of his poems in English translation. In 2004, CNN's "Inside Africa," featured another story on Reesom Haile, prompted by his death in 2003. The segment included Reesom Haile reciting excerpts from his poems in Tigrinya and me reading the translations and adding commentary. My translations of Eritrean poetry also include the following:

2017   "My Washington Agenda," "Bitter and Cold," "Adam, You Original," "No Regrets," poems by Reesom Haile translated from Tigrinya, *Imagine Africa* (volume 3), ed. Bhakti Shringapure (New York: Archipelago Books), 7-10.

2016   "Asmara by Night," "Her Photo," poems by Reesom Haile translated from Tigrinya, *Capitals: An Anthology*, ed. Abhay K, (New Delhi: Bloomsbury Publishing), 11-12.

African Anthem," poem by Reesom Haile translated from Tigrinya, *Centres of Cataclysm* (Hexham: Bloodaxe Books), 227.

"Shakespeare, Enough," "To My Graceful People," poems by Reesom Haile translated from Tigrinya, *Modern Poetry in Translation*, 2, 90-92.

2015   "Before the Birth of Toys," poem by Reesom Haile translated from Tigrinya, *Modern Poetry in Translation*, 2, 88-89. Also included in "Engaging Children in World Poetry (MPT Education Pack for Primary Schools)."

2013   "African Anthem," "Eritrea's Daughter," "Poverty," poems by Reesom Haile translated from Tigrinya, *Modern Poetry in Translation*, 25-28.

"Knowledge," "Dear Africans," poems by Reesom Haile translated from Tigrinya, *The Broadview Introduction to Literature* (Calgary: Broadview Press, 2013), 504-07.

2012 "Unjust Praise," poem by Ghirmai Yohannes translated from Tigrinya, with Ghirmai Negash, "The Written Word" (BBC broadcast for 2012 London Olympics: poem to represent Eritrea).

"Like a Sheep," poem by Ghirmai Yohannes translated from Tigrinya, with Ghirmai Negash, lyrics for music by Carine Tripet, http://www.youtube.com/watch?v=D5uOdOXeE-0w&feature=youtu.be.

2011 "Knowledge," "Development," "Under Consideration," "Learning from History," "Your Head," "Speak Out," poems by Reesom Haile translated from Tigrinya, www.zocalopoets.com.

"What Can I Call You," oral poem by Weldedingel translated from Tigrinya, with Ghirmai Negash, *The Dirty Goat* 25, 155.

"Negusse, Negusse – The World Falls Apart," oral poem translated from Tigrinya, with Ghirmai Negash, *The Dirty Goat*, 25, 157-67.

"Son and Father," anonymous oral poem translated from Tigrinya, with Ghirmai Negash, *The Dirty Goat*, 25,153.

"Naqra," poem by Fessahazion Michael translated from Tigrinya, with Ghirmai Negash; "Who Said Merhawi Is Dead," poem by Solomon Drar translated from Tigrinya, with Ghirmai Negash; "The Invincible," poem by Mussa Mohammed Adem translated from Tigre, with Ghirmai Negash; "Singing Our Way to Victory," poem by Mohammed Osman Kajerai from Arabic, with Ghirmai Negash; introduction, *Voices*, (http://voiceseducation.org/content/eritrean-war-poetry).

"Garden Eritrea," "Learning from History," "The Next Generation," "Desta," "Knowledge," poems by Reesom Haile translated from Tigrinya with an introduction, *Voices* (http://voiceseducation.org/content/reesom-haile-quotable-poet-eritrea).

"The Dead of Night," "Are They Watches?" "Jesus' Last Words," poems by Reesom Haile translated from Tigrinya, *Modern Poetry in Translation* 3.14, 140-42.

"Unjust Praise," poem by Ghirmai Yohannes translated from Tigrinya, with Ghirmai Negash, *The Ecco Anthology of International Poetry* (New York: HarperCollins Publishers,

2010), 419. Republished @ http://www.poets.org/viewme-dia.php/prmMID/21822. Academy of American Poets, "Po-em-A-Day," September 1.

2009 "Our Path," poem by Reesom Haile translated from Tigrinya, http://www.poemsfor.org.

"Voice," poem by Reesom Haile translated from Tigrinya; video poetry with Mark Oliveiro, *Silliman's Blog: a weblog focused on contemporary poetry and poetics*, http://ronsil-liman.blogspot.com/ 5/17/09) / http://www.youtube.com/watch?v=9AkWQ8rm9Qc.

"Desta," poem by Reesom Haile translated from Tigrinya, *Fire in the Soul: 100 Poems for Human Rights* (Rotherham: New Internationalist Publications), 74.

"The Tithe of War," poem by Solomon Tsehaye translated from Tigrinya, with Ghirmai Negash, *Fire in the Soul: 100 Poems for Human Rights* (Rotherham: New Internationalist Publications), 156.

2008 "African Leaders," "Angel Fiqriel," "Tell the President," "Her Picture," poems by Reesom Haile translated from Ti-grinya, *Per Contra* 9 (Spring issue), http://www.percontra.net/13hailecantalupo.htm.

"Under the Sycamores," oral poem by Zeineb Yassin trans-lated from Tigre, with Dessale Berekhet, *Per Contra* 10 (Fall issue), http://www.percontra.net/archive/12yassin.htm.

"Love in the Daytime," "I Love You II," "Ferenji and Habe-sha," "Whose Daughter," Talking About Love," poems by Reesom Haile translated from Tigrinya, *Bending the Bow: An Anthology of African Love Poetry* ed. Frank Chipasula (Carbondale: Southern Illinois University Press), 123-27.

"Silas," "Let Us Divorce and Get Married Again," poems by Beyene Hailemariam translated from Tigrinya, with Ghirmai Negash, *Bending the Bow: An Anthology of African Love Poetry* ed. Frank Chipasula (Carbondale: Southern Illinois University Press), 128-129.

"Go Crazy Over Me," poem by Saba Kidane translated from Tigrinya, with Ghirmai Negash, *Bending the Bow: An An-thology of African Love Poetry* ed. Frank Chipasula (Carbon-dale: Southern Illinois University Press), 150.

"Juket," poem by Said Mohammed Osman translated from Tigre, with Ghirmai Negash, *Bending the Bow: An Anthology of African Love Poetry* ed. Frank Chipasula (Carbondale: Southern Illinois University Press), 208.

"Breaths of Saffron on Broken Mirrors," poem by Abdul Hakim Mahmoud-El-Sheik translated from Arabic, with Ghirmai Negash, *Bending the Bow: An Anthology of African Love Poetry* ed. Frank Chipasula (Carbondale: Southern Illinois University Press), 248-50.

2007 "War and a Woman," "'Your Father,'" poems by Saba Kidane translated from Tigrinya, with Ghirmai Negash; "Remembering Sahel," poem by Paulos Netabay translated from Tigre, with Ghirmai Negash, *UniVerse,* http://www.universeofpoetry.org/eritrea.htm.

"Freedom's Colors," poem by Angessom Isaak translated from Tigrinya, with Ghirmai Negash; "Abeba," poem by Ribka Sihatu translated from Tigrinya, with Ghirmai Negash; "Your Father," poem by Saba Kidane translated from Tigrinya, with Ghirmai Negash; "Naqra," poem by Fessahazion Michael translated from Tigrinya, with Ghirmai Negash; "Like a Sheep," poem by Ghirmai Yohannes translated from Tigrinya, with Ghirmai Negash; "The Invincible," poem by Mussa Mohammed Adem translated from Tigre, with Ghirmai Negash; "Breaths of Saffron on Broken Mirrors," poem by Abdul Hakim Mahmoud El Sheikh translated from Arabic, with Ghirmai Negash; "A Song from the Coast," poem by Ahmed Omer Sheikh translated from Arabic, with Ghirmai Negash; "Singing for the Children of Ar," poem by Mohammed Mahmoud El-Sheik (Madani) translated from Arabic, with Ghirmai Negash, *Fascicle* 3, http://www.fascicle.com/issue03/main/issue03_frameset.htm.

2006 "Wild Animals," poem by Meles Negusse translated from Tigrinya, with Ghirmai Negash, *Modern Poetry in Translation* III: 5, 17-20.

"Remembering Sahel," poem by Paulos Netabay translated from Tigre, with Ghirmai Negash, *Rattapallax* 13: 50-51.

"Help Us Agree," poem by Fortuna Ghebreghiorgis translated from Tigrinya, with Ghirmai Negash, *Two Lines* XIII, 154-57.

"Next Time Ask," poem by Ghirmai Yohannes translated from Tigrinya, with Ghirmai Negash; "Juket," poem by Mohammed Said Osman translated from Tigre, with Ghirmai Negash, *Dragonfire* (http://www.dfire.org/x2264.xml).

"The Tithe of War," poem by Solomon Tsegaye translated from Tigrinya, with Ghirmai Negash, *War, Literature and the Arts*, 18:1&2, 169-70

"Wind and Fire," poem by Mohammed Osman Kajerai translated from Arabic, *War, Literature and the Arts*, 18:1&2, 167-68.

2005 "Unjust Praise," poem by Ghirmai Yohannes translated from Tigrinya, with Ghirmai Negash, *Words Without Borders* (http://www.wordswithoutborders.org/).

2004 "If I Had," "Mothers Like Mine," poems by Reesom Haile translated from Tigrinya, www.unicef.no.

"Knowledge," "Desta," poems by Reesom Haile translated from Tigrinya, www.modestaproposta.net.

2003 "Incompatible," "I Cut His Hair," "Old Sayings," "Thread and Culture," "My Donkey Says," "To a Pen," poems by Reesom Haile translated from Tigrinya, *Titanic Operas* 2, http://archive.emilydickinson.org/titanic/material/cantalupotrans.html.

2002 "Freedom of Speech," "Four Dots," poems by Reesom Haile translated from Tigrinya, *A.bacus*, 17-18.

2001 "Living," "Am I?" "Let Him Through," poems by Saba Kidane translated from Tigrinya, with Ghirmai Negash, *The New York Times*, 3/25, section 14, 10.

"They Don't Eat People," "Mirror," "On Her Watch," "Dear Hand," "Tell It Like It Is," "Love in the Daytime," "Y2K," "Four Dots," "Man and Button," "I Cut His Hair," "Whose Daughter," "To a Pen," poems by Reesom Haile translated from Tigrinya, *Exquisite Corpse* 8.

"Tigrinya," "Dear Africans," "Democracy," "Thy Brother's Envy," "Democracy," "Ova, Signora," "Knowledge," "The Camel," "Voice," poems by Reesom Haile translated from Tigrinya, *Drunken Boat* 3, http://www.drunkenboat.com/db3/haile/haile.html.

"Alphabet Soup," "Exposure," "Mother Courage," "To Rome," "Bush Afrique." poems by Reesom Haile translated from Tigrinya, *Al Performance* (Spring), 65.

2000   "To Our Bread," "Believe It or Not," "Esh," "Eyes in Front," "The New Houses," poems by Reesom Haile translated from Tigrinya, *Samizdat* 6, 8.

1999   "Desta," "Our Language," "Learning from History," "Knowledge," "The Next   Generation," poems by Reesom Haile translated from Tigrinya, *about.com*,   http://poetry.about.com/od/multilingualpoems/ss/tigrinyapoems.htm.

"Desta," "Our Language," "Learning from History," "Knowledge," "The Next Generation," poems by Reesom Haile translated from Tigrinya, *Light & Dust Anthology of Poetry,* http://www.thing.net/~grist/ld/haile/rht-eng.htm/.

"Sister," "Ova Signora," "Foreign Aid," "Voice," "Your Head," poems by Reesom Haile translated from Tigrinya, *Left Curve* 23, 28-29.

2   "Asmara Declaration on African Languages and Literatures," Charles Cantalupo, Kassahun Checole, Mbulelo Mzamane, Nawal El Saadawi, Ngũgĩ wa Thiong'o, Zemhret Yohannes (http://www.africa.upenn.edu/Govern_Political/asmrlit.html). Accessed 29 August 2016.

We writers and scholars from all regions of Africa gathered in Asmara, Eritrea, from January 11 to 17, 2000, at the conference titled Against All Odds: African Languages and Literatures into the 21st Century. This is the first conference on African languages and literatures ever to be held on African soil, with participants from east, west, north, Southern Africa and from the diaspora and by writers and scholars from around the world. We examined the state of African languages in literature, scholarship, publishing, education, and administration in Africa and throughout the world. We celebrated the vitality of African languages and literatures and affirmed their potential. We noted with pride that despite all the odds against them, African languages as vehicles of communication and knowledge survive and have a written continuity of thousands of years. Colonialism created some of the most serious obstacles against African languages and literatures. We noted with concern the fact that these colonial obstacles still haunt independent Africa and continue to block the mind of the continent. We identified a profound incongruity in colonial languages speaking for the continent. At the start of a new century and millennium, Africa must firmly reject this incongruity and affirm a new beginning by returning to its languages and heritage.

At this historic conference, we writers and scholars from all regions of Africa gathered in Asmara, Eritrea, declare that:

1. African languages must take on the duty, the responsibility, and the challenge of speaking for the continent.

2. The vitality and equality of African languages must be recognized as a basis for the future empowerment of African peoples.

3. The diversity of African languages reflects the rich cultural heritage of Africa and must be used as an instrument of African unity.

4. Dialogue among African languages is essential: African languages must use the instrument of translation to advance communication among all people, including the disabled.

5. All African children have the unalienable right to attend school and learn in their mother tongues. Every effort should be made to develop African languages at all levels of education.

6. Promoting research on African languages is vital for their development, while the advancement of African research and documentation will be best served by the use of African languages.

7. The effective and rapid development of science and technology in Africa depends on the use of African languages and modern technology must be used for the development of African languages.

8. Democracy is essential for the equal development of African languages and African languages are vital for the development of democracy based on equality and social justice.

9. African languages, like all languages, contain gender bias. The role of African languages in development must overcome this gender bias and achieve gender equality.

10. African languages are essential for the decolonization of African minds and for the African Renaissance.

The initiative that has materialized in the Against All Odds conference must be continued through biennial conferences in different parts of Africa. In order to organize future conferences in different parts of Africa, create a forum of dialogue and cooperation, and advance the principles of this declaration, a permanent Secretariat will be established, which will be initially based in Asmara, Eritrea.

Translated into as many African languages as possible and based on these principles, the "Asmara Declaration" is affirmed by all participants in Against All Odds. We call upon all African states, the OAU, the UN, and all international organizations that serve Africa to join this effort of recognition and support for African languages, with this declaration as a basis for new policies.

While we acknowledge with pride the retention of African languages in some parts of Africa and the diaspora and the role of African languages in the formation of new languages, we urge all people in Africa and the diaspora to join in the spirit of this declaration and become part of the efforts to realize its goals.

Asmara, 17th of January 2000

3   See note 11, page 9 above.

4   Contracted for publication by Random House, Inc., Pantheon Books in 2002, *Wizard of the Crow* did not appear in print until 2006.

5   Horace, *"Epistula ad Pisones"* or *"De Arte Poetica,"* ed. and trans. H. R. Fairclough, *Horace: Satires, Epistles and Ars Poetica* (London: William Heinemann, Ltd.; Cambridge: Harvard University Press, 1970), l.361, 480. Further references to this source are noted parenthetically in the text as *Ars Poetica.*

6   Jonathan Swift, "Verses on the Death of Dr. Swift, D.S.P.D.," *The Writings of Jonathan Swift*, ed. Robert Greenberg & William B. Piper (New York: W. W. Norton & Co., 1973), ll. 253-60, 536.

7   "[T]he premier commercial center and political capital of British America.... Philadelphia was also the acknowledged nexus of literary America.... [b]y 1775." Neil Baldwin, *The American Revelation* (New York: St. Martin's Press, 2005). 31.

8   For example, Shakespeare's plays were not collected for publication – and then not all of them – until 1623, in the *First Folio*. The first folio of Shakespeare's most famous literary contemporary, Ben Jonson, only appeared seven years earlier, in 1616. Furthermore, even twenty-four years later in *Wit's Recreation*, an anonymous poet mocked Jonson's desire for his work to appear in published form: "Pray tell me Ben, where doth the mystery lurke / What others call a play, you call a worke." See David Loewenstein. *The Cambridge History of Early Modern Literature* (Cambridge: Cambridge University Press, 2002) 115. *The World Factbook* (CIA) lists literacy in Eritrea at 58.6% (https://www.cia.gov/library/publications/the-world-factbook/geos/er.html). Although literacy rates in Elizabethan English are more difficult to ascertain, see Richard L. Greaves. *Society and Religion in Elizabethan England*. (Minneapolis: University of Minnesota Press, 1981). 334.

9   Charles Cantalupo and Ghirmai Negash, *Who Needs a Story? Contemporary Eritrean Poetry in Tigrinya, Tigre, and Arabic* (Asmara: Hdri Publishers, 2005), back cover. Further references to this source are noted parenthetically in the text as *Story*. Belew Kelew is the pre-Axumite site of a stele in southern Eritrea near the town of Senafe.

10   Said Abdulhay, email to Charles Cantalupo, 8 March 2008.

11   Cf. Charles Cantalupo, *Joining Africa: From Anthills to Asmara* (East Lansing: Michigan State University Press, 2012), 1-124, *passim*.

12   See Ghirmai Yohannes, *Who Needs a Story – Contemporary Eritrean Poetry in Tigrinya, Tigre, and Arabic* (Asmara: Hdri, 2005), 80.

ጽውጽዋይ ጽሒፈ

መዓልትን ለይትን ደኺሙ
ረሪካ ዘይድቅስ ጽር ሓሳባት ሓዚለ
ተጨኒቐ! ውሻጠ ኣእምሮይ ሓሊበ፣
ሓሳብ ንሓሳብ ኢጋጭዬ - ቃላት ኣብ ሽክናይ ሓቛኑ፣
ዘዘጽዓየለይ መሪጸ ብልበይ ዛንታ ቀዊደ፣
ብርዐይ ወረቐተይ ኣዋሃይደ-ተ-ዋ-ዲ-ደ፣
ትማሊ ምሸት ተኣንቲተ - ጽውጽዋይ ክጽሕፍ ሃቀነ።

        ግንከ ከንቱ'ዩ ነይሩ ዘየድሊ ድኻም፣
        ግዜኻን ሓንጐልካን "ንብላሽ" ምብኻን፣
        ከመይሲ!...............
        ጽውጽዋይ ምጽሓፍ ኣይመድለየንን ነዓይ፣
        ዋላ ኣይፈለጥ ምዕራፍ መወዳእታይ፣
        እንኹ'ንዶ ባዕለይ ጽብ'ቕቲ ጽውጽዋይ።
             ኸላ ሎሚ'ስ ንዒቻያ - መዚጊያ ነብሰይ፣
             ጽውጽዋይ ከሰኩስ - ጽውጽዋይ ምጽሓፈይ።

13   Philip Sidney, *Astrophil and Stella* (1591), *The New Oxford Book of Sixteenth Century Verse*, ed. Emrys Jones (Oxford and New York: Oxford University Press, 1992), 303.

14   William Butler Yeats, "The Circus Animals' Desertion," *W. B. Yeats: The Collected Poems*, ed. Richard Finneran (New York: Macmillan Publishing Company, 1983), 346. Further references to this source are noted parenthetically in the text as *Yeats*.

15   Alemseged Tesfai, *Against All Odds: African Languages and Literatures into the 21st Century*, dir. Charles Cantalupo (Asmara: Audio Visual Institute of Eritrea, 2007; distributed by African Books Collective), 23:33-24:44.

57

4

Return to Rome

Petrarch would never have wanted only Latin to say this:
Barbara pyramidum sileat miracula Memphis.[1]
He'd use Italian. Thus, in English: "Barbaric Memphis,
Praise of the pyramids as if they were miracles should stop."

I saw a monument in Arezzo, built in the 20s
By Mussolini to Petrarch as if he wrote in Latin:[2]
Rome's nursing she wolf beside him, standard Mother and Child,
Medieval knights and heroic nudes inscribed with the paunchy
Dictator's fantasy: *"Roma caput mundi"* [3] –a nightmare.
But something else carved near Petrarch sounded much more
      creative.
I read the words *"Nostro Capo Roma"* out loud to myself,[4]
Honoring Petrarch as first to write his poetry the way
Poets in Europe and anywhere must follow: in their own
Language like Petrarch's Italian and not anyone else's,
Faking what should come directly from the sense of their own
      tongue.

Petrarch would never have wanted only Latin to say this
(Pliny the Elder derived it from a Greek common saying):
Africa semper aliquid novi [5] –but in Italian

Non-Native Speaker

He might say, translated into English: "Something new always
Comes out of Africa," and he might have said it of my friend
From Eritrea in Rome for doctors there to save his life.

Thirty-year veteran of fighting Ethiopia, my friend
Struggled for freedom and triumphed, standing by his small nation
Fighting the US and Russians, too, their proxy wars feeding
Geopolitical fires still burning, with Eritrea
Still forced to fight for its life, depending only on itself
And no one else in a world that barely knows Eritrea,
Where it appears on the map or who might live there like my friend:
Battlefield graduate of the only university
Found to be credible – revolution; marrying there, too;
His fighter wife and he raising their son – dealing with the day
Bombs hit their valley and shrapnel nearly blinded him for life.

Two decades later my friend served as a Marxist Medici,[6]
Helping the writers and artists of Asmara to survive.

I hadn't visited Rome for twenty years, but I had come
When I was younger and searching for a spiritual home.
Ten times at least I had stayed there, hoping never to depart.
But if I now had a place away from home and my children,
Barbara, Bethlehem, and whatever else I had become,
Might I say Africa? Eritrea? Now where I traveled
Even more frequently since my last trip long ago to Rome?
Why was I calling Asmara, "Rome's Rome?"[7] What was I feeling?
"Africa's Africa" back in my old spiritual home?

Thirty-five years ago with my parents, on my first visit,
Speeding through Traforo tunnel,[8] I looked out of the back seat
Into the darkness, but what if I could see myself walking
Now on the sidewalk and holding hands with Barbara amidst
Bellowing traffic that sounded like Fellini's in *Roma?*[9]
I was obsessed with religious art, and would I have even
Recognized I was myself and almost my father's age then?
What would I think of four children, our belonging to no church,

What we were wearing to dinner, what we thought of the Forum –
Seeing an arrogant nation like our own come to ruin
(Hopelessly commonplace feeling, therefore, seeming all too true),
And the idea of an endless chain of history in things
Equally there to exalt: my favorite being the frescoes
Up on *secondo* of Rome's *Palazzo Massimo alle
Terme*,[10] and Barbara's being little churches with paintings
Filling the ceilings, and maybe work by Caravaggio
Off in a corner and waiting to be patiently worshipped?[11]

Now that I came back to Rome, I walked through set after set of
Dreams less forgotten and more real than the past I remembered.

One afternoon when we met my friend and after espressos,
Several times as we walked and let him choose the way to go,
We would be stopped at a corner or enjoying some baroque
Detail we never before had noticed – typical of Rome –
When he would say to me, "*La città eterna*," with a smile.
"*Roma*," I answered him, "*La città eterna*," and later
Three times at dinner we toasted, "To the *città eterna*."
As we were walking I felt like we were walking forever:
As if the afterlife – "The eternal city" – could be true;
As if it started already here and now and continued
Simply with walking together in *la città eterna*.
It didn't matter he lost a lot of weight and he shuffled,
His pants too baggy as if he could be merely another
African immigrant hustling me, a tourist, around Rome.

Petrarch would never have wanted only Latin to say this:
Carthago delenda est, or "Carthage has to be destroyed."[12]
Petrarch would use his Italian to embellish such a curse,
As I imagined it booming in the air of a painting
By the Italian Michele Cammarano,[13] whom we found
Coincidentally next day after seeing my good friend.

Following him to *Piazza Cinquecento*,[14] half-circling
Termini Station, and thinking "*Cinquecento*" referred to

Art or more simply the 1500s, I heard the story
How in Dogali the Eritreans, thousands and well-armed,
Slaughtered five hundred Italian soldiers, put there to quickly
Conquer the country in 1887 with no one
Able to stop them, which Cammarano's painting depicted.
Shocked by the massacre and in mourning, Italy tried to
Honor the casualties, with a granite middling obelisk,
As my friend showed us, where we could see the *memento mori*[15]
Set on a pedestal glass and garbage strewn, though it couldn't
Dampen our wanting to see it closer and the inscriptions:
Surnames Italian – *cinquecento*, dead in Dogali.
Then I remembered when I was there, and in Eritrea
That little hilltop and monument seemed much less important[16] –
With its inscriptions, Tigrinya and Italian side by side –
Than the few camels and two historic bridges in the dust.
In the same spirit of "*Roma caput mundi*" on Petrarch's
Monument, and in the 1920s, too, Mussolini
Ordered the obelisk moved from right in front of the station
To a small park on the side. *Eroi* failing to survive
Africa,[17] meeting the eyes of Romans, wasn't a vision
Fascism wanted to face, yet neither did Cammarano's
Painting, which took up a whole wall of the *Arte Moderna*'s[18]
Room twenty-three in the "Giordano Bruno" *salone*.[19]
Finishing in 1895, supposedly after
Five years of living in Eritrea, did Cammarano
Paint what he saw near Massawa, or what Italy had dreamed
Africa always would look like from *la città eterna*?
White gloves and uniforms, sashes, scarves, and earnest Italians
Mustached and falling down hills too green and under a blue sky?
Falling in foregrounds where coal black Eritreans blend into
Still blacker horses: an apelike mass with leopard skins and tails;
Brute force with scimitars, spears and Colonel De Cristofori[20]
Plunging his sword as if he alone could never be destroyed?

1   Martial, "*De Spectaculis Liber*," "On the Spectacles," *Epigrams,*
     vol. I, ed. and trans. D. R. Shackleton Bailey (Cambridge: Harvard
     University Press, 1993), 12.

2   Arezzo's monument to Petrarch was built in 1928. The sculptor was Alessandro Lazzerini di Carrara (1888-1942). As a poet and a major humanist scholar, Petrarch, or Francesco Petrarca (1304-1374), revolutionized Italian and European poetry by being among the first to write in his vernacular language, Italian, instead of Latin.

3   "Rome, capital (head) of the world."

4   "Our leader Rome," Francesco Petrarca, *Il Canzoniere, The Canzoniere, or Rerum vulgarium fragmenta,* ed. and trans. Mark Musa (Indianapolis: Indiana University Press, 1999), 1.20, 84. Musa translates the phrase, "the head of us all, the city Rome."

5   Pliny the Elder, *Naturalis Historia, Natural History,* ed. and trans. H. Rackham (Cambridge: Harvard University Press, 1940), VIII: xviii, 32-33.

6   The Eritrean revolution, like many wars of independence in Africa, modeled itself on the principles of Karl Marx (1818-1883), the German philosopher and economist. After the war, Eritrea's ruling party, the People's Front for Democracy and Justice (PFDJ), maintained the same ideology. Princes of the Medici family ruled Florence in the 15th century and were among the greatest patrons of the arts.

7   Italy first occupied Eritrea in 1889 and soon thereafter made Asmara its capital in 1897. The city became known as "La Piccola Roma" because it developed a large Italian population and, even more so, because of its extensive Italian Modernist architecture, which has survived intact for the most part despite the end of the Italian occupation in 1941 and the many decades of war that followed. Cf. *Asmara: Africa's Secret Modernist City,* Edward Denison, Guang Yu Ren, & Naigzy Gebremedhin (London & NewYork: Merrell Publishers, 2007).

8   Built in the first decade of the 20th century, the Traforo Umberto I is Rome's most famous tunnel. Roughly a quarter mile long, it is located in the center of the city, under the Quirinale Hill.

9   *Roma* (1972), a film by Frederico Fellini (1920-1993) – a major post World War II Italian filmmaker – presents a semi-autobiographical and episodic account of a young man's shock and wonder when he moves to Rome from his native Rimini. Cf. https://www.youtube.com/watch?v=tVLGveU5jbU. Accessed 7 December 2016.

10   A branch of the National Museum of Rome (*Museo Nazionale Romano*), the *Palazzo Massimo alle Terme* is a museum of ancient art

housed in a 19th-century palace near Rome's main train station. The second floor features frescoes from the Livia and Farnesina villas.

11 Michelangelo Merisi da Caravaggio (1571-1610) came to Rome in the early 1590s and became the city's most famous and painter by 1600. His gleaming, visual realism portrayed intense, often emotional physicality and/or spirituality, depending on the subject, which could be sacred or secular. The paintings can be found in the chapels of Rome's baroque *chiese* (churches) of San Agostino, San Luigi de Francesi, and Santa Maria del Popolo.

12 This famous phrase relates specifically to the 2nd and 3rd-century Punic Wars, of which there were three, between Rome and Carthage. In the end, the northern African city was destroyed. While the exact phrase, *"Carthago delenda est,"* has no one ancient source, close variations expressing the same sentiment recur in Plutarch, Pliny the Elder, Livy, and the Roman statesman, Cato the elder. Cf. Charles E. Little," "The Authenticity and Form of Cato's Saying *"Carthago Delenda Est,"* *The Classical Journal* 29, no. 6 (1934): 429-35. http://www.jstor.org.ezaccess.libraries.psu.edu/stable/3289867. Accessed 7 December 2016.

13 Michele Cammarano (1835-1920) traveled from Italy, his birthplace, to the city of Massawa in Eritrea, where he lived for five years, after being commissioned by the Italian government to commemorate the battle of Dogali (1887).

14 The *Piazza dei Cinquecento* is a large and busy square directly in front of Rome's main railway station.

15 The literal meaning of *memento mori* is "remember you must die." The term refers to art or objects that are to remind a viewer of death.

16 Eighteen miles west of Massawa atop an arid hilltop in a mostly barren landscape, the Dogali monument is one of many sites in Eritrea commemorating the wars it has fought for independence.

17 "Heroes."

18 Containing Italy's largest collection of modern and contemporary art, the *Galleria Nazionale d'Arte Moderna* (GNAM) or National Gallery of Modern Art was founded in Rome in 1883, four years before the battle of Dogali, and commemorated the unification of the Italian national state.

19 Giordano Bruno (1548-1600) was a pioneering Italian philosopher accused of heresy by the Roman Catholic Church and burned at the

stake in Rome's Campo de Fiori. There is irony in the placement of Cammarano's "Battle of Dogali" in the Giordano Bruno room. His advocacy of the cosmology of Copernicus, displacing the earth from the center of the universe, and disputing of fundamental Roman Catholic dogmas, which ecclesiastical authority still maintained, could be considered analogous to the way that the Italian defeat in Dogali defied Italy's military and colonial might.

20   Tommaso de Christofori (1841-1887) died in combat, allegedly hand to hand, on January 26, 1887, along with most of the Italian soldiers he commanded.   Cf.   http://3.bp.blogspot.com/-tOHJ6Ba1BV8/U2kxlQUsgkI/AAAAAAAAKxs/u2A7l8bWoMI/s1600/DSCN2190.JPG. Accessed 7 December 2016.

5

The Reluctant Translator

I *was in a quandary.* Why had my translation of a short story originally written in Tigrinya, "The Girl Who Carried a Gun" by Haregu Keleta provoked nearly as many questions and comments
in the few months that it had been posted as all of the Eritrean poetry
I had translated and published, including three books, over the last
fifteen years?[1] *Who were the EPLF? What did they do? Were there
a lot of Eritrean women soldiers? The story is autobiographical,
right? When did the Eritrean against Ethiopia take place? And
who were the ELF? Why the Marxist elements in the story? Where
is Eritrea? Can you tell me more about its history?*

The same questions could have been prompted by many of the
poems I had translated,[2] but they had not been. For example, Eritrean history appeared in most of them since contemporary Eritrean poetry was rarely personal or individual, despite its sometimes
sounding autobiographical when it was not – like Haregu Keleta's
short story, too. Furthermore, most of the poets I had translated
were formerly EPLF, that is, Eritrean People's Liberation Front soldiers or "fighters" (as they preferred to be called), and ELF (Eritrean
Liberation Front) soldiers, too, before the EPLF defeated it in a civil
war.[3] In addition, Eritrea's location in the Horn of Africa and its
war with Ethiopia had figured in a lot of the poems. Also, many of
the poems I had translated revealed an Eritrean revolution that was
Marxist, and I also had translated Eritrean women poets who fought
in the armed struggle.

One answer to my quandary was that if contemporary Eritrean poetry and "The Girl Who Carried a Gun" presented roughly the same subject matter, to most readers the short story was a more inviting, accessible, transparent, and attractive literary form than poetry. Actually, one of my closest colleagues in Eritrea, Zemhret Yohannes, head of Eritrea's Research and Documentation Center and of the Eritrean publishing house, Hdri, had been telling me this for years, repeatedly urging me to publish an anthology of Eritrean short stories as a companion volume to my anthology, *Who Needs a Story? Contemporary Eritrean Poetry in Tigrinya, Tigre, and Arabic*. Reluctantly, I finally agreed to try by translating a few stories as a test to see if they would attract any interest.

But I was primarily a poet. In comparison with my abilities and desires to communicate through images, formally rhythmic language, rhyme / alliteration / assonance, poetic forms, and lines of print that usually end long before a page's right margin, my skills in constructing and understanding prose narrative felt like a disability. Writing or translating poetry for nearly forty years, I had to admit, of course, that I knew for nearly as long – once I moved beyond writing teenage protest songs against the Vietnam war – that poetry was generally perceived, in English at least, as marginal and less inviting and accessible than prose fiction. But as a poet I have never fully understood or, at least, accepted why this was the case. My incomprehension, furthermore, was reinforced when I first began in 1998 to witness and understand that poetry – contemporary or traditional, oral poetry – in Eritrea was central, enjoyed and understood by nearly everyone, especially in public in performance.[4]

Now, however, after my experience with Haregu Keleta's short story, had I finally to concede, bowing at least to the Western gods of prose fiction in the literary marketplace,[5] that no Eritrean poem, at least in my translation into English, could ever state as clearly or accessibly something like this from "The Girl Who Carried a Gun?" "[A] few months of military training made my soft body hard. I had muscles. My skin grew darker. I could run up and down the mountains. I sprinted over the sand. The oppression of Eritrea and especially of its women changed me into a fighter – far from a girl who was afraid to go outside."

Claudia Moreno Parsons began her provocative essay, "Into the Landscape of Humanity," with:

> Is poetry the answer to war? Of all the systems of communication we have, one of the most effective in considering and talking about the horrors of war is poetic language. That most ancient form, poetry, can tell the truth about war in a way that other forms of language do not. The ability to extract threads from the complex mass, to lay images before us one at a time – teaching us, in a sense, the aesthetic of war....[6]

"Talking about the horrors of war," was poetry unique? Was there also "truth about war" that was unique to poetry and not to "other forms of language," particularly literary language? In either case, was such a unique quality believable? Desirable? Furthermore, could there be an "aesthetic of war" only about its "horrors?" An "aesthetic of war" without glories? Could there be any aesthetic without beauty?

But if poetry was not "the answer to war," what was? Did "the answer," and whether it was poetry or not, depend on place, history, and language? Could an attempt to ascertain "the answer," any answer, defer questions of class, race, and gender?

Alternating between "yes" and "no" in trying to resolve such questions, I am distracted by a vision of the authors of *Gilgamesh, Exodus, The Iliad, The Aeneid, Beowulf, La Chanson de Roland, El Cid, Sundiata,* and other,[7] ancient warlike epics getting ready to approach the stage for their laurels, pre-written acceptance speeches tucked into their robes. Yet I see closer to the stage, a group of British, young men, as if they have been secretly tipped that their names are going to be called instead: Wilfred Owen, Siegfried Sassoon, Isaac Rosenberg, and a few more, among them a faintly smiling and older Thomas Hardy.[8] Unlike the epic poets, this group appear more up-to-the-minute, as if they know that the audience could care less about and even dislike most epic performers and their vaunting lines about war and its heroism, violence, death, and "the glory that was Greece, / ...the grandeur that was Rome," as Edgar Allan Poe wrote in "To Helen,"[9] or Babylon, Egypt, England, France, Spain, Mali, wherever.... Then I see Oliver Stone[10] and Kathryn Bigelow[11] approaching the podium together to open the proverbial envelope and smiling at the group in the front rows, yet I catch out of the corner of my eye several of the epic war poets leaving their seats and pulling on their beards as they head for the exits.

"[T]alking about the horrors of war...poetry *can* [my emphasis] tell the truth about war in a way that other forms of language do not," again as Parsons contends, but the nature of that truth was debatable, at least between traditional epic poets and, to take only one example, the greatest British poets of World War I, yet nearly most poets, epic and lyric, who came after them. Although not an epic poet, Horace sounded as if he was being straight and meant his famous line, "*dulce et decorum est pro patria mori,*[12] "It is sweet and right to die for your country," despite his own possible dereliction of warlike duties, whereas the line's most famous citation, in Wilfred Owen's eponymous poem, was ironic, meaning the opposite of what it said. That is, it meant anything but "sweet and right" when invoked amidst

...An ecstasy of fumbling...
...yelling out and stumbling,
And flound'ring like a man in fire or lime...
...drowning...
...guttering, choking, drowning.
...the white eyes writhing in his face,
His hanging face, like a devil's sick of sin;
...at every jolt, the blood
Come gargling from the froth-corrupted lungs,
Obscene as cancer, bitter as the cud
Of vile, incurable sores on innocent tongues....[13]

Dying in war was neither sweet nor right, according to Owen, his peers, and nearly all poets since, at least most who were published and read, whether – to name particularly American conflicts – they wrote about World War II, Korea, Vietnam, Afghanistan, and Iraq out of direct or, as in the writing of Ammiel Alcalay, historical experience. Yet who wanted to be so patronizing as to imagine that ever more shocking technological advances in the weaponry of war, typified by Owen's portrayal of a poisonous gas attack on a World War I battlefield, were something beyond or worse than "the horrors of war" as understood by ancient or medieval poets, who imagined an array of supernatural kinds of violence and killing: if not as shocking and even seeming contrived to us, still indicating a desire to add to the horror of – what postmodern warfare seemed more and more obsessed to avoid – an ultimate reality of the immediate physicality of one human killing another human being to survive?

Nevertheless, living in the midst or in the shadow of war at least as much as what could be readily imagined about ancient epic poets, most modernist and postmodernist epic poets, even romantic epic poets like Williams Wordsworth's *The Prelude* (1805)[14] or Walt Whitman's *Song of Myself* (1855)[15] simply "would prefer not to" engage it, in Herman Melville's famous phrase in "Bartleby the Scrivener."[16]

Still, poets who did, from *In Parenthesis* (1937)[17] by David Jones to Ammiel Alcalay in *from the warring factions* (2002)[18] or in his translations of Semezdin Mehmedinovic, *sarajevo blues* (1998),[19] could no more than Owen find anything but irony in Horace's famous Latin tagline. Yet in *The Great War and Modern Memory* (1975), Paul Fussell suggested that such cynicism and nihilism in Jones, at least, had its limits, since his poem "associate…[d] the events of front-line fighting…with Arthurian legend, Welsh and English folklore, Old Testament history, Roman Catholic liturgy, Norse myth, Chaucer, *The Rime of the Ancient Mariner*, the poems of G. M. Hopkins, and even the works of Lewis Carroll,"[20] becoming what Fussell called "appliquéd literariness" (*The Great War*, 153). As if to avoid any such literariness and its inevitable nostalgia for the heroic values of ancient poetic epic if not actual war or, perhaps, to create a different kind of literariness free of such blandishments, Alcalay in *from the warring factions* also created and even appliqued himself a phalanx of texts. In Parsons' words, "Lines are quoted verbatim from sources as disparate as political speeches, documentaries, UN documents, poets both contemporary and ancient, and the 19th-century Pequot orator William Apess. Alcalay turns the straightforward business of war – the news reports, the magazine articles, the speeches – into a new form" ("Landscape of Humanity"). The occasional and usually unpredictable deployment of mostly long-lined free verse reinforced the text's aura of a new kind of verbal expression and literary style, albeit formally descended from the projectivist poetics of Charles Olson and in content akin to the anti-*dulce et decorum est* tradition of poetry relating to war. Bringing "these disparate elements together into one long, epic poem," Alcalay, in his own words, even "needs[ed]…to confound the whole notion of a narrator, or a single self" (*warring factions*, 152).

With ancient epic and lyric praise of war and its values of heroism, violence, death, and glory having metamorphosed into most romantic, modernist and subsequent epic and lyric poetry's – with few notable exceptions – abhorrence and even avoidance of war and any praise for its values, had we reached a kind of end of the history of poetry as far as the topic of war and its representation was concerned? Did the sociocultural norms, however varied, of people who read and/or hear poetry uniformly require there be nothing "sweet and right" about it anymore? Had a 20th century of two world wars, the Cold War, many other wars of national liberation, and a 21st of continuing global and local terror and violence waged in the name of nations, insurgencies, ethnicities, and religions made the representation in poetry of war – if it's not one or two thousand years or more in the past and in the form of medieval or ancient epic – impossible to conceive of except, in terms like Simone Weil's? "Force employed by man, force that enslaves man, force before which man's flesh shrinks away;" where "the human spirit is shown as modified by its relations with force, as swept away, blinded by the very force it imagined it could handle, as deformed by the weight of the force it submits to;" where "[t]he bitterness…is… undiluted. No comforting fiction intervenes; no consoling prospect of immortality; and on the hero's head no washed out halo of patriotism descends?"[21] Moreover, had we reached an end to any serious contemporary poetry about war through not only a near universal abhorrence of war itself but also of any poetic artifice – unless it also was a kind of anti-artifice like Alcalay's – being devoted to it?

The answer to all four questions was *yes* – at least for the present. Fussell's *The Great War and Modern Memory*, Alcalay's war writings, and, most persuasively, the virtual absence of any great contemporary poetry about war in the last two hundred years unless it conformed to Weil's terms reinforced this conclusion.

On a smaller scale, I also knew this to be the case first hand: not as a poet who would write about war any differently through direct or historical experience, but as a translator of contemporary poets who could say Horace's Latin *"Dulce et decorum est pro patria mori"* without any irony in their minds or voices and translate it the same into their own languages and poems. Furthermore, these poets embraced and expressed a level of force and violence as profligate and apodictic as anything in Weil while also revealing war as not only about fighting but also friendship, love, natural beauty, and other perennial issues of life. Also, these poets neither expressed doubt and self-consciousness about their abilities to convey "the horrors of war," as if they could be beyond comprehension or adequate representation, nor any need for a new kind of poetics or anti-poetics to recount such conditions. Thus as a translator, despite the historical and literary record established by Fussell, Alcalay, and others, including my own predisposition, I was challenged to find – discover, rediscover? – the words and poetic forms in English that could represent and embody such an outpouring of verbal art and genuine emotion, in this case, in Tigrinya, Tigre, and Arabic, three languages spoken in Eritrea. As if to accentuate this quandary, the close verbal equivalent for the word "poet" in Tigrinya, *"getamay,"* could be translated not only as "joiner" but also as "challenger."[22]

But meeting this challenge is not my point. A reader can judge whether I have for him or herself by reading individual translations or my books, *War and Peace in Contemporary Eritrean Poetry* (2009*)* and *Who Needs a Story: Contemporary Eritrean Poetry in Tigrinya, Tigre, and Arabic* (2005).[23] I would add, nevertheless, that while many literary journals published poems from the anthology, *Who Needs a Story*, the same editors rejected most of its poems about war as a positive and praiseworthy, "sweet and right," and *necessary* means of Eritrean nationalism and liberation, when there was no other way to achieve independence from Ethiopian annexation and colonization, whatever the original language I translated from: neither elegant Arabic –

I sing for the children of Ar,
Of a love in the forest and caves
Of Golujj – a painting finished

With the barrel of a gun – the soldier,
Abraham, shot, carrying out the body
Of his hero, Mahmuday;

Story, 119

Homeric Tigre –

He sees his enemies like sorghum bending
And breaking, their heads spilling out all red.
Never missing the target, his bullets
Fall like rain hitting the lake, and it floods
As in the days of Noah, only with blood....
He throws the trees and rocks out of his path
And grabs his weapons – nobody's laughing.
Fields planted thick with mines, impossible
Desert sand and heat, crocodiles swarming
The rivers and gaping valleys in his way
Reveal him close and watching overhead
Before he leaves them choked with too many dead.

Story, 89

nor baroque Tigrinya –

...we still need to see him back with us
...in this brutal place
Of too many heroes and martyrs yet
...Like a pearl? A stately shade tree needing
Our protection? A pillar of light? Gold?
A compass? A diamond? The riches of
Grass or flesh. The mighty lion? Words
And comparisons cannot say enough....

Story, 47, 49, 51

Or can they "say enough?" Have they already said too much? Can two, three, four millennia – Virgil and Homer back to *Exodus* and back to *Gilgamesh* – of such poetry have sufficed? The problem is not poetry itself or what the poetry is about – war. Nevertheless, is the positive spin on "the horrors" the only problem? Or is that group of young nihilist, anti-war poets self-assuredly winking at each other in the front row of the awards ceremony also about to be disappointed at the end of the sentence "And the award goes to?"

Of course, they are. On this imaginary occasion, they are as delusional as the epic poets because it is not about poetry. And not even about prose. It's about film. They are at two removes. So am I – and Claudia Moreno Parsons, Ammiel Alcalay, and many more as well. Together we're in good company, but the audience and the academy aren't really interested in us. War, yes. But poetry, much less poetry about war, its praises or its horrors, without or with occasional beauty? No.

Such a conclusion was obvious to most, but was it to a true believer in the power of "[t]hat most ancient form, poetry," to "tell the truth about war in a way that other forms of languages do not?" I wanted to agree wholeheartedly with Parsons that "[o]f all the systems of communication we have, one of the most effective in considering and talking about the horrors of war is poetic language" and its "ability to extract threads from the complex mass, to lay images before us one at a time – teaching us, in a sense, the aesthetic of war," but again, *I was in a quandary*. In theory I could agree "[T]hat most ancient form, poetry, can tell the truth about war in a way that other forms of language do not." But in practice? When I considered the lackluster critical reception of all my translations of Eritrean war poetry in comparison with the much stronger response to an experience from the same war recounted in a single short story? If only I didn't translate it, I could still be happy in my state of denial.

Then again, maybe I should have attributed this *cri de couer* not so grandly to poetry itself but, frankly, to my own translations. To be in a state of denial about the merit of one's own literary work, that is, its lack of merit, although common, was the worst of reasons for questioning the value of an entire literary enterprise, in this specific case, the efficacy of contemporary poetry about war. I should confess that in translating Eritrean poets who wrote about war, I could never wholly escape the feeling that my job was impossible, at least quixotic – and not only because they wrote lyrically and positively without irony, doubt or self-consciousness about horrific violence and a dying heroically in battle. This sinking feeling even stayed with me as I steeled myself to the challenge of trying to find an English language and diction that had not been used for a century or two, with the exception of Rudyard Kipling[24], that might convey the genuine emotions that these poets embodied in their work. Moreover, I could accommodate poetry that was without irony and positive about war – from poetry that was ancient to its pre-modern dying gasps in English – and, as I learned to be open to the possibility of poetry without irony and positive about war in the 20th century and beyond, I even began to feel that I could find the language to express this. In praise or blame, the language was the same. After all, the language of modernist and postmodernist poetry, albeit it profoundly anti-war, was rich, regardless. To take the examples of Jones or Alcalay, they both produced rhetorically difficult, elaborate texts, applying modernist – in the case of Jones – and postmodernist – in the case of Alcalay – radical literary experimentation to express war's shattering of traditional experience and understanding.

Ultimately, however, my greatest insecurity about my translations of contemporary Eritrean war poetry was that, regardless of its war traumas, neither modernist nor postmodernist, experimental poetic forms became the way to translate them. My first impulse was to use them, believe me. But when I applied such widely accepted 20th and 21st-century aesthetics or poetics to translations of Eritrean poets and shared the results, they rejected them outright as incomprehensible and barely related to their work in style or content. The poetry was no more radical and experimental in an expected modernist or postmodernist way than it was negative and ironic about war. Nevertheless, I should have known better. I had experienced a similar rejection when I first started translating Eritrean poetry, specifically Reesom Haile's, several years before.

But what if, after recognizing the unique difficulty of translating war poetry that was largely positive about the experience (an obstacle that translating Reesom Haile's work never presented, since he neither participated in nor wrote directly about the Eritrean revolution), I had persisted with my translations as I saw fit rather than as the original Eritrean poets did? Would the work have garnered any more editors' interest? Would the benefits – publication, greater circulation, and more critical attention – of my translations' falsifications have outweighed the notion that we were no more at an end of the history of poetry about war than we were at an end of history itself, to recall the original, infamous phrase?[25]

What if *I was not in a quandary?* What if I was not in a state of denial about poetry's limits? What if my translations of contemporary Eritrean war were not even horrible? Could there be another reason for readers' avid curiosity about "The Girl Who Carried a Gun" in comparison with their comparatively complacent response to translations of Eritrean poetry? What if I went back to the most obvious reason: that the short story was a more inviting, accessible, transparent and attractive literary form than poetry to most readers?

The form of the short story was international, all but universal, familiar, and probably the most accessible of all literary forms. Most any reader could respond to it immediately and feel secure based on his or her having read many short stories before.

But African language poetry in translation? It was as proportionally limited as the short story was widespread. In short, there was an endemic failure to translate and publish African language poetry.[26] No continent had less of its indigenous language poetry published. Every major international journal – in print or online – was complicit in this failure, since their publishing African language poetry was minimal if at all. With only a few exceptions, every major African literature anthology was similarly complicit. And the translators were few, especially if high quality literary translation was the criterion.

Consequently, besides translations of African language poetry being subjected to the standard marginalization that nearly all poetry, at least in the West, suffered in comparison with prose fiction, the fact that there were so few translations made them even stranger and more forbidding – or at least less familiar and easy to talk about. I could attest to that personally. It was a new experience for me, as I did not doubt it would be for most Western readers. After decades and decades of reading contemporary poetry, I never heard or read contemporary poetry like Reesom Haile's or poems by Eritrean poets about war. When I first did, I hardly knew how to describe it, and I knew even less about how to translate it. Reading the translation of an Eritrean short story was different. The content might vary from story to story, language to language, but the form was familiar, accessible, and totally recognizable, even when its viewpoint could seem still foreign and strange, as in "The Girl Who Carried a Gun," which was also neither negative nor ironic about the experience of being a soldier in a war.

Thus, "poetry" could be and poetry still "is the answer to war," but the answer changes. "[P]oetry can tell the truth about war in a way that other forms of language do not," but the truth changes, too. "[O]ther forms of language" tell it as well, but better or worse, uniquely or not – who can really tell? Also, who can tell how translating and reading more African language poetry as well as poetry – for example, from Gĩkũyũ, Acoli, and Swahili in East Africa; from Mandinka, Akan, and Yoruba in West Africa – would affect and change the writing of war poetry in the West?

Regardless, "the truth about war" according to contemporary Eritrean poets who fought during Eritrea's revolution compared to "the truth about war" according to an Eritrean woman who similarly fought and wrote a short story about an Eritrean woman fighter during the war remained roughly the same. It was sweet and right to die for your country. For them to think differently throughout Eritrea's thirty year armed struggle for independence, as if such a truth could only be ironic, the nation would not exist. Contrary to a popular automobile bumper sticker in the United States that stated "war is not the answer," in Eritrea war was the answer – it was the answer of Eritrea's poets and writers of prose fiction and nonfiction, too, at least throughout that war.

Readers of the poems in English translation were put off by such a conclusion. But it did not seem to bother readers of the English translation of the short story. Both the poems and the short story embodied an ethic, perhaps also an aesthetic, about war that was, frankly, outdated and objectionable to most English-language and nearly all Western readers of more than popular literature. Still, the short story by Haregu Keleta was more popular with them than all the war poetry famous in Eritrea, albeit in Eritrea only, and that I had translated, by Isayas Tsegaiaye, Solomon Tsehaye, Fessahazion Michael, Ribka Sibhatu, Fessehaye Yohannes, Solomon Drar, Saba Kidane, Paulos Netabay, Mussa Mohammed Adem, Mohammed Osman Kajerai, Mohammed Mahmoud-El-Sheikh (Madani), Ahmed Mohammed Saad, Ahmed Omar Sheikh, and more.[27]

If they wrote short stories about war instead of poetry, would this still have been the case? Probably not, but like it or not, these poets and their local readers and audience found two propositions like "war is the answer" and "poetry is the answer to war" to be compatible. In the West and much of the world today, neither answer would be considered tolerable, but it was a foundation in the history of poetry out of which our contemporary poetry emerged and, therefore, an "answer to war" that still should be more familiar than foreign. These Eritrean poets and writers in a *tegedelti* tradition, the Tigrinya word for Eritrean fighters, echoed a tradition embodied in the Latin, "*Dulce et decorum est pro patria mori,*" which had been translated for millennia upon millennia and continues to be translated: a tradition that now extended, again through translation, to include languages and traditions that we had not known before but that we should know if we really did believe that "poetry is the answer to war" – however different the poetry, the answers, and the wars could seem.

1   Haregu Keleta, "The Girl Who Carried a Gun," trans. Charles Cantalupo and Rahel Asgedom Zere, *Words Without Borders* (October 13, 2013), http://wordswithoutborders.org/article/the-girl-who-carried-a-gun. Accessed 7 December 2016.

2   See note 1, page 48 above.

3   Cf. Dan Connell, Tom Killion, "Civil Wars," *Historical Dictionary of Eritrea* (Lanham: Rowman & Littlefield, Scarecrow Press, 2010), 150-152.

4   Cf. pages 13-14 and 114 below.

5   Cf. Carmen Mccain, "Words Without Borders Draws Attention to African Women Writing in Indigenous Languages," *Daily Trust* (12 October 2013), AllAfrica, http://allafrica.com/stories/201310120164.html (subscription). Accessed 7 December 2016.

6   Claudia Moreno Parsons, "Into the Landscape of Humanity," *Warscapes* (12 March 2014), http://www.warscapes.com/reviews/landscape-humanity. Accessed 7 December 2016. Further references to this source are noted parenthetically in the text as "Landscape of Humanity."

7   Respectively, epics of Iraq, Israel, Greece, Rome, England, France, Spain, and Mali.

8   Wilfred Owen (1893-1918), Isaac Rosenberg (1890-1918), and Siegfried Sassoon (1886-1967) were British poets who fought in World War I and wrote poetry about it. Owen and Rosenberg died in the war. Thomas Hardy (1840-1928), one of England's greatest novelists and poets, was their senior by over two generations, but he wrote about the war, too.

9   Edgar Allan Poe, "To Helen," *The Collected Works of Edgar Allan Poe*, vol. 1: Poems, ed. Thomas Ollive Mabbott (Cambridge: Harvard University Press, 1969), 163-171.

10   The director, producer, and screenwriter, Oliver Stone, created a trilogy of films based on the Vietnam War: *Platoon* (1986), *Born on the Fourth of July* (1989), and *Heaven and Earth* (1993).

11   Kathryn Bigelow won the Academy Award for best picture with her film, *The Hurt Locker* (2009), focusing on an American explosives and bomb dismantling unit during the Iraq war.

12   Horace, *Odes and Epodes*, ed. and trans. Niall Rudd (Cambridge: Harvard University Press, 2004), III.2.13, 144.

13   Wilfred Owen, "Dulce et Decorum Est" (1917), *The Collected Poems of Wilfred Owen*, ed. C. Day Lewis (New York: New Directions, 1963), 55.

14   William Wordsworth, *The Prelude: or Growth of a Poet's Mind* (1805; 1850), *The Prelude: A Parallel Text*, ed. Jonathan Wordsworth (New York: Penguin Books, 1996).

15   Walt Whitman, *Song of Myself* (1855; 1856; 1860; 1867; 1891-92), *Walt Whitman: The Complete Poems* (New York: Penguin Books, 2005).

16   Herman Melville, "Bartleby, the Scrivener" (1853), *Melville's Short Novels*, ed. Dan McCall (New York & London: W. W. Norton, 2002), 11.

17   British poet and painter, David Jones (1895-1974) fought in World War I, and his epic *In Parenthesis*, derives from both his wartime experience and his Modernist poetic aesthetic, employing lyric, discontinuity, collage, prose, and diverse diction.

18   Ammiel Alcalay, *from the warring factions* (Los Angeles and New York: re: public / UpSet Press, 2012). Further references to this source are noted parenthetically in the text as *warring factions*.

19   Semezdin Mehmedinovic, *sarajevo blues*, translated by Ammiel Al-calay (San Francisco: City Light Books, 1998).

20   Paul Fussell, *The Great War and Modern Memory* (New York: Oxford University Press, 1975), 146. Further references to this source are noted parenthetically in the text as *The Great War.*

21   Simone Weil, *The Iliad, or, the Poem of Force,* translated by Mary McCarthy (Wallingford: Pendle Hill, 1983), 6.

22   Cf. note 22, page 11 and pages 31-32 above.

23   See *War and Peace in Contemporary Eritrean Poetry* (Dar es Salaam: Mkuki na Nyota,2009) and *Who Needs a Story? Contemporary Eritrean Poetry in Tigrinya, Tigre, and Arabic* (Asmara: Hdri Publishers, 2005), with Ghirmai Negash. Cf. http://voiceseducation.org/content/eritrean-war-poetry, http://wlajournal.com/18_1-2/cantalupo-trans.pdf, http://www.universeofpoetry.org/eritrea.shtml. Accessed 7 December 2016.

24   A major British writer whose works spanned the late 19th and early 20th centuries, Rudyard Kipling (1865-1936) wrote journalism, short stories, novels, autobiography, and poetry.

25   Francis Fukuyama, *The End of History and the Last Man* (New York: Free Press, 1992), *passim.*

26   Cf. Charles Cantalupo, "Translating African Language Poetry: Is There Enough," *Modern Poetry in Translation* 3:16 (2011), 119-24; "Literature, Power, Translation, and Eritrea" below; and "Africa Antetranslation" below.

27   All of these poets are included in *Who Needs a Story? Contemporary Eritrean Poet in Tigrinya, Arabic and Tigrinya.* All of them are also discussed *War and Peace in Contemporary Eritrean Poetry.*

6

Literature, Power, Translation, and Eritrea

In memoriam: Beyene Haile and Isayas Tsegai[1]

Eritrea's famous stele at Belew Kelew and its inscription strike me as an archaeological, beginning of Eritrean literary production – be it written or oral – and it has never stopped.

In most other African countries, literary (again oral and written) composition of the highest critical standard in African languages has been frequently derailed, most notably by the imposition of colonial languages. Eritrean literature has also suffered the occasional imposition of colonial languages – both European and African – although to a lesser extent than countries likes Nigeria, Senegal, South Africa, Kenya, and many more African nations. In most other African countries, literature in colonial languages becomes the standard, but the example Eritrea defies this. Yet precisely such compositions by African writers in European languages are what has been published as African writing up till now with rare exceptions by editors and publishers – European, American, and African – and what has been featured in literary conferences and festivals, and this is still the case.

The conference held in Asmara, Eritrea, in January 2000 – Against All Odds: African Languages and Literatures into the 21st Century – and the statement that ratified at its conclusion – the "Asmara Declaration on African Languages and Literatures"[2] – are recent exceptions to this rule. Eritrea has always been an exception to it. Thus, neither the conference nor the declaration's emergence in Eritrea is merely coincidental.

Yet as one of the conference's organizing chairs, however, I can attest that the recognition of the fact of Eritrea's longstanding African language literary history was not widespread, at least in the project's planning stages, which went back nearly five years before it occurred. On the contrary, Eritrea's literary tradition was barely known, and only for the most part by Eritreans. Ngũgĩ wa Thiong'o himself, one of the conference's presiding chairs and, perhaps, the world's greatest advocate for African language and literature recognition and development, was not much aware of Eritrea's longstanding African language literary tradition until 1999 when he first visited the country.

Nevertheless, Ngũgĩ's African language literary accomplishments had been widely known and acclaimed at least since 1986, when he shocked Africa's and the world's literary and publishing establishment by proclaiming, "his farewell to English as a vehicle for...my writings" (*Decolonising*, xiv), embracing the African languages of Gĩkũyũ and Kiswahili instead. Subsequently, Ngũgĩ's statement radically altered African literary history. Furthermore, Ngũgĩ's critical writings after *Decolonising the Mind* continued to argue ever more persuasively for and in his fiction powerfully to exemplify African languages as a primary means for African literature production, which also won him near universal critical acclaim.

Yet again as one of the conference's organizing chairs, I must attest that Ngũgĩ, his advocacy of and his writing in African languages were the cause célèbre and the biggest reason, in addition to the organizers' unflagging efforts, why Against All Odds: African Languages and Literatures into the 21st Century received international and institutional, financial, and intellectual support to take place in Asmara in 2000. The project vitally depended on his renown and credibility to attract large amounts of funding and in kind support from the Ford and Rockefellers foundations, the World Bank, universities, nations, and other institutions and NGOs. A host of African international writers and scholars rode into town on this wave of support and, as the saying goes, the rest is history.[3]

This outline of the development and international financial support of Against All Odds, nonetheless, demonstrates a profound and fundamental incongruity. The African language writing and advocacy beginning in the 1980s of one man was far more widely known and appreciated than the long, thousands of years long, African language literary history of an entire nation and even of a region.

Still, the project would have been doomed had this incongruity in its development not changed. In May 1998, the bubble burst with the outbreak of war again between Eritrea and Ethiopia. I had first conceived the title of the project, "Against All Odds," to signify the literary achievement of 20th-century African writers despite all of the political and social problems that contemporary Africa had to face. With the outbreak of war and as a consequence the near-fatal decrease in international support that the project received, I saw its title transformed or extended from characterizing Eritrea's political struggle for independence, and African writers struggle to be heard, to signifying everything the project itself had to struggle against – including the war – if it was ever to succeed.

Furthermore, I realized that Against All Odds happened not merely because a kind of global coalition had converged with a brilliant and charismatic African writer as its leader, although this helped. Our real and greater power was local. Most of the national, international, academic, and corporate institutions and foundations that said they wanted to support us did not, and if they did, again it was with a lot less funding than we were originally promised. War or no war, we needed a lot more help if we were to continue.

Most of it came from one source: Eritrea. Eritreans mobilized, performing all the work such a gathering required: students and faculty from the university, the unions of Eritrean youth and women, local writers, musicians, dancers, businesses, clubs, state and city workers, and the *tegedelti*, that is, Eritrea's veterans of war. Moreover, inside Eritrea, the conference's happening was never "against all odds" – only outside. Of course, the historic example of Eritrea's confidence that it would win its thirty-year struggle for independence sustained our project, too. Whatever the odds, Eritreans had dealt with infinitely worse. How could they let us fail, mere child's play in comparison? Against what odds? As is said in Tigrinya,

Dehan dehan. Or in Italian, *Non si preoccupi.* No problem.

Still, I wondered? Where did this attitude, or philosophy, this spirit, this resolve come from? Again, one answer was obvious: the Eritrean revolution; its indomitable nationalism; its unprecedented struggle to triumph in winning independence. But surely that did not come out of a vacuum. The "wind of change" sweeping other African nations in the third quarter of the 20th century towards independence as well as popular Marxist insurgencies and revolutions worldwide also provided some context and inspiration for the Eritrean struggle, too.[4]

But where else might I find its source? Might it be in Eritrea's literature, again oral or written? If so, this may also not be a surprise, but it is a story that is only beginning to be told. The stories of African literatures in colonial languages and even those of literary latecomers to African languages like Ngũgĩ and others may be more widely known. This is a reality, yet it is a misconception that must change. And it is changing, thanks to Against All Odds, Ngũgĩ's example and support, the "Asmara Declaration," Eritrean writers and their translation, Hdri Publishers, Africa World / Red Sea Press, East African Educational Publishers, Mkuki na Nyota Publishers, and others.[5]

Ghirmai Yohannes (San Diego) concludes in his now famous poem, "I...have a story / That nobody knows and it's great – / I am the story" (*Story*, 79). In *War and Peace in Contemporary Eritrean Poetry*, I write that all of Eritrea's poets clearly demonstrate that they have a story, too. "If 'nobody knows' them, or if they are only known for the most part to Eritreans, then" the "purpose" of my book is "to make them known." Furthermore, "Eritrea can be truly known, only when" its literature is "known."[6] Or in other words, as the journalist and scholar, Said, laments, after Eritrea's armed struggle, "the other face of Eritrea" still needs to be known because "the world [has] never seen or heard our voices except through the gun."[7] On a more individual but related note, the historian, Alemseged Tesfai attributes his literary motivation to a desire for the history of Eritrea in the 1940s and 1950s to sound as a distinct, clear voice to fill a silence and a kind of vacuum of Eritrean historical knowledge when various countries are claiming Eritrea has no history of its own that is separate from theirs and thus falsely substantiating the rationale of Eritrea's annexation.[8]

Precisely with such an Eritrean voice more widely and clearly heard, what is not Eritrean but what is all too frequently attributed to Eritrea might be replaced or, at least, more seriously and widely challenged and discredited, or at least balanced. Words like "secretive," "isolated," "belligerent," "remote," "unverifiable," "unrepresented," "unresponsive," "negative," "arms trafficking," "starving," "underreported," and more, applied to Eritrea as if only such words could describe it, might someday not be the most often used descriptors in headlines and news stories. Perhaps I should restate, "not... the most often used." I cannot say, "never used" – literature has its limits, too.

Yet I have asked before and I ask again: "What nation can ever be known without" its literature being "known" (*Eritrean Literature*, 115)? Furthermore, is a nation even conceivable, or little beyond that, without its literature, both for its inhabitants and for anyone else who would recognize it? The incisive yet near primal eloquence of Isayas Tsegai in his poem, "I Am Also a Person," answers both questions, re-enacting in personal terms a situation in which any denial of the existence of Eritrea by either an individual within it or the surrounding world is impossible.

When I saw the world didn't care
If I was stripped of everything,
Even my dignity,
And beaten like a slave
Less than human,
I lost all sense of peace except in saying
I am also a person. I'm an Eritrean.

Story, 9

Embedded within such lines or functioning as a kind of critical premise or *a priori* for their assertion is a reality, famously phrased by Thomas Hobbes in his 17th-century, philosophical and literary masterpiece, *Leviathan*, about how the life of a human being can be "solitary, poore, nasty, brutish, and short" (*Leviathan*, 186). While Hobbes imagines such a condition to be the only alternative to a strong nation and its government, history provides many examples of situations – and the present supplies more – in which people suffer such Hobbesian conditions precisely because of government. Can any nation on earth say that it cannot be held responsible for such misery at some time in history, although debate about to what degree is undeniable, too?

Literature should never be allowed to veil or deny such a human reality. Literature, however, presents the reality of a nation in addition to, even as a part of, such painful facts of history. Furthermore, the reality of a nation as realized through its literature can outshine the all too human and all too common, historical failures of human politics and governance.

Notwithstanding caveats against literature's covering up and/or exposing any and all of the gruesome sides of the history of nations, their authors inevitably seem to prevail, and their names achieve a kind of unique indelibility that only the rarest political leaders attain. Or as Shakespeare writes in sonnet 55, "Not marble, nor the gilded monuments / Of princes, shall outlive this powerful rhyme" (*Riverside Shakespeare*, 1759). Think of England and its famous authors along with William Shakespeare: Geoffrey Chaucer, John Milton, William Wordsworth, Jane Austen, Alfred Tennyson, Virginia Wolf. Think of France: Michel de Montaigne, François Rabelais, Moliere, George Sand, Gustave Flaubert, Marcel Proust. Think of Italy: Petrarch, Dante Alighieri, Torquato Tasso, Giacomo Leopardi. Think of Ireland: James Joyce, W. B. Yeats, Samuel Beckett. Think of Rome: Ovid, Virgil, Horace, Juvenal. Think of Greece: Homer, Sophocles, Euripides, Sappho. Think of the United States: Ralph Waldo Emerson, Nathaniel Hawthorne, Henry David Thoreau, Edgar Allan Poe, Emily Dickinson, Edith Wharton, Henry James, T. S. Eliot, Ezra Pound, Ernest Hemingway, William Carlos Williams…. The lists can go on and on. The names are familiar. But try to come up with as many names of prime ministers, kings, queens, presidents, and the like when these writers live and write. Other than for the rare historian, few or none can. If this is not literature as power, what is? Not that the political powers that be or the supreme responsibility of good governance should be denigrated. Without it, writers no more than anyone else can survive Hobbes's state of nature. Still, the names and the works of the writers and other artists remain more widely recognized than all but a comparative handful of political leaders.

Admittedly, such catalogues of writers are Eurocentric. Which African nations and cultures can or will assert themselves similarly in terms of their writers when their political leaders may be forgotten? Such a question may be difficult, challenging, ignorant, insensitive, and even insulting. But can it be inspiring, too?

The question reminds me of a meeting with Kassahun Checole and Ngũgĩ wa Thiong'o when we were planning Against All Odds, particularly how we would use $250,000 from the Ford and Rockefeller foundations to fund African-language writers to come to Asmara: a lot less than we had been promised before the war, but enough – for which we were grateful – to carry out at least part of our plan. Kassahun begins:

> "You know, now we may have a problem. Whom should we invite? I can think of three or four in Tigrinya and many more in Amharic but . . . ."

> Now Ngũgĩ interrupted, "Yes, I have several names of Gĩkũyũ writers, both in Kenya and in here. Of course there are many Swahili and South Africans."

> I wrote down the names Kassahun and Ngũgĩ suggested and said, "Who else?" Neither Ngũgĩ nor Kassahun spoke. Hoping they weren't expecting me to add any names, I said, if only to break the silence, "I'm trying to remember the name of the writer in Chichewa whom I heard in Malawi."

> "We will need help," Kassahun sighed, smiling and shaking his head.

> "Yes," Ngũgĩ answered, rubbing his hand on his forehead. "Who do we have in Mande, Akan, and Hausa?"

> "And Yoruba, Sotho, Wolof, and Xhosa," Kassahun added.

> "We have so many, too many, but who are they? Where are they?" Ngũgĩ responded, his voice trailing off, "It's a mystery so far...."

> *Joining,* 195-96

The episode directly relates to the question of *why* African writers in European languages dominate what has been published as African writing up till now. The answer is, quite simply, that not enough writers in African languages are known beyond their local, national, and regional surroundings.

In the case of Eritrea, where its literature thrives is obvious: Eritrea. Beyond this, Eritrean literature thrives in a good number of international journals, in print and online, and in books that since roughly the beginning of the 21st century have mostly included translations of Eritrean poetry, both contemporary and traditional, as a Google search can readily demonstrate.[9] Not as widely disseminated but still important, Carlo Conti Rossini, Nefa'e Ethman, Enno Littmann, Jacques Faitlovitch, and Johannes Kolmodin document a thriving Eritrean literature in early 20th-century collections of Eritrean poetry.[10]

Still, this is not enough. It barely scratches the surface of what can be known about Eritrean literature. (The same can be said for archeology in Eritrea.) From the time of the stele in Belew Kelew until now, the amount of literature, including orature or oral literature, must approach the inconceivable – not that all or even much of it is known. Fiction, nonfiction, poetry, drama – Eritrean literature has it all. There is plenty. I say this with total confidence, even though I only know the literature, for the most part, through translation. How can there not be? Where there is language, there is literature. Where there are nine languages or more, there are nine literatures or more. Thus, the opportunities for writers and scholars in Eritrean languages and literatures are innumerable. One outstanding example is Hdri's anthology of Tigre language stories, poetry, tales, curses, blessings, and more, titled *Mieras* (2010).[11] The book is monumental and begging for literary critical and scholarly attention *and translation* as soon as possible.

Yet again, how can such an achievement and many more equally laudable, Eritrean literary projects become known outside of Eritrea? Or is it time once more in describing such an endeavor to dust off that old phrase used to characterize Eritrea's 30-year armed revolution as well as the little African literary revolution that took place in Asmara in January 2000? Is a project to make Eritrean literature more widely known "against all odds," too? I have had reasons to think so, but I am not going to make the same mistake as I did back in the late 1990s and in 2000 when I tried to describe what can happen when Eritreans are involved. Still, difficulties remain.

One example would be my own efforts to publish *War and Peace in Contemporary Eritrean Poetry*, before it came out from Mkuki na Nyota Publishers in Dar es Salaam in 2009.[12] The book was rejected by just about every publisher in the United States and England who publish titles in African literature, as well as by a clutch of publishers whom I thought should be publishing on African literature, and nearly all stated the same reason in their rejection letters – the topic was too narrow. Allegedly, there really was not enough – subject matter or readership – to warrant such a book. Such an editorial judgment went against my own thinking, which I stated in the first sentence of the book's "Foreword": "To discuss the entire contemporary poetry" – not to mention all of the poetry, much less all of the literature – "of most if not all countries requires more than a book, and Eritrea is no exception" (*Eritrean Poetry*, xi).

To expand this assertion: the African language poetry and literature of nearly every country of Africa, or of most African languages – be they national or transnational or regional – warrant book length studies like mine. Nor is such an approach necessarily unique to Africa.

For instance, Michael Naydan, translates and publishes books of Ukrainian poetry and fiction. His multiform efforts have created a kind of critical mass that unprecedentedly and unmistakably establishes Ukrainian literature in the annals of world literature, as it has never been before. Moreover, through translation he has majoritized a previously minoritized literature: minoritized, I should add, by a political history of brutal proportions and intensity, again not unlike many of examples of African language literature, particularly Eritrea's. For example, of the 1500 writers Stalin executed in the 1930s, at least half, 750, are Ukrainian.

A plethora of literary talent, they are, nevertheless, as Naydan recalls, an "executed Renaissance."[13] The recognition and critical study of African language literature is at the beginning of uncovering any number of examples of "an executed Renaissance" of writers or poets and storytellers. Yet working in African language literature and its translation is a part of the struggle to prevent such executions from continuing.

A major achievement in establishing once and for all the power of Eritrean literature and in beginning to make it known to the world is the first book by Ghirmai Negash, *A History of Tigrinya Literature in Eritrea*, subtitled "The oral and the written, 1890 – 1991 " (1999).[14] It is a model of what can and should be done for the literature of any African language in any African nation or region. The first, the pioneering, and thus far the only book of its kind on the subject, it is a 240-page testimony, providing the evidence for why Ghirmai Yohannes / San Diego's lines, "I ... have a story / That nobody knows and it's great – / I am the story" (*Story*, 79) can represent the historical consciousness, the supreme confidence, and the justifiably high ambition of contemporary Eritrean literary practice.

Another major achievement by Ghirmai has followed: one that will rewrite African literary history of the 20th century. He has translated *The Conscript*, a novel written in Tigrinya by Ghebreyesus Hailu, initially in 1927, and first published in 1950.[15] The novel is undoubtedly great, yet its translation is momentous for the literary world. In translation, moreover, *The Conscript* provides an example of how literature can most reveal its power.

The Conscript tells the story of an Eritrean whom the Italian colonial army conscripts and sends to Libya to quell a colonial uprising in that country. Hailu depicts his character's emotional struggles and develops a plot that leads him to refuse combat against Libya's Arab freedom fighters. He realizes that he should not be fighting the colonized instead of the enemy he has in common with them: the colonizers, in this case the Italians.

The book is a postcolonial long before the term became popular *and* written in an indigenous African language – two vitally important "firsts" in African literary history.[16] With all due respect, the longstanding chorus of assertion that Chinua Achebe's *Things Fall Apart* (1958) written in English is the first modern African novel should pause and at least think twice.[17] This most basic premise of 20th and 21st-century African literary study is challenged and undone. Hailu writes *The Conscript* in Tigrinya over thirty years before Achebe's achievement. Not to question either its monumental stature or its unique literary power, the fact remains that *The Conscript* predates the publication of *Things Fall Apart* (1958) by almost a decade. Furthermore, *The Conscript* in Tigrinya predates Ngũgĩ wa Thiong'o's first African-language novel in Gĩkũyũ, *Caitaani mũtharaba-Inĩ* (*Devil on the Cross*) in 1980 by over fifty years.[18]

Hailu's narrative maintains a strong momentum: Tuquabo's passive and sentimental home life in an Eritrean village deepens into a scenery that transforms his psyche as he arrives in a sweltering Massawa to board a ship to Libya. Eventually he realizes that he is on a journey to hell, into a heart of darkness. Two horrific days in the Libyan desert include an even more horrific battle. He survives all but almost to die of thirst. Hailu devotes an entire chapter to it. Finally, Tuquabo returns to his homeland. He is a forsaken and guilt-ridden shadow – or is it simply a mature version? – of his former self.

The Conscript also contains a kind of proto-anthropological study of Libyan Arab culture in contrast to Habesha. Does its characterization raise questions about whether Tuquabo is truly Eritrean or unwilling and unable to distinguish between Habesha culture in Eritrea and Habesha culture in Ethiopia? Such self-consciousness and sensitivity, albeit pertinent in the present, can be irrelevant to the true identity of Tuquabo as Hailu presents him. He is born in an Eritrean village. He is raised there, and it is the home to which he returns at the end of the story. Hailu offers a distinctive portrait of Asmara and Eritrea, a specific place in a specific time. He portrays the life of a man, a father, a mother, and a citizenry who cherish and have a unique sense of their homeland. At the novel's outset, when Tuquabo departs for Massawa on his way to Libya, he feels he is on a fateful and long journey while he also suffers the pangs of being away from home. Where he is leaving from, passing through, and going to are all distinct and different places. Furthermore, Tuquabo can be endearing, engaging, charming, and shrewd, yet most credible in his general reticence, nearly always communicating through understatement.

A less local and regional or more pan African analysis of Hailu's Tuquabo reveals a stunning contrast with Achebe's Okonkwo in

Things Fall Apart. Both characters embody a crucible for the culture from which each emerges. Differing from Achebe's creation, Tuquabo's awakening to the evils of empire provokes his rebellion and survival rather than his destruction, in fact, his self-destruction. Tuquabo resolves on anything but Okonkwo's obsession with tradition that he fashions into a delusion of his macho prowess and indigenous exceptionalism as his people's hero manqué. Instead, Tuquabo is an everyman, a distinctly Eritrean one at that.

Ghebreyesus Hailu's *The Conscript* stands as a vital and important, pioneering and major work of fiction that comes from Africa in an African language in the 20th century. Ghirmai Negash's translation reinforces such an unprecedented achievement and is readily accessible to students, scholars, and general readers and enjoyed for generations to come, in and outside Africa. *The Conscript* is a timeless and unforgettable work of literary beauty for Eritrea, Africa, and for the world.

Such high praise for *The Conscript*, including a call for it to be a basis for the rewriting of 20th-century African literary history, is based on its translation. In addition to *The Conscript*, nearly my entire engagement with Eritrean literature as well as with my Eritrean colleagues yet with any and all African language literature is based on translation. It is my lifeline, although this dependency is not unique to either Eritrea or Africa. I depend on the translation of all literature except English language literature. Albeit my first love to whom I remain faithful, it is still limited and not fully comprehensible without further knowledge of the literatures of Europe from its beginnings until now, the ancient Greeks and Hebrews, Eastern cultures, African cultures, as I have been arguing, and more – all of which I can know only through translation.

In the case of *The Conscript*, if it is to change, to rewrite, to correct African literary history – to replace inaccurate old knowledge with more accurate new knowledge – it must be through translation. Similarly, to turn momentarily to another scholarly discipline, a likewise corrective effect on African and world political history would result through a translation of Alemseged Tesfai's *Aynfelale* ("Let Us Not Separate"), *Kab Matienzo ksab Tedla Bairou* ("Eritrean Federation with Ethiopia: From Matenzo to Tedla"), and *Ertra akab FedereSn nab GobeTan Sewran* ("Eritrea: from Federation to Annexation and Revolution").[19] Again similarly, an understanding of the traditional poetry of Eritrea, as an element of the traditional poetry of Africa, yet as an element of the legacy of poetry to the world, would result through the translation of Solomon Tsehaye's monumental *Massen Melqesn Qeddamot* on the subject.[20] And again, a better understanding of the art of the novel, the African novel, the Eritrean novel, and the novel in world literature would result from the translation of works like Beyene Haile's.

Take, for example, the novel he writes in his late teens in 1958, *Abidu Do Tibluwo*, now translated and published *Mezghebe: Would You Say He Was Mad*, the *bildungsroman* and portrait of a young artist, written in the same year as the publication of Achebe's *Things Fall Apart*.[21] In the 1970s, as Alemseged Tesfai can recall, the work is widely denounced for its lack of Marxist principles, which in retrospect can seem misguided, although it is, at least, in keeping with the times. Fortunately, however, *Abidu Do Tibluwo*'s story does not end there. Its new translation heralds a rewriting of 20th-century African literary history once again, and the voice that summons such a project is again Eritrean. Moreover, with the publication of the translations of both *The Conscript* and *Mezghebe* in 2013, it is an *annus mirabilis* yet a new beginning for Eritrean, African, and world literature.

Or is this to claim too much for the importance and the potential of the translation of literature in Eritrea from its indigenous languages? Are there not enough speakers, readers, or writers of its major languages? Are there more in London in Shakespeare's England, or in Dante's Italy, or in Virgil's Rome, or in Homer's Greece, or in King David's Jerusalem or in Edgar Allan Poe's America? No. And would anyone argue that such works as Shakespeare's plays, Dante's *Divine Comedy*, Virgil's and Homer's national epics, the psalms of David and the Bible as a whole, and the writing of Edgar Allan Poe, should not have been translated; that they have only local interest; that the world would be better off if they merely remained in their own original languages? Isn't the world unimaginable, vastly impoverished, and terribly misunderstood without them. Still the world, except in their respective native countries, only knows them through their translation.

Thus, the prospective outcome of African language literature translation and its publication is exceedingly bright.

But its current state is dim. Consider this survey of poetry alone – not to mention fiction and literary nonfiction – in journals, books, and on websites.

The UK's *Poetry Translation Centre* (http://www.poetrytranslation.org/): translations from nine African countries but only three in indigenous African languages.

Words Without Borders (http://www.wordswithoutborders.org/): eighteen poets in translation but only one from an indigenous African language (Ghirmai Yohannes' "Unjust Praise" in Tigrinya). Seven in Arabic but ten from French and Portuguese.

The UK's *Poetry Society* (http://www.poetrysociety.org.uk/): next to nothing.

The USA's *Poetry Foundation* (http://*www.poetryfoundation.org/*): Nothing.

The UK's *SOAS Poetry Translation Centre* (http://www.soas.ac.uk/cts/): translations from six of the fifty-four African countries; 11% of African countries, but roughly 0.2% of Africa's languages.

The literary journals *Wasafiri* (http://www.wasafiri.org/) in the UK and *Callaloo* (http://www.callaloo.tamu.edu/) in the USA, which claim a strong connection to African cultures: next to none.

Wild Berries Inside and Behind the Yard: An Anthology of Contemporary Botswana Poetry (2008):[22] no African language poetry, although 2% of the country is English speaking and 78.2% Setswana speaking.

The Trickster's Tongue (2006):[23] nearly 400 pages of African poetry, and only one selection of indigenous language poetry – Yoruba. Nevertheless, the book includes the translation of inscriptions in Greek and Latin from Carthage, with an assertion that they should be recognized as African due to their geographical location in Tunisia.

Gods and Soldiers: The Penguin Anthology of Contemporary African Writings (2009):[24] Of the thirty items, only four are translated, and those from the French. There is no mention of an African language.

The Penguin Book of African Poetry (2008):[25] the most popular anthology of African poetry and currently in its fifth edition. First published in 1963, it is all in English and contains few translations of African language poetry.

The *American Literary Translators Association*, ALTA (http://www.utdallas.edu/alta/): After thirty-five annual conferences, it has still not included a single scholarly session on translations from African literature.[26]

There is more poetry translated and published, to take one example, from a single country with one language like Romania than a continent with fifty-four countries and thousands of languages.

Such a vast imbalance or incongruity can be attributed to a similarly large misperception and the widespread inability to recognize a basic fact. African literature exists primarily in African languages, which require translation. To speak of the relationship of one continent's languages and literatures to another's and to the rest or the world, how could this *not* be the case – still Africa is the exception to such a common sense notion. Of all the continents, Africa has the least amount of translation from its languages' literature, excluding Antarctica, of course, although there is probably more widespread knowledge about penguins than about African language writers. Well-known political formulae attribute this wild imbalance, like countless other African problems, yet all too often as if they are unique to Africa, to the destructive nature of colonialism and neocolonialism, which persist, of course. Still have such remedial efforts as these analyses provide done much to change the situation? If one African-language book was published and/or translated for every time these arguments have been made and agreed to – time and time again – the problem might be closer to being resolved.

I foresee a day, nevertheless, when reading African authors who only write in English, French or other colonial languages will look as obtuse as someone only reading authors who write in Latin during the European Renaissance? I foresee a day when there will be as many books and handsome volumes on the shelves of African language literature – both in the original and in translation – as there are of beloved English and European vernacular Renaissance literature. In the role of Secretary of State and delivering a lengthy policy speech in Kenya, Hillary Clinton can assert that although "the story of Africa is told in stereotypes and clichés about poverty, disease, and conflict...the story we also need to tell, and tell it over and over again, is that many parts of Africa are rising to 21st-century challenges.... We have seen the changes, and we know what is happening right now."[27] But do we know, and what do we know about Africa, if we do not recognize that it must come from Africa first and in Africa's languages and their translation?

Eritrean literature in African languages and their translation, nevertheless, is a bright and ever more glowing exception in a world and a literary world that has not yet realized that African literature in the future and in part already lives primarily in translation like the rest of the world's literatures. There are more translations of poets from Eritrea in print and online than from any other country of Africa. Their work is the subject of songs, documentaries, radio broadcasts, articles, websites, and books. But Eritrean literature in translation has only begun with its contemporary poetry, a sampling of traditional oral poetry, a few plays, essays and short stories, an early 20th-century novel and a handful of outdated, colonial collections. The challenge to do much more remains.

Is it against all odds? Maybe to writers and scholars from outside Eritrea, but how can it be for Eritrea itself, where its literatures in all their languages are alive and thriving day in and day out. Eritrea's being a leader in Africa in promulgating a long, brave, and exemplary ancient and modern tradition in the development of its languages and of their literature, oral and written, has for too long gone either unrecognized, especially externally, or taken for granted, internally. Yet a recent essay by Ngũgĩ wa Thiong'o suggests just how far ahead Eritrea is of the norm for Africa.[28] In Kenya, for example, Ngũgĩ laments that recently "Parliament voted to ban African languages in public places", an unconceivable prohibition in Eritrea, unless one could imagines "public places" utterly silent or devoid of people. Ngũgĩ also observes that "in most African countries before but more so after independence the majority is denied access to their languages because the state has marginalized them to the point of official invisibility. English, French and Portuguese take the pride of place in the body politic" – yet another unthinkable state of affairs in contemporary Eritrea. Ngũgĩ wonders, is it "not too much to ask that demonstration of competence in at least one African language be made a condition for promotion?" Should someone "be allowed to stand for councils and parliament without showing a certified competence in an African language?" And should not "a knowledge of one or more African languages…be a requirement at all levels of graduation from primary to colleges?" Requiring competence in at least one African language for promotion in school, graduation, and serving in public office? Such competence is universal in Eritrea: a given, established, historical, and undeniable matter of fact. It is not hope but a reality.

But Eritrea must set yet one more African example. Every great nation offers its literature to the world, beginning with the original, but it requires translation. Eritrea's unique and notable beginning in the translation of its literature notwithstanding, how can this effort continue to, in Ngũgĩ's word, "thrive"?

Walter Benjamin, provides two ways to proceed to meet this challenge, one ideal or philosophical, and one more practical. First, the ideal: "It is the task of the translator to release in his own language that pure language which is under the spell of another, to liberate the language imprisoned in a work in his recreation of that work."[29]

By "pure language" Benjamin can mean a language that does not really or literally exist – at least as we commonly understand what language is – but is a kind of current of common understanding that flows freely from one human being to another, at least in writing, regardless if they speak the same language, even because they do not speak the same language or come from the same place, time, or people. Furthermore, the translator is inspired by the language "of another," even while not quantitatively understanding much or any of it, but qualitatively understanding a purer, more revealed sense of his or herself in that other language than could be known in his or her "own language." Still, this greater understanding cannot merely rest as an intimation from the other language but must be actively "liberated" not merely through listening but recreating or liberating from the other language through its *translation* a greater language that is still his or her own but greater than it has ever been. Thus a great translation increases the scope and power of the translation's language beyond what it was before the translation, for example, the way a translation of the Bible will inevitably and profoundly enrich the language it is translated into. The greatest translation of the Bible in English, the King James version, published in 1611, has famously had a profound effect on the history of English, including its' literary history.[30] Ngũgĩ once said to me that the most influential and beautiful book in Gĩkũyũ was its translation of the Bible. And as for the Bible's original language, while it cannot be literally enriched from the language of its translation, if only due to the temporal limitation of the original having come first, the original's language is inevitably better understood, or more fully interpreted and comprehended, in terms of style, content, or both than before it was translated. This, too, can be a property of what Benjamin calls the "pure language" that both an original and its translation not only share but also aspire to.

Approaching the subject of translation in a more practical and less philosophical way, Benjamin also writes:

> a...basic error of the translator is that he [sic] preserves the state in which his [sic] own language happens to be instead of allowing his language to be powerfully affected by the foreign. Particularly when translating from a language very remote from his [sic] own he [sic] must go back to the primal elements of language itself and penetrate to the point where work, image, and tone converge. He [sic] must expand and deepen his [sic] language by means of the foreign language.
>
> "The Task," 81

Testifying for such a process based on my own experience, I recall the middle of February 1999 when I am in London and receive an email from Reesom Haile, containing the poem, "*Alewuna, Alewana*," the first poem for translation that he ever sent me, both in the original Tigrinya in Latin letters and with a half literal / half doggerel version in English.

In the Tigrinya version, nearly every line seemed to rhyme. Also, the singsong version in English settled on abstractions and generalities without a single image.

"Maybe you are right about Tigrinya being too difficult to translate," I said to Kassahun when I told him about the email as we emerged from the Piccadilly Tube station to walk to the British Council headquarters, International House, for our meeting [to discuss its offering financial support for Against All Odds].

"Still, you can try. You poets only speak your own language to yourselves anyway," he replied as I thought about the rhythm of the poem I had heard in Asmara – "eZM! Z-eEZM! eZM! Z-eEZM! eBUM! Z-eEZM! eBUM! Z-eEZM!" It made the jostling Piccadilly crowds seem unreal, and I felt like a ghost passing among them. Even as we sat with the director of the British Council, well known for his work in African literature and whose rumpled demeanor enhanced his OBE status and supreme position in Britain's cultural bureaucracy[31], his words and promises of support seemed no more substantial than the steam rising at first from the surface of our tea in comparison with the original Tigrinya rhythm I kept hearing behind my eyes. I worried about getting it into English instead of getting more than verbal support for our project from the patronizing director.

Joining, 181

The scene took place at the same time as the war between Eritrea and Ethiopia was revealing Against All Odds' wide ranging NGO and international funding as too much empty rhetoric. But

101

...in translating the poetry of Reesom Haile, I was finding the opposite....an independent voice steeped in Eritrean oral poetic traditions and, as the poet Rimbaud – who may have lived in or at least passed through Eritrea in the 1880s – demanded, "absolutely modern,"[32] yet in a way I had never experienced and had to learn. For example, "*Alewuna, Alewana*" in Reesom's eponymous poem meant "we have, we have," the "u" and the "a" signifying gender, respectively men and women. Since the words recurred so frequently in the poem, in my first translation I set up a kind of grid, with "We have" positioned at the corners and key points, as in concrete poetry. Next I had them feed into the poem's second recurring words – "men" and "women" – via the poem's third most recurring word, "Who," which led to a verb describing what men and women could do to rebuild Eritrea: sacrifice, gather, provide, lead, grow, study, persist...and so on. Along the lines of the innovative 20th-century [American] poet Charles Olson,[33] I imagined the poem as a kind of field of energy filled with the poet's spontaneously projected language.

When I emailed my translation back to Reesom, he rejected it in an email the same day. As I read past the rejection and Reesom explained what he was looking for instead, I thought of Kassahun...[Checole's] contention about the 20th century... writers collected in the book *Black Lions*:[34] that they were modern but in ways that still weren't recognized. I also recalled what Zemhret Yohannes said in our first meeting: that he looked for a parallel between tradition and change. I had to find an English approximation for the poetic process of writing in Tigrinya....

The poetry Reesom wanted had few critical equivalents in English, especially not modern: spontaneous, fresh, oral, unforgiving, accessible, and public without becoming empty words, broken promises, and sinking expectations: a kind of daily bread or common currency for all kinds of people – writers, children, artists, young professionals, working people, the elderly, government people – to create a universal rapport of give-and-take.

Joining, 184-85

This incident marks the beginning of my experience in translating poetry from Eritrea: trial, error, and failure; a wrong first step precisely because I was relying on my own language and only on the poetic tradition that I knew, both in terms of history and composition or techniques, however informed and current. To cite Benjamin's terms once more, the language of my translations had "to be powerfully affected by the foreign...[which was so] very remote from my own...[and I had to] go back to the primal elements of language itself...[to] expand and deepen" what I wrote. Still, how could I not, confronted with a poem so monumentally ambitious, calling for yet another kind of rewrite of history, in this case, through the repeated assertion of "We have...we have...we have...we have," profoundly reversing the most popular misconception of Africa, as well as of Eritrea, that it was a place that did not have: that did not have medicine; did not have money; did not have governance; did not have languages; did not have freedom? With "*Alewuna, Alewana*" Reesom Haile (*Voice*, 44-45)) created a new icon not only of Eritrea but also of all of Africa.

After this initial experience, Eritrean poets continued to confront me – unknowingly and not deliberately I should add – with a style and a content that further required I change any preconceptions I had about their work that were not at least in part derived from their experience and language as much as from my own. For example, I had to move from an understanding of poetry's existing for the most part despite a surrounding culture, which is an American experience, to a culture in which poetry appeared central, as in Eritrea, appealing across a broad social, educational, and political spectrum. A recognition of which position for literature and poetry was better or worse was not so much my concern, nor is it now, as simply realizing this difference and letting it affect the way I would write a translation.

Only the process did not stop there. I felt powerless and even regretful when I began to realize that through this linguistic cultural exchange of writing translations of Eritrean poetry my own poetry began to change. I neither sought nor wanted it to change and even tried to resist. I had written and published six long poems, four of them in my book of 2004, *Light the Lights*, totaling over 3700 lines in all, which I considered to be a kind of epic recounting the cultural shift I had made in coming to African cultures from Western cultures.[35] I staked my literary reputation on this. Critics called it experimental, urgent, imagistic, wild, churning, visceral, surreal, and dynamic. It garnered critical praise, professional recognition, and promotion. But nearly all of the writing predated my translating Reesom Haile and later the poets of the anthology, *Who Needs a Story*, after which I found myself unable to write poetry as I had been, even if and when I wanted to. In sonnet 111, Shakespeare wrote about a person's "nature" being "subdued / To what it works in, like the dyer's hand" (*Riverside Shakespeare*, 1769): the way through immersion that a hand becomes the same color as the cloth or leather it is dying. Translating Eritrea's poetry "subdued," dyed my poetry in a way I never expected and that even now I am not able to fully explain. I tried to explain, nevertheless, in these opening lines from the poem, "*Fognatura*." Written on a visit to Asmara, they described a process of casting off one's cultural moorings, not necessarily intentionally, but being buoyed up, nevertheless, by the *plus ultra*, Latin for "further beyond," where literature and power cannot be attained without translation.

> Traveling, passing the portals
> Of dissociation and older
> Than anyone I see, alone
> And in a language not my own,
> Why end up here again? Abstract
> Except for the pangs of leaving
> Home? The reasons have no effect.
> The eloquence of the unknown
> Takes over.
>
> *War*, 37[36]

---

1   I dedicate this essay to these two major, contemporary literary artists because they both had died recently and roughly a month apart, as I

was preparing and about to deliver the lecture upon which this text is based. Written before their deaths, it presents their respective work as vital and prime examples of truth and beauty in Eritrean literature. The embodiment of its aspirations, their work should never die. Beyene Haile (1941-2012) – novelist, poet, playwright, painter, and educator – was one of Eritrea's greatest writers and artists and its most avant-garde. He wrote three novels: *Abidu'do Teblewo* (1965) or "Mezghebe – Is He Mad?," *Deqwan Tebereh* (2003) or "Tebereh's Shop," and *Titsbit Bahgu* (2006) or "Setting the Bar." Only *Abidu'do Teblewo* has been translated into English. His narratives can be complex, employing collage, stream of consciousness, magical realism, ambiguity, and other experimental, Modernist techniques to focus on artistic and intellectual life, including politics. Isayas Tsegai (1956-2012) was a soldier, poet, dramatist, theater and film director, and producer. His first book of poetry *Lemin Leminey* became known as one of the greatest poetic, lyrical expressions to come out of Eritrea's revolutionary struggle for independence. His work as a dramatist and theater director, including children's theater, was pioneering and precedent setting in post-war Eritrea's cultural development. His films *Milenu, Timali, Guya,* and *Fikrin Kuinatin* earned him the appellation of father of Eritrean cinema.

2   See pages 53-55 above.

3   Cf. note 14, page 10 above.

4   Applied to Africa, the phrase, "wind of change," is identified with the British prime minister, Harold Macmillan. Addressing the South African Parliament on February 3, 1960, he said, "The wind of change is blowing through the Continent. Whether we like it or not, this growth of national consciousness is a political fact."

5   See African Books Collective for the most up-to-date and comprehensive listings of Africa-based publishers: http://www.african-bookscollective.com/. Accessed 22 February 2017.

6   See Charles Cantalupo, *War and Peace in Contemporary Eritrean Poetry* (Dar es Salaam: Mkuki na Nyota, 2009), pages 115-17. Further references to this source are noted parenthetically in the text as *Eritrean Poetry*.

7   Said Abdulhay, email to Charles Cantalupo, 8 March 2008. See note 11, page 56 above.

8   Alemseged Tesfai, lecture, Penn State University, Schuylkill Campus, 13 April 2010.

9 See note 1, page 48 above.

10 An Eritrean, Nefa'e Ethman helped Enno Littman produce his groundbreaking scholarship on Tigre literature early in the 20th century. During the same period, Carlo Conti Rossini published Eritrean oral poetry, including *Canti Popolare Tigrai* (Tigrinya Popular Songs). Jacques Faitlovitch, and Johannes Kolmodin also produced early 20th-century collections of Eritrean and Ethiopian literature.

11 Mussa Aron and Dessale Berekhet, *Mieras* ("Heritage: a treasure collected from the traditions of the Tigre peoples") (Asmara: Hdri Publishers, 2011).

12 See "The Story on *Who Needs a Story.*" pages 31-57 above.

13 Michael Naydan, "Ukrainian Avant-Garde Poetry Today: Bu-Ba-Bu and Others," *Slavic and East European Journal*, 2006: 50 (1), 455.

14 Ghirmai Negash, *A History of Tigrinya Literature in Eritrea: The oral and the written* (Leiden: CNWS Publications, 1999; rpt. Africa World Press: Trenton, 2010). See note 32, page 12 above.

15 Ghebreyesus Hailu, *The Conscript* (1927), *Hadde Zanta*, trans. by Ghirmai Negash (Athens: Ohio University Press, 2012).

16 "Postcolonial: Occurring or existing after the end of colonial rule; of or relating to a former colony. In later use also: of or relating to the cultural condition of a former colony, esp. regarding its relationship with the former colonial power." *Oxford English Dictionary.* (http://www.oed.com.ezaccess.libraries.psu.edu/view/Entry/263746?redirectedFrom=postcolonial#eid. Accessed 20 December 2016.)

17 Chinua Achebe, *Things Fall Apart* (1958), Norton Critical Edition, ed. Francis Abiola Irele (New York: W.W. Norton & Co., 2008).

18 Ngũgĩ wa Thiong'o, *Caitaani mũtharaba-Inĩ* (1980), *Devil on the Cross* (London: Heinemann Publishers, 1982).

19 Alemseged Tesfai, *Aynfelale* ("Let Us Not Separate") 1941 – 1950 (Asmara: Hdri Publishers, 2001). Cf. *Kab Matienzo ksab Tedla Bairou* ("Eritrean Federation with Ethiopia: From Matenso to Tedla Bairu") 1951 – 1955 (Asmara: Hdri Publishers, 2005). Cf. *1956-1962, Ertra akab FedereSn nab GobeTan Sewran* ("Eritrea, from Federation to Annexation and Revolution"), *1956-62* (Asmara: Hdri Publishers, 2016).

20 Solomon Tsehaye, *Massén Melqesn Qeddamot* ("Oral Poetry of Our Ancestors"), (Asmara: Francescana Printing Press, 2012).

21   Beyene Haile, *Abidu Do Tibluwo* (1958), trans. Huriy Ghirmai: *Mezghebe: Would You Say He Was Mad?* (London: Azab Publishers, 2013).

22   *Wild Berries Inside and Behind the Yard: An Anthology of Contemporary Botswana Poetry*, ed. Jen Hamilton Emery (Gaborone: Macmillan Botswana Publishing Co., 2008).

23   *The Trickster's Tongue: An Anthology of Poetry in Translation from Africa and the African Diaspora*, ed. Mark Angelo de Brito (Leeds: Peepal Tree Press, 2006).

24   *Gods and Soldiers: The Penguin Anthology of Contemporary African Writings*, ed. Robert Spillman (London: Penguin Books, 2006).

25   *The Penguin Book of African Poetry*, ed. Gerald Moore and Ulli Beier, fifth edition (London: Penguin Books, 2007).

26   Accessed 17 June 2013.

27   Hillary Clinton, "Remarks at the 8th Forum of the African Growth and Opportunity Act". 2009, http://www.state.gov/secretary/rm/2009a/08/126902.htm. Accessed 17 June 2013.

28   Ngũgĩ wa Thiong'o, "Linguistic Power-sharing: Culture and the Freedom of Expression," *Sunday Times*. 2012 Literary Awards, June 21, 2012 (http://bookslive.co.za/blog/2012/06/25/speaking-my-language-Ngũgĩ-wa-thiongos-address-at-the-2012-sunday-times-literary-awards/). Accessed 17 June 2013.

29   Walter Benjamin, "The Task of the Translator" (1923), trans. Harry Zohn, *Theories of Translation: An Anthology of Essays from Dryden to Derrida*, ed. R. Schulte and J. Biguenet (Chicago: University of Chicago Press, 1992), 80. Further references to this source are noted parenthetically in the text as "The Task."

30   *The Bible: Authorized King James Version* (1611), ed. Robert Carroll & Stephen Prickett (Oxford: Oxford University Press, 2008). Further references to this source are noted parenthetically in the text as *KJV*.

31   "OBE" is an abbreviation for Order of the British Empire and is awarded by the United Kingdom to citizens with major achievements in the arts, sciences, and society.

32   Arthur Rimbaud, *Une Saison en Enfer (A Season in Hell)*, (1873); *A Season in Hell and Other Works / Une saison en enfer et oeuvres diverses*, ed. and trans. Stanley Appelbaum, (New York: Dover Publications, 2003), 43.

33   See note 18, page 11, above.

34   *Black Lions: the creative lives of modern Ethiopia's literary giants and pioneers*, ed. Reidult Knut Molvaer (Lawrenceville & Asmara: Red Sea Press, 1997).

35   *Light the Lights* presents close-ups from a variety of points where three continents – America, Europe, and Africa – collide and join, yet all thirteen poems of *Light the Lights* connect with Africa. They are poetic re-enactments of evolutionary evidence that all human beings have origins in Africa. The poetry of *Light the Lights* is also a reversal of the cultural journey of St. Augustine, the 3rd-century bishop of the African city of Hippo who traveled to Rome to become one of Western civilization's most important and influential writers. Thus *Light the Lights* is a cultural journey beginning in the United States, returning to ancestral and intellectual roots in Europe, yet continuing to find them in Africa" (http://africaworldpressbooks.com/light-the-lights-by-charles-cantalupo/).

36   Charles Cantalupo, *Where War Was – Poems and Translations from Eritrea* (Tanzania: Mkuki na Nyota, 2016), 31. Further references to this source are noted parenthetically in the text as *War.*

7

Literature, Translation, and National Development in Eritrea

S hould encouraging and investing in literature be among Eritrea's development aspirations? What is the role of literature in the way forward for Eritrea, particularly in education? The challenge of such questions, although they might not sound poetic, is worthy of Eritrea's traditional oral poets, the *getamo* and *getemti*[1] among their festive *massé* and funereal *melkes*,[2] who are also known for the challenges they hurl at their audiences as well as at each other. What is literature's responsibility to society, and particularly what is Eritrean literature's responsibility to Eritrea?

Writing on the death of the Anglo-Irish poet W. B. Yeats, the British poet, W. H. Auden asserted, "poetry makes nothing happen,"[3] to go against the grain of leftist political activism in the arts in the 1930s. The line recurred to me three quarters of a century later as I sat in an important, local official's office waiting to speak with him. A similarly important official burst out of its doors, saw me, and said to my colleague, "Who is that?" in Tigrinya. My colleague replied, "That is Charles Cantalupo. He translates Eritrean poems." "Poems," the official replied dismissively. "We need bread not poems." At that moment I should have said to my colleague, "Please translate

Auden's classic line to him in Tigrinya, 'Poetry makes nothing happen,'" but I kept quiet.

Contrary to Auden, however, I think that poetry and literature make plenty happen. Furthermore, it can be like bread, a daily bread. While I have almost always thought this way, for me it has become more than a mere assertion, Romantic ideology, or a tenet of sentimental humanism – particularly since I started coming to Eritrea in 1995 and seeing that Eritrea embodies the development of literature. Thus a question like what is the role of Eritrean literature in the development of Eritrea becomes an anagram of a question just as important and challenging: what is the role of Eritrea in the development of Eritrean literature. To go forward, they go together, because here they have always gone together. Eritrean literature's responsibility to Eritrea has been and should be inseparable from Eritrea's responsibility to Eritrean literature – "as it was in the beginning, is now, and ever shall be." I apply the ancient doxology to a literature of ancient origins.

Such a substantial record can here only be recounted in part, but it provides a canon of powerful texts and contexts and a way forward for critical, educational development. A tool of the trade in teaching literature is the anthology of primary texts: an anthology of American literature, English literature, French literature, Italian literature, and most substantial national literatures. The first entry in an anthology of Eritrean literature to mark a beginning of Eritrean literary history – be it oral or written – could be the inscription on a stele at least three thousand years old in a place called Belew Kelew in the southern part of the country. I have tried to translate its Sabean script. It says something like "strug l agains al od s wi..." (*War*, 31). Also on the stele, there is a sun and quarter moon with words that can say "Adulite. / Join here and write" – "Adulite" suggesting pre-Axumite.[4]

From the time of the stele in Belew Kelew until now, how could the amount of literature, including orature or oral literature, not be voluminous, even if much of it, like Eritrea's archaeological heritage, remains to be discovered? Just because we do not know them, at least not yet, does not mean that we do not search for them. Yet subsequently we find them, and we find more and more. Fiction, nonfiction, poetry, drama – how could Eritrea not have it all? Even though I only know the literature, for the most part, through translation, how can I not ask such rhetorical questions? How can they not be a given for any contemporary national literature with an ancient tradition? Greece? China? Egypt? India? Where there is language, there is literature. Where there are nine languages or more, there are nine literatures or more.

As a result, the opportunities for writers and scholars in Eritrean languages and literatures are innumerable. A literary tradition reaching as far back as the stele of Belew Kelew, as the Bible, and as the Koran demands and deserves more. This is the challenge. I remember hearing it in Seghenyetti, resounding in Tigre through the valley of the sycamores, bringing in the new millennium in January 2000, when Zeineb Yassin, Mother Zeineb declared,[5]

> I'm burning
> To boil you
>
> Like raw,
> Delicate meat
> In liberation.
>
> But I'm too ancient
> For the army.
>
> Too helpless
> To be the minister
> Of education
>
> And too bold
> In this damn world.

War, 57

Eritrean literature like all great literature must be "bold / In this damn world." As an aspiring nation, Eritrean knows this lesson all too well. It is vital to the way forward, too.

Many a milestone of Eritrean literature succeeds its beginning in an ancient stele. To take a few examples, they appear in the early 20th-century collections of Eritrean poetry by Carlo Conti Rossini, Nefa'e Ethman, Enno Littmann, Jacques Faitlovitch, and Johannes Kolmodin.[6] The first of a three-volume project by Solomon Tsehaye, *Massén Melqesn Qaddamot*, reveals a 250-year old poetic tradition still alive in the present.[7] For Solomon, to anthologize and to study Tigrinya's highest form of traditional poetry provide a "knowledge of history, culture, language, politics, religion," and more, and is "also very entertaining."[8] The aim is to teach and delight, as in the famous formulation of *prodesse et delectare* by the ancient Roman poet, Horace (*Ars Poetica*, 478). Yet the poetic genre of *massé* and *melkes* become a search for meaning in the past as well as an expression of identity, values, ethics, psychology, and a comprehensive vision of the world, as Tsehaye affirms. This Eritrean, timeless, and universal tradition particularly resonates in the poem, "What Shall I Call You," a masterpiece from the 1860s by the oral poet, Weldedingel.[9]

What if I call you the
Mountain where we live?
I remember people begging
"Help us up! Help us down!"

And the same people complaining,
"He's too strong! Too strong!

Let them try
To take your place – at least, try!
                                        War, 77

A record of more such literary transformations of the original stele at the beginning of Eritrean literary history can be found in Ghirmai Negash's *A History of Tigrinya Literature in Eritrea* (1999).[10] Eritrean literature and orature in Tigre, Arabic, and other languages, even Italian and English, should generate similar critical studies. Recovered by scholars, how could such primary texts not reinforce, articulate, and provide the recognition of an Eritrea ever more aware, bold, aspiring, and positive about the truth and beauty in its future? The sempiternal presence of the stele in Belew Kelew, the self-determination in the lines of Mother Zeineb, the community consciousness of the *getemti* in their *massé* and *melkes*, and the inscrutable poetic and political power of the elegy by Weldedingel form an historic and literary context for a modern nation of Eritrea to emerge. A dynamic process, it reveals a new nation yet a long-standing literary culture that is a paragon of African literature and languages. Not that such a recognition is universally acknowledged: the verbal art of Eritrea like Eritrea itself has had to struggle to be heard. The key fact, however, is that both have struggled together, and neither could be or would be silenced. Alemseged Tesfai's trilogy of Eritrean history is the most powerful documentation of this fact. *Aynfelale* ("Let Us Not Separate," 2001), *Kab Matienzo ksab Tedla Bairou* ("Eritrean Federation with Ethiopia: From Matenzo to Tedla," 2005), and *Ertra kab FedereSn nab GobeTan Sewran* ("Eritrea – From Federation to Annexation and Revolution," 2016) reveal an indomitable national eloquence that would not be denied despite any number of historical developments that lined up against it.[11] The development of Eritrea and the development of its literature are a dynamic process. They go hand in hand and can be seen as their mutual *raison d'être*.

Furthermore, the tradition represented by the stele in Belew Kelew continues and is renewed to an unprecedented degree. For example, the recent publication of translations of two 20th-century novels, *The Conscript* (2013) and *Mezghebe* (2013) marks a new beginning for Eritrean, African, and global literature as well.[12]

The well-known British newspaper, *The Guardian*, published an article called "What You Need to Know about Eritrea."[13] It failed to mention Eritrean literature. I have said it before, and I say it again: "What nation can ever be known without" its literature being "known?"[14]

For over two decades, I have been witnessing and writing about the powerful the role of literature in Eritrea's development. Those fragments on the stele at Belew Kelew – "struggle…against all odds…win…join here…write" – echo over and over, and certain experiences spontaneously generate to become their own momentous stele. For example, I never imagined, much less experienced, such an intimate yet public connection between a poet and his audience, yet a vast audience, as when I first heard Reesom Haile perform his poems at the Expo Festival in 1998.[15] Awash in a flood of humanity that flowed towards where he stood, I could not believe at first that a poetry reading would be the source of such a spectacle. But there he stood: tall and thin, with a much-grayed Afro, hollow eyes, a long sharply angular face, and wearing a dark tweed sport jacket with a classic white Eritrean blanket or *gabi* draped over his shoulder and wrapped around him. As the applause and the cheers for the first poem he read began to recede, he reached his long arm out to the crowd and, as he formed a wide swirl with the icon-like dark gold fingers of his hand, slowly intoned, *"Alewuna"* (*Voice*, 45). The multitude all around responded in near ecstatic unison but in the exact same tone, *"Alewuna."* The poet countered with *"Alewana"* the same way, again as did the crowd, which triggered another performance *prestissimo staccato* of his most famous poem interrupted roughly every ten or twelve syllables with the more slowly pronounced refrain, *"Alewuna, Alewana,"* echoing back and forth, back and forth. What does that mean, I asked the person next to me. "'We have.' It means 'we have, we have,'" he said. I witnessed for my first time, as I would time and time again, the lyrical banishment of any sense of Eritrea as a "have not" – a place of deprivation, denial, poverty, and loss. How could I not also feel Reesom's poem in Tigrinya like a new kind of anthem for all of Africa to embrace? Still, I did not know the source of the poetry's inspiration until, shaking Reesom's hand after the reading and trying to congratulate him on his extraordinary performance, he interrupted me and said, "It is the people who make the performance in Eritrea." Reesom Haile believed that his country, Eritrea, was best known through its languages – in his case, Tigrinya – and specifically through Eritrea's literature. From the first moment I heard him performing his poetry at the Expo cultural festival in Asmara to an audience of thousands in August 1998, I knew he was right. Thus was I initiated in the belief that the development of Eritrean literature and the Eritrean people went hand in hand: *"Dehai, dehai,"* "Voice…voice!" (*Voice*, 13).

My initiation received near immediate confirmation since I was primarily in Asmara to work on the conference, Against All Odds: African Languages and Literatures into the 21st Century.[16] Several chapters of my memoir, *Joining Africa*, tell the whole story about the conference, and my eponymously titled documentary about it is also available.[17] A major outcome of the conference, the "Asmara Declaration on African Languages and Literatures," is now historic. Yet its originating in Eritrea could not be more fitting and, in retrospect, is hardly a surprise. In most other African countries, the composition of literature in colonial languages becomes the norm. But it never does in Eritrea. Thus, Eritrea is recognized as a leader in the literature of African languages – both historically as well as currently: a fact also testified to at conference of hundred of scholars in Nairobi at Kenyatta University in 2014 called From Asmara 2000 to Nairobi 2014: New Horizons and Trends in African Languages and Literatures.[18]

In the early stages of planning for Against All Odds, President Isaias Afewerki of Eritrea agreed to serve as Against All Odds' honorary chair and to be joined by Meles Zenawi, prime minister of Ethiopia, and Yoweri Museveni, president of Uganda. Against All Odds would be a summit of language, politics, and power. A long list of universities, foundations, NGOs and corporations accepted our invitation for support: Penn State, New York University, the University of Iowa, the University of Asmara, Addis Ababa, Makerere; the African Literature Association and the African Studies Association; many 5-star NGOs and Fortune-500 corporations; the Economic Commission of Africa, the OAU (Organization of African Unity, as it was then called); UNICEF, UNESCO, and UNDP. Even Oprah Winfrey expressed interest in doing a telecast from the conference. I was in negotiations with her Harpo Productions.

But on May 6, 1998 in the one-street, hot and dusty, border town of Badme, any discussion about African languages and literatures could not be heard through all the gunfire between Eritrean and Ethiopian troops determined to decide who would own the place. A kind of dirge drowned out the praise song of Afro optimism about an imminent African Renaissance that Against All Odds would generate:

Back to war.
Shut the door.

Forgive, forget before?
Now remember twice –

Then and now,
Shut the door.

War, 28

The halcyon days of gathering an unprecedented cultural coalition to support Against All Odds all too quickly revealed its fair weather friends. I did not know at the time, however, that I was about to witness yet again how the nation of Eritrea and the literature of Eritrea, yet now including literature from all over Africa, would go forward together.

Cities being bombed, trench warfare, massive attacks, counterattacks, ethnic cleansing, redeployment, strategic withdrawal, total victory – the news threatened to make the conference no more substantial than a dream. The war that began in 1998 burst the bubble of Against All Odds, and the immediate decrease in international support nearly killed the project. Alemseged Tesfai, was reporting absolute carnage on the battlefields of southern Eritrea.[19]

Up to this point, the development plan of Against All Odds depended on the positioning of Ngũgĩ wa Thiong'o as its spearhead. Widespread critical, national, pan-African and international recognition of his advocacy of and his writing in African languages were certainly the cause célèbre and the biggest reason for Against All Odds' initial success in garnering international support. But such a development resulted, nevertheless, in a conundrum. It depended far more on the international critical recognition of one man's roughly twenty-year African language writing and advocacy than on any recognition of the thousands of years long, African language literary history of Eritrea. Furthermore, only the latter, of course, and not the former could provide the multifaceted and generous local support, in kind and financial, logistics and venues for such an historic gathering to take place and succeed after all too much of its global support withdrew.[20] Thus, May 6, 1998, while marking the first day of the outbreak of yet another horrific war in Eritrean history, also became one more moment to recognize the literary and national development in Eritrea moving forward hand in hand.

The way forward for Eritrea in literature and national development pulled me along again in 2002, leading to the publication in 2005 of *Who Needs a Story: Contemporary Eritrean Poetry in Tigrinya, Tigre, and Arabic*.[21] It was a book of firsts for Eritrea, Africa, and the world: the first book to include poems from three of Eritrea's major languages in their original scripts of Ge'ez and Arabic; the first to feature poets who for the most part have never been translated and have remained unknown outside of Eritrea; the first to gather in a single volume Eritrea's most accomplished contemporary poets; and the first to be produced in Africa by a publisher making its first foray into the international bookseller's market.

Who Needs a Story remains unique in a world where literary anthologies of contemporary American poetry, Irish poetry, French poetry, British poetry, in short the poetry of most developed nations are abundant. The opportunities to create unique literary anthologies of contemporary poetry in other indigenous African languages are similarly abundant. But where are they?

As Ngũgĩ wa Thiong'o observed in a recent interview when I asked him why African language literature still had to struggle to be heard, Against All Odds and the "Asmara Declaration" notwithstanding,

> The conference we had in Eritrea, where we produced the "Asmara Declaration in African Languages and Literatures:" even for me, an advocate of literature in African languages – I was totally amazed…. It was a beautiful thing to see. But to get the resources, even within Africa, or to get the gathering going again, there is a problem. These days the resources that go… to promote African literature are given on the condition that it is not written in an African language: a prize to encourage African writers but they cannot write in their African languages if they want to submit their work. Governments in Africa and financial institutions like the World Bank have policies that are aligned to ensure that European languages

remain the dominant languages of education, intellectual production, and literary production.[22]

"But not Eritrea," I answered Ngũgĩ, as I also recalled the exception of the World Bank funding the construction of the amphitheater around a sycamore near Seghenyetti where Mother Zeineb and so many others performed at the Against All Odds conference a decade and a half before.

Many more public examples besides what I have recounted about seeing Reesom Haile first read in 1998, chairing Against All Odds, and editing *Who Needs a Story*, which are only personal, testify to the synergy between national and literary development in Eritrea: from the literary instruction, production, and translation that thrived at 'university of the revolution' in the field during armed struggle to the robust list of Eritrean authors, old and new, being published by Hdri and others.

To cite only one more example, I witnessed the profound inseparability of Eritrea from its literature – but also the anguish were this not the case – on July 24, 2012 at the funeral of Isayas Tsegai in Asmara's Patriots Cemetery. The day after the 56-year old soldier, poet, theater director, dramatist, and father of Eritrean cinematography had died unexpectedly,[23]

Thousands and thousands of men and women...
...have gathered to form a long procession from the church –
Orthodox under the Eritrean flag – as they follow
Body and flowers in two black minivans through the stucco
Walls of the graveyard: the men in Western clothes and the
women
Wrapped in traditional white and gauzy dresses with ribbons
Hemming their similar shawls. The men and women stay separate,
Never together until they reach the grave, where I'm hoping
Not to be visible. But instead my friends say I should be,
Pushing me into the front row, nodding, "Look. You should
see it."
Was that the message, the din of weeping, wailing, the crackling

Eulogies straining the metal speakers strung up on high poles;
Bricks lining six open graves, a growing mountain of flowers
Next to Isayas; his rest in peace or chaos all the same,
Like the wind, red clay and sunshine – indistinguishably hard,
Too bright and cold while the children who had joined the
    Isayas'
Theater group break through the crowd to throw themselves in
    his grave –
All while the Orthodox priests in day-glo shimmering vest-
    ments,
Waving their censers and loudly chanting barely could be
    heard?
After the funeral, mourners filled the restaurants, cafés,
And all the bars in Asmara. Joining is the only choice.

War, 50

Symbiotic, synergistic, simply reciprocal, the development of Eritrean literature in Eritrea *and* the development of Eritrea in Eritrean
literature can seem to defy standard critical terminology to characterize it. *A priori*, deductive, one-size-fits-all approaches that usually apply to the literature of developing countries do not seem to fit
a relatively continuous three thousand year old, indigenous language
tradition. To the waves of colonization that Eritrea has suffered –
from the Egyptians to the Turks to the Italians to the English to Ethiopia's Haile Selassie to its Marxist Dergue[24] – Eritrean literature has
acted, as Reesom Haile worded it, "Like a flywhisk" – "*esh!...esh!*"
(*Wheel*, 158).[25] The stele in Belew Kelew, Weldedingel, Gebreyesus
Hailu, Beyene Haile, and all the fighter writers in the field – seen in
their continuity – do not fit in a formulation like this from Frantz
Fanon:

> The colonial situation calls a halt to national culture….there
> is not and there will never be such phenomena as new cultural
> departures or changes in the national culture. Here and there
> valiant attempts are sometimes made to reanimate the cultural
> dynamic and to give fresh impulses to its themes, its forms,
> and its tonalities. The immediate, palpable, and obvious in-
> terest of such leaps ahead is nil.[26]

This is not a picture of Eritrea. The resounding of such Eritrean voices through the centuries also defies the subaltern characterizations of Antonio Gramsci[27] and Gayatri Spivak[28] – merely oppressed, barely if ever heard, outside or below the power structure. Fredric Jameson insists that "All third world texts are necessarily...allegorical," where "the story of the private individual destiny is always an allegory of the embattled situation of the culture and society."[29] This would require that texts by Weldedingel, Gebreyesus Haile, Beyene Haile, Alemseged Tesfai, Reesom Haile, and many others be considered as little more than medieval or like John Bunyan's *Pilgrim's Progress* from a Western perspective.[30] Still, to cast aspersions on either the art of allegory itself or *Pilgrim's Progress* would be similarly misguided.

Yet Jamison also decries any nationalism in literature. It should be "liquidated" (*Social Text*, 65). Whether such an imperious call for extermination should include the rich, world legacy of national literary epics like *Gilgamesh, Exodus, The Iliad, The Aeneid, Beowulf, La Chanson de Roland, El Cid, Sundiata*, and more, the reciprocal development of Eritrea and Eritrean literature is precisely what has saved the nation from liquidation, which is still a threat. Fanon also has observed that "national consciousness...is the most elaborate form of culture" (*Earth*, 1592). Were the "national consciousness" of Eritrean literature during the nation's thirty year armed struggle for independence and ever since to be lost, Eritrea itself would be "liquidated." As Alemseged Tesfai has said, "Eritrean history is a struggle between forces that have been trying to write off Eritrea as a nation, to simply ignore it as something that did not exist, and the heart of Eritreans that refused to bend to these forces of destruction."[31] The struggle of Eritrean literature has been coterminous, and it is not transnational in the now popular, critical sense that economic, social, and political boundaries among nations pose more of hindrance than a help to the creative spirit. He or she and all of us require "the uniforms" of one nation or another's to "guard you while you sleep," as Rudyard Kipling trenchantly put it,[32] which in all good faith should instill a singular national allegiance, which transnationalistic theory barely considers.[33] But such global politics notwithstanding, as Ngũgĩ again has contended with alarming simplicity and directness, "To be part of African literatures, we write in African languages" (*Transition*, 21). Consequently, to be a part of Eritrean literature is to write in Eritrean languages. From Belew Kelew till now, the continuity and the constant is the art of the Eritrean word.

The national literature of Eritrea defies the standard critical terminology of postcolonial studies because it is a time-limited mode of analysis, tied to colonialism like a Procrustean bed. Moreover, Eritrea's millennia-long literary tradition in indigenous languages sustains itself regardless of colonialism or not. The postcolonial critique, furthermore, is more timely than timeless: it must end, however reluctant its legions of adherents to admit this in the *schadenfreude* of their all but interminable iterations. I witnessed such an end and a much different sentiment two years ago at the "Asmara 2000 to Nairobi 2014" conference at Kenyatta University. Speaking in a plenary session, the Kenyan scholar and translator of African languages, Jayne Mutiga, asked the nearly two hundred similarly young African language scholars, "Have any of you ever been colonized?" They roared back, "No!" – to which she responded, "Neither have I."

The interdependence between the development of Eritrean literature and the Eritrea's development does not, of course, guarantee either the former's critical quality nor the latter's success. The former cannot be bound but must be freed by the latter. Nor can it insist that the former merely represent the latter or that it is the ultimate criterion. Again, they are co-equals. The representation, particularly if it is deliberate, of a national cause, as in Eritrea, or of similarly reductive formulations that would reduce literature to other causes like class, race, gender, and ideology is more likely to hinder rather than to help in the creation of aesthetic excellence or beauty. On the contrary, a long literary tradition commingled with a long national history – including nations with more than one major language – defies such artless, comparatively timely and superficial representation, which is precisely the strength of nations and/or languages with powerful literary traditions: Greek to Ge'ez; Hebrew to Hindu; English, Italian, French, German, American, Chinese, and many more, including Eritrean.

No one speaks more than a few of these languages, at best, but many have enjoyed and learned from literature in all of them through the process that bestows on a national literature a form of recognition second only, perhaps, to the embrace of its own nation: translation. In 1827, Goethe famously observed that "National literature is now a rather unmeaning term; the epoch of world literature is at hand, and everyone must strive to hasten its approach."[34] But world literature consists of national literatures or literatures in languages that are spoken by more than one nation. As no nation, including Eritrea, can be known without its literature, literature cannot be known beyond its geographical origin and its rudimentary understanding without translation. Both the question of what is the role of Eritrean literature in the development of Eritrea and the question of what is the role of Eritrea in the development of Eritrean literature must include "translation" in their answer.[35]

Knowledge of literature depends on translation. Take Dante: for all who read him, comparatively few read him in Italian. To take an even greater example: for all who read and know the Bible – in its myriad of translations – its readers in actual biblical languages, like Hebrew, or later translations, long-standing translations like the Septuagint Koine Greek or the Vulgate in Latin, are miniscule. No national or regional literature could function any differently. Even literature in an international language like English, which admittedly has many readers worldwide, still has such limits: as Charles Baudelaire had to be the first to translate Edgar Allan Poe into French and Julius Nyerere the first to translate Shakespeare's *Julius Caesar* into Swahili. For Against All Odds, Alemseged Tesfai performed a variation on this theme. He translated an English translation of a work by Ngũgĩ originally in Gĩkũyũ into Tigrinya.

As a non-native speaker, I plead for more translations of Eritrean literature and of all African language literature. They have to be translated, and they have to be translated beautifully. How else to know them – including any effort to know one, or a few, or however many more any individual can know, African or non-African notwithstanding – like so many of the world's great literatures, except through translation? When and how can this happen?

Widespread recognition of Africa's – and Eritrea's – political, economic, and social problems is a given, but the role of literature in national development yet its responsibility to develop national literature should be widely recognized, too. Moreover, a way forward, beyond the seemingly endless, critical litany of such problems and the partisan polarities they generate can become apparent precisely through such recognition. Not that they should be denied. On the contrary: they have been narrated, performed, sung, heard, seen, and read in Eritrean languages as well as in other African languages for decades, centuries, and millennia; as do they continue, including new kinds of problems. In a poem, "To My Graceful People," Reesom Haile clearly recognizes this:

> To please or displease, praise or condemn,
> Frighten or fear, adore or dismiss –
> We've been in this abyss.
> Together we break out.
>
> Enough polarizing
> Who lives or dies?
> End it. Let peace rise.
> *Modern Poetry*, 91

The national development of Eritrea has recognized and depended on such a literary reality, but worldwide, even pan-African recognition is for the most part lacking due to both the overbearing tendency only to focus on Eritrea's political, economic, and social problems and to the lack of translation of its literary masterpieces. Their role, in their original languages, in Eritrea's national development is a also given. Yet their role, through translations, in Eritrea's international recognition and the international understanding of Eritrea is yet to be seen. When will that day come? All too often Eritrea is discussed, again like many African nations, as if it has no literature. Yet Eritrean literature, to use Matthew Arnold's famous phrase from *Culture and Anarchy*, is "the best which has been thought and said," about Eritrea.[36] For two decades, therefore, the recognition of the power of Eritrean literature has been my passion:

...the words have their own spell or, less dramatically: listen
First and say nothing and listen, listen...something is in it
Faraway from any words I know yet taking me back to
Where they begin and then mixing in and...what? Is it joining,
Freeing them? Deepening, purifying them to be my own?
Origins different but still the feeling, I'm this person, too,
And not a stranger? This land is not strange? Neither of us is
Dead? We connect through the words that lead us only
    together
Back to them or through the dread of being silenced before
    this?
Tell me that hieroglyph. Is it over five millennia?
Now hear me say it in your way true to mine and with love,
    too.
Something is missing? It's close...and like that sycamore, just
    as
Anciently singing four seasons simultaneously – lyrics
Translating into the names I hold most dearly and against
Fear that my loved ones are taken from me, yet as in a dream
I can't cry, whisper or breathe? But even then, what is that
    stele:
Towering at the beginning, sun and quarter moon inscribed;
Trying to read it...the dust, or tears, or too much light in my
    eyes?[37]

1   See note 21, page 11 above, and see page 21 above.

    Two major genre of traditional Eritrean oral poetry are *massé* and
    melkes. *Massé* are poetry, performed by highly respected oral po-
    ets, the *masséniyas*, is produced at social gatherings and is usually
    reserved for special occasions of importance in society. Typical set-
    tings where the *massé* poems are performed are during the com-
    memoration of local chiefs or national figures and during marriage
    ceremonies.... The *melkes* shares most of the features of the *massé*
    form, but, unlike the generally festive and prototypically panegyric
    content of the *massé*, the poems in this category are exclusively per-
    formed to mourn a dead person, during a funeral.

2   See Ghirmai Negash, *A History of Tigrinya Literature in Eritrea: The oral and the written* (Leiden: CNWS Publications, 1999; Africa World Press: Trenton, 2010), 99.

3   W. H. Auden, "In Memory of W. B. Yeats" (1939), *The English Auden*, ed. Edward Mendelson (New York: Random House, 1977), 242.

4   The Axumite empire revolved around Axum (or Aksum) in northern Ethiopia, stretching from Arabia and Yemen to Sudan and Egypt at various times from the 1st to the 9th-century CE. "Adulite" culture derives from the ancient Red Sea port city of Adulis, designating an era from the 9th-century BCE to the 5th-century CE.

5   Veteran fighter in Eritrea's armed struggle for independence and mother of nine, Zeineb Yassin – popularly known as Mother Zeineb – died at the age of 87 in 2005. Born in Afabet in 1918, she joined the Eritrean People's Liberation Front (EPLF) in 1977, challenging the tradition of a male-only fighting force and exemplifying equal rights for women in Eritrea. A well- known oral poet, she was also famous for saying "Even the stones are burning," when asked to describe the course of the war in her village. "Under the Sycamores," translated from Tigre, is based on a transcription of her performance on 1/15/2000 at the Against All Odds literary festival and conference in Eritrea.

6   See note 10, page 106 above.

7   Solomon Tsehaye, *Massén Melqesn Qeddamot* ("Oral Poetry from our Ancestors"), (Asmara: Hdri Publishers, 2013).

8   Solomon Tsehaye, "A Conversation with Solomon Tsehaye," *Issayas' Blog* (Issayas Tesfamariam). http://kemey.blogspot.com/2013/09/a-conversation-with-solomon-tsehaye.html. Accessed 29 August 2016.

9   A 19th-century, Tigrinya oral poet, Weldedingel is believed to have composed the original poem for a chief's funeral in the 1860s.

10   Cf. note 23, pages 11-12 above.

11   See note 19, page 106 above.

12   Cf. pages 92-95 above.

13   Mark Tran, "What you need to know about Eritrea – the Guardian Briefing." *The Guardian*, 17 August 2015, https://www.theguard-

ian.com/world/2015/aug/17/inside-eritrea-migrant-crisis-guardian-briefing. Accessed 29 August 2016.

14 See page 87.

15 Cf. pages 13-14 above.

16 See note 14, page 10 above.

17 Cf. Charles Cantalupo, *Joining Africa: From Anthills to Asmara* (East Lansing: Michigan State University Press, 2012), 125-235. Cf. Charles Cantalupo and the Audio Visual Institute of Eritrea, *Against All Odds: African Languages and Literatures into the 21ˢᵗ Century,* a documentary (East Lansing: Michigan State University Press; Oxford: African Books Collective, 2007).

18 From Asmara 2000 to Nairobi 2014: New Horizons and Trends in African Languages and Literatures (http://news.psu.edu/story/323905/2014/08/25/academics/distinguished-professor-cantalupo-travels-africa-invited-keynote). Accessed 29 August 2016.

19 Alemseged Tesfai, "A Defeat Denied: A Report from the Alitena-Mereb (Tsorona) Front," 20 March 1999 (http://www.dehai.org/conflict/articles/alemseged_egrimekel.html). Accessed 29 August 2016.

20 Cf. pages 84-85 above.

21 See "The Story on *Who Needs a Story*" above.

22 Ngũgĩ wa Thiong'o, "African Literature – Says Who? An Interview with Ngũgĩ Wa Thiong'o," Charles Cantalupo, *Transition* 120 (2016), 14. See the entire interview below. Further references to this source are noted parenthetically in the text as *Transition.*

23 See note 1, page 104-05 above.

24 See note 1, page 29 above.

25 Cf. page 20-21 above.

26 Frantz Fanon, *The Wretched of the Earth* (1963), *The Norton Anthology of Theory and Criticism,* ed. Vincent B. Leitch (New York: W. W. Norton, 2001), 1587-88. Further references to this source are noted parenthetically in the text as *Earth.*

27 Marxist literary philosopher and critic, Antonio Gramsci (1891-1937) focused on the relationship of literature, political power, and the life of the intellectual. Gramsci coined the term "subaltern" to refer to the majority colonized as opposed to the minority colonizer

and oppressor, with an overriding exhortation that the former should take back the power that the latter had unjustly seized.

28 Gayatri Chakravorty Spivak (1942-) is a literary scholar, theorist, translator, and critic, whose work invokes principles of deconstruction, feminism, postcolonialism, and Marxism to understand literature, philosophy, and politics.

29 Frederic Jameson (1934-) is an American contemporary Marxist literary theorist and scholar. Cf. Fredric Jameson, "Third-World Literature in the Era of Multinational Capitalism," *Social Text* 15 (1986), 69. http://www.jstor.org.ezaccess.libraries.psu.edu/stable/466493. Accessed 29 August 2016. Further references to this source are noted parenthetically in the text as *Social Text.*

30 John Bunyan (1628-88) was an English, Baptist writer and preacher whose most famous work, *Pilgrim's Progress* (1678), has never been out of print since its first publication. The work harkens back to early English Renaissance and medieval literary allegory, with many characters and settings that have the name of Christian virtues and vices

31 Alemseged Tesfai, *Against All Odds: African Languages and Literatures into the 21ˢᵗ-Century*, writ. & dir. Charles Cantalupo (Asmara: Audio Visual Institute of Eritrea; East Lansing: Michigan State University Press; Oxford: African Books Collective, 2007), 24:58-25:19.

32 Rudyard Kipling, "Tommy" (1890), *Rudyard Kipling's Verse* (New York: Doubleday and Company, 1940), 397.

33 Transnationalism, a popular term in late 20ᵗʰ and early 21ˢᵗ-century postcolonial studies, argues that individual national identities, borders, and even nations themselves can be politically and personally irrelevant and even delusional and destructive due to widespread, global immigration.

34 Cited by Ngũgĩ wa Thiong'o, *Globalectics: Theory and the Politics of Knowing* (New York, Columbia University Press. 2012), 44. Further references to this source are noted parenthetically in the text as *Globalectics.* German author and leading historical figure, Johann Wolfgang von Goethe (1749-1832) produced major works in a variety of genre, including drama, lyric and epic poetry, and prose.

35 Cf. "Literature, Power, Translation, and Eritrea," above. Cf. "Africa Antetranslation" below.

36   Matthew Arnold, *Culture and Anarchy* (1869), ed. J. Dover Wilson (Cambridge: Cambridge University Press, 1932), https://archive.org/stream/matthewarnoldcul021369mbp/matthewarnoldcul021369mbp_djvu.txt. Accessed 29 August 2016.

37   Charles Cantalupo, "Africa Antetranslation," *Minor Heroics* (2016), unpublished manuscript, 52.

8

Africa Antetranslation

In January 2000 in Asmara, Eritrea, a conference called Against All Odds: African Languages and Literatures into the 21st Century gathered writers, scholars, cultural activists, educators, NGOs, civic groups, students, publishers, artists, children, and thousands of Eritrean citizens for seven days to devote themselves to the art of the African word.[1] Conducted in African and other languages – including Arabic, Akan, English, Ewe, French, Gĩkũyũ, Italian, Kiswahili, Mandinka, Saho, Shona, Tigrinya, Tigre, Yoruba, Urhobo, and Zulu – Against All Odds created an environment in which African languages, performances (music, film, drama, readings, dance, and visual arts), and literary scholarship were a constant presence. While there had been many conferences on African literature, this was the first ever to focus primarily on African languages. Against All Odds concluded with the "Asmara Declaration on African Languages and Literatures," a declaration of African language independence, establishing once and for all an end to the hegemony of European languages in African literature. In the words of the "Asmara Declaration"'s preamble, "At the start of a new century and millennium, Africa must affirm a new beginning by returning to its languages."[2]

Since Against All Odds took place in January 2000, the role of African languages in Africa and the world has greatly increased. Ninety percent of the African language titles distributed by African Books Collective have been published in the 21st century. From UNISA in South Africa to Mkuki na Nyota in Tanzania to Hdri in

Eritrea and throughout the continent, the numbers of books by African language writers are more and more impressive. *Ecclesiastes* (12.12) states, "Of making many bookes there is no end" (*KJV*, 760), and books by African language writers are still, relatively speaking, at their beginning, but the enterprise is firmly established. Examples are many. In the case of one specific writer who is seminal to this development, Ngũgĩ wa Thiong'o, his Gĩkũyũ magnum opus, *Murogi wa Kagogo*, or *Wizard of the Crow*, which was in progress in 2000, is now published in Gĩkũyũ and English,[3] and it is a milestone of both African and world literary history. In the case of one specific language, newly published translations of two novels originally written in Tigrinya—*Hadde Zanta* [*The Conscript*], written by Gebreyesus Hailu in 1927 and published in 1950,[4] and *Abidu Do Tibluwo* [*Mezghebe – Is He Crazy*],[5] written at age sixteen by Beyene Haile in 1958 – can now challenge the longstanding chorus of assertion that Chinua Achebe's *Things Fall Apart*, published in 1958 and written in English, is the first modern African novel.[6] To interchange Eritrean fiction with Eritrean poetry, in 2005 Hdri published *Who Needs a Story? Contemporary Eritrean Poetry in Tigrinya, Tigre, and Arabic.*[7] Containing thirty-six poems by twenty-two contemporary poets and produced in two local and two global languages, *Who Needs a Story* was the first anthology of contemporary poetry from Eritrea ever published. Yet there is a need for an anthology of African language poetry and its translation like *Who Needs a Story* for every African nation. Furthermore, the poetry of every African nation requires book-length critical studies about it.

The very title of the conference, "Against All Odds," signified a kind of call to arms and a salvo of African language literary publications has resulted. In 2014, the title of the Zimbabwe Book Fair, "Indigenous Languages, Literature Art and Knowledge Systems of Africa" resulted from, according the organizers, the overwhelming number of submissions on the subject of African languages.[8] They are now in popular demand, if not in all cases then far more than they were fifteen years ago. Popular contemporary music, mobile phone apps, and greeting cards thrive in African languages, as do they flourish more and more on the web in general. Gmail is available in Zulu, Afrikaans, Swahili, and Amharic. A Google email alert on the term "African languages" provides at least one story a day, usually more. Even the "Asmara Declaration"'s worry over "colonialism and neocolonialism creat[ing]... some of the most serious obstacles against African languages and literatures" must adapt to such a new reality, asking whether digitalism, capitalism, and consumerism's embrace of African languages will dilute their profound and unique vitality, intellect, and continuity. Yet another affirmation of Against All Odds' legacy that indicates it beat the odds foretells an ever brighter future for African languages and literatures. Another large conference, From Asmara 2000 to Nairobi 2014: New Horizons and Trends in Africa Languages and Literatures took place at Kenyatta University.[9] With this, a new generation has emerged to lead the language struggle from the Cape to Asmara to Nairobi and beyond.

But as a non-native speaker, after Against All Odds and the progress of the last fifteen years, for me the translation of African language literature has become all but paramount. It still remains a matter of beating the odds. Thus, I plead for more African literary translation. As African language literature forges ahead, its translation lags far behind.[10] Two directives from the formative essay by Walter Benjamin "The Task of the Translator" (1923) can point the way to assure that African language literary translations achieve long overdue greatness and worldwide dissemination. First, Benjamin insists, "It is the task of the translator to release in his own language that pure language which is under the spell of another, to liberate the language imprisoned in a work in his recreation of that work" ("The Task," 80).[11] Benjamin's diction or choice of words, albeit his translator's, is revealing. The lowly, invidious word, "task," precipitously transforms itself into a visionary, romantic, and revolutionary act "to release...[the] pure...under the spell of another...to liberate the imprisoned." Yet the sentence performs in microcosm the way a great literary translation begins: mundanely identifying words in two different languages that equal or approximate each other; whereupon "the spell" of literary style and understanding, to take a famous example like the Bible, transform the Hebrew, Aramaic, or Greek into a text that can be considered to contain the greatest truth and beauty in the language into which it is translated.

Benjamin's second point returns to the translator's "task," its failures and chances for success. He focuses on what precedes and is required to aspire to a "pure language...of ...recreation" so that a literary text in one language becomes a literary text in another language. *Before* the "release" and liberation that result in the metamorphosis and flight of the once lowly "task" of translation,

> a...basic error of the translator is that he [sic] preserves the state in which his [sic] own language happens to be instead of allowing his language to be powerfully affected by the foreign. Particularly when translating from a language very remote from his [sic] own he [sic] must go back to the primal elements of language itself and penetrate to the point where work, image, and tone converge. He [sic] must expand and deepen his [sic] language by means of the foreign language.
>
> "The Task," 81[12]

Benjamin outlines a state or condition that I would name "antetranslation," i.e., "before translation." An antechamber is a small room before and that leads to a main room. To move from an antechamber to a main room is straightforward, but from antetranslation to translation? Not necessarily, as Benjamin contends. There can be forward movement or not. A "basic error of the translator" can result in antetranslation becoming a permanent condition, and antetranslation fails to become translation. Moreover, antetranslation becomes a condition of antitranslation, the "e" changing to "i," resulting in either a poor translation or no translation.

Describing "the task of the translator," Benjamin hardly focuses on the craft or the necessary mechanics of translation. Practically speaking, for antetranslation to become translation, particularly literary translation, the translator's "task," which Benjamin leaps over, is to move from reading or hearing "the foreign language" not only to the language of translation, but also from one set of grammatical and stylistic or rhetorical structures to another. The former observation might be obvious, overly obvious, but the latter, at least, intimates the art of literary translation itself. Antetranslation leads to poor translation or no translation unless an individual who is interested in literature in a foreign language translates it and realizes that it requires extensive thought and analysis, rhetoric and/or poetics, cultural identification and contextualization, yet many drafts and edits if there is any chance that the translation will have real merit. Still, Benjamin does not mention such literary necessities in "The Task of the Translator." Or, perhaps, they go without saying.

Instead, Benjamin asserts that what results in poor translation, so that it is no more than antetranslation or even antitranslation, derives from the translator's insecurity and defensiveness about whether his or her own language and presumably its national and cultural constructs can survive an even-handed and open-minded encounter and existential verbal and intellectual exchange with another language. The "error" of the translator is a belief that his or her language is originally "pure," whereas for Benjamin it is not. The possibility of a language being "pure" depends instead on the effect of the language to be translated on the original; an effect, furthermore, that propels the original language not only outward to encounter the language to be translated, but also inward so that the original language confronts and penetrates "the primal elements" of itself, including the status of whether it can even be original instead of a mere point where it converges with another language to be translated. No one language but the convergence of languages is the only original. Yet Benjamin's avowal is not meant as a truism of the history of languages but as a vital, critical premise for their contemporary and continuing translation and as a key to their well-being.

With exceptions, African language literature is in a state of antetranslation. Most translations are poor, and Benjamin provides a fascinating if general and theoretical reason why this is the case. But the greater problem is not merely one of quality, as Benjamin would have it, but also of quantity. There are far too few translations. Either way, African language literature is stuck in antetranslation, and such a status quo is untenable.[13] Yet at this moment in the history of African literary translation Benjamin's viewpoint is either taken for granted, after over ninety years since it was first published, or mostly forgotten. Either poor translation or no translation is the rule. Neither the need for translation nor the need for translation of the highest critical quality is widely recognized. Furthermore, the *de rigueur* explanation for the profound neglect of African language literature and similarly the disregard for its translation is not what Benjamin asserts but the historical, continuing, and all but incalculably adverse legacy of colonialism and neocolonialism. Political and social conditions are primarily to blame. Precisely such a contention results in African language literatures *remaining* in a condition of antetranslation, either untranslated or poorly translated.[14]

Even the world's most eloquent and powerful advocate for African languages and their literary translation, Ngũgĩ wa Thiong'o, considers their lack of standing or status in comparison with other languages in the world primarily as a result of their political, social, and economic repression. His landmark book *Decolonising the Mind* (1986) in fact focuses not on an individual mind but on "social forces…. imperialism in its colonial and neo-colonial phases…. [Its] control [of] the economy, politics and, and cultures of Africa" (*Decolonising*, 4). Crucially for Ngũgĩ, such "control" also extends to repressing "the choice of [African] language and the use to which language is put" in "creative initiative" and "self-definition," which he also describes not as individual but as "communal." One could even say that in Ngũgĩ's terms, imperialism and colonial/neocolonialism commit roughly the same "basic error" as Benjamin's translator. Delete his particular concern with language, and colonialism/neocolonialism is absolutely devoted to preserving its own state and not being "affected by the foreign."

The accuracy of Ngũgĩ's analysis is not the question, although the widespread acceptance of his scenario nearly three decades after its publication makes it sound simply historic and objective rather than critical and partisan. The question is how much further have African languages, particularly their literary translation, come from Ngũgĩ's undeniable milestone in African literary criticism? And what has prevented them, even if it might include some of the terms of Ngũgĩ's own argument, from coming further than they have?

The only literary analysis from an African perspective equal to or, perhaps, even more significant than Ngũgĩ's about African languages in *Decolonising the Mind* is Chinua Achebe's, roughly ten years earlier, in an "An Image of Africa: Racism in Conrad's *Heart of Darkness*" (1977). Joseph Conrad is "a thoroughgoing racist,"[15] according to Achebe, for his "dehumanization of Africans and Africa" (*Darkness*, 344) particularly because Conrad denies "language" to the "'rudimentary souls' of Africa. In place of speech they... [make] 'a violent babble of uncouth sounds.' They 'exchange... short grunting phrases'" and, at best, a few phrases of broken English: "Catch 'im....[g]ive 'im to us....eat 'im.... Mistah Kurtz – he dead'" (*Darkness*, 341).

Again, the accuracy of Achebe's *J'accuse* is not the question. The widespread rebuttals when he first stated it have subsided to a contrarian trickle. Like Ngũgĩ's analysis of oppressive political and social conditions as a result of colonialism, Achebe's viewpoint is a critical given and objective about not only Conrad's style and content of literary representation, its own superlative use of language notwithstanding, but also a historic reality. Still, the question remains, to repeat: how much further have African languages, particularly their literary translation, come since this undeniable milestone in African literary criticism? Has Achebe's powerful indictment of Conrad especially for his denigrating and racist characterization of Africans as having only "rudimentary" and "uncouth" language skills *and*, even worse, no languages of their own become a catalyst for any number of demonstrations of African languages' performative and literary power, including in translation, to move beyond antetranslation? Or could there be anything about Achebe's argument that might be counterproductive to such an ideal outcome?

Reinforcing his argument about Conrad's racism in denying language to Africans in *Heart of Darkness*, Achebe disparages Conrad's "lavish[ing] a whole page quite unexpectedly on an African woman who has obviously been some kind of mistress to Mr. Kurtz and now presides (if I may be permitted a little liberty) like a formidable mystery over the inexorable imminence of his departure" (*Darkness*, 340). To quote this Conrad passage at length precisely because there could be a good reason, hitherto unrecognized, why Conrad lavished so much on it or, at least, why a current reader should:

> She walked with measured steps, draped in striped and fringed cloths, treading the earth proudly, with a slight jingle and flash of barbarous ornaments. She carried her head high; her hair was done in the shape of a helmet; she had brass leggings to

the knee, brass wire gauntlets to the elbow, a crimson spot on her tawny cheek, innumerable necklaces of glass beads on her neck; bizarre things, charms, gifts of witch-men, that hung about her, glittered and trembled at every step. She must have had the value of several elephant tusks upon her. She was savage and superb, wild-eyed and magnificent; there was something ominous and stately in her deliberate progress. And in the hush that had fallen suddenly upon the whole sorrowful land, the immense wilderness, the colossal body of the fecund and mysterious life seemed to look at her, pensive, as though it had been looking at the image of its own tenebrous and passionate soul.

She came abreast of the steamer, stood still, and faced us. Her long shadow fell to the water's edge. Her face had a tragic and fierce aspect of wild sorrow and of dumb pain mingled with the fear of some struggling, half-shaped resolve. She stood looking at us without a stir and like the wilderness itself, with an air of brooding over an inscrutable purpose. A whole minute passed, and then she made a step forward. There was a low jingle, a glint of yellow metal, a sway of fringed draperies, and she stopped as if her heart had failed her. The young fellow by my side growled. The pilgrims murmured at my back. She looked at us all as if her life had depended upon the unswerving steadiness of her glance. Suddenly she opened her bared arms and threw them up rigid above her head, as though in an uncontrollable desire to touch the sky, and at the same time the swift shadows darted out on the earth, swept around on the river, gathering the steamer into a shadowy embrace. A formidable silence hung over the scene.

She turned away slowly, walked on, following the bank, and passed into the bushes to the left. Once only her eyes gleamed back at us in the dusk of the thickets before she disappeared.

Darkness 60-61

Achebe objects to Conrad's "withholding" "human expression" (*Darkness*, 341) or language from the woman, since she does not speak. Her being "some kind of mistress to Mr. Kurtz" and a "formidable mystery" become additional terms of disparagement. But is this all she amounts to?

Generally, a character's "silence" can be readily associated with the state of being oppressed and powerless due to race, class, or gender, but the examples in literature are too numerous to mention when a response of "silence" signifies cunning, wisdom, and power itself – with all these variations on the trope of "silence speaks" providing testimony that "silence," literally, speaks volumes. As in the well-known phrase of Cicero: *"cum tacent, clament,"* 'they cry out in silence.'[16] Or as John Keats writes in "An Ode on a Grecian Urn," a poem also about stunning visual but silent beauty, "Heard melodies are sweet, but those unheard / Are sweeter: therefore, ye soft pipes, play on...."[17] Closer to the Congo where Conrad's story takes place, could the extraordinary power and beauty of sculpture like the Kongo *nkisi n'kondi*, for example, the Mangaaka, albeit in a visual rather than a verbal language, ever be in doubt? What if the African woman in *Heart of Darkness* is an example of such "unheard" power, too?

At one point in his essay, Achebe himself seems perfectly content to acknowledge the power of African artistic expression that remains silent. Rightfully indignant at Conrad's portrayal of Africans as "savages...merging into the evil forest or materializing out of it simply to plague Marlowe and his dispirited band" (*Darkness*, 346), Achebe invokes "just north of Conrad's River Congo...the world's greatest masters of the sculptured form....the Fang people" (*Darkness*, 347). Achebe recounts a story of one of their masks being shown "to Picasso and Matisse, who were greatly affected by it.... The revolution of 20th-century art was under way! ... The event... marks the beginning of cubism and the infusion of new life into European art, which had completely run out of strength" (*Darkness*, 346). Not surprisingly, perhaps, Achebe says nothing of Fang language, literature, or orature, or of their translation in Conrad's time or the present. Nor are their translations, from the past or from the present, much in evidence now. Yet speaking of the Congo now, as more and more translations of its indigenous language literatures emerge, the silence of over five million people who have died in its modern wars must always be powerfully heard, too.

Again, there is no question that Conrad's portrayal of Africans in *Heart of Darkness* is racist in denying them language, but just who is denying whom in this passage? Could there be any other reasons besides Conrad's racism for her not speaking in such a dramatic moment? At other times, a reader is told, "she talk[s]... like a fury to Kurtz" (*Darkness,* 61), according to his only other partner on the river, the Russian in patches. Achebe may scorn the "African woman" in *Heart of Darkness* as "obviously...some kind of mistress to Mr. Kurtz," but she is, again according to the Russian, not merely vulnerable in the relationship. She wields significant power and not only sexually. Anything but devoid of "human expression," when she speaks to Kurtz, she "kick[s]...up a row" and makes "mischief" for him—even though, according to the Russian, who admonishes Marlow, "You don't talk with...[Kurtz]—you listen to him" (*Darkness,* 53). Apparently she does more than merely "listen." Furthermore, not only does Kurtz understand her – he'd better, at his own peril, understand what she says, according to the Russian. Obviously she speaks an African language that Kurtz knows but the Russian does not, who can only say, "I don't understand the dialect of...[her] tribe" (*Darkness,* 61). He also comments at the end of this scene, "I really think I would...shoot her," suggesting the outcome, certainly not desirable, if she spoke out in Lingala, Mongo, or Kikongo. Might she, therefore, have a good reason for not speaking in this particular scene?

Conrad himself calls her silence "formidable." And why not? First, it threatens the Russian, makes another crew member "growl," and the other agents or "pilgrims" onboard "murmur." Clearly, she makes them afraid. More than mere catering to the ogling male gaze—the crew is, after all, only men—her portrayal is as more than a mere object with little or no power in comparison with those who eye her. The crew and, perhaps, even a reader can hardly feel much power over her. Second, considering the slow unfolding and powerfully visual drama of the entire encounter within the "immense" (60) and "colossal" riverscape, its "silence" – also described by Conrad as "the hush that had fallen suddenly upon the whole sorrowful land" – forcefully compounds the moment's suspense. To accentuate this, the only actual sound that Conrad mentions in the entire passage is the "low jingle" of what she is wearing when she walks (*Darkness,* 61).

Conrad himself even seems to signal his narrative's awareness of her status, or lack thereof, as an African and as a woman if not explicitly as a victim of "racism," which must reduce her to "silence." In his words, she may be "proud" (*Darkness,* 60), "superb," "passionate," "stately," "magnificent," and "tragic" (*Darkness,* 61), but also she is "savage" (*Darkness,* 60) "wild-eyed," "ominous," "pensive," "tenebrous," "fierce," "dumb," "struggling," "half shaped," "brooding," "inscrutable," and "uncontrollable" (*Darkness,* 61) – whereupon she disappears. The fact is that for all her stunning appearance, and whether she speaks or not, once Kurtz is taken onboard "The Nellie," how can she be sure she won't be next? As Conrad writes, "her life... depend[s]... upon the unswerving steadiness of her glance," staring down and calling the bluff of the ship, so that she can quickly escape. This would be her situation not only in Conrad's fiction, but also, realistically, if the encounter were nonfiction or historical. Where is the example of an African man or woman dramatically confronting and speaking out against King Leopold's Belgian, apocalyptically brutal colonial enterprise and surviving? However extravagant Conrad's fiction in *Heart of Darkness,* such a scene would render it even more like fantasy. Yet this is the exact same brutal world of colonialism that she challenges silently and with great effect, if not wholly successfully, at least effectively. After all, she has made its greatest exponent, whose "making" (*Darkness,* 49) "[a]ll Europe contributed to" its "universal genius" (*Darkness,* 72) and "emissary of pity...science, and progress" (*Darkness,* 35) not only her lover, but also the only white man whom she considers worthy to know her language.

Writing in *Literature, Modernism, and Dance,* Susan Jones focuses on another aspect, besides the silence, of the power of the African woman in *Heart of Darkness*: her movement. She "presents a positive, celebratory aesthetics that privileges the *grace* of...human action."[18] Her "measured steps," according to Jones, have the power of dance. "The woman stops, turns, and fixes her eyes on the men in the boat, returning their gaze, and flings her arms up in a sublime gesture before proceeding, as before, with measured steps." Her "movement" is

> a form of kinetic communication beyond language. The woman's physical confidence and expressivity does not simply inspire anxiety in the...onlooker—it engenders admiration. Conrad presents the action of the African woman...as a manifestation of...and an expression of grace...where the reader/viewer is invited...to experience wonder, awe, erotic desire, but also approbation and fear.
>
> "Dance," 153

Next to space and movement, the silence of dance is its third dimension, and the profound silence of the woman partakes of the same elemental power.

Another obvious source of the African woman's power in *Heart of Darkness* is her physical beauty: "gorgeous" (*Darkness,* 60), "treading the earth proudly," "her head high," "a crimson spot on her tawny cheek, "magnificent," her "passionate soul," "[h]er long shadow" (*Darkness,* 61), "the unswerving steadiness of her glance," her gleaming eyes. She is also beautifully attired: "draped in striped and fringed cloths" (*Darkness,* 60), "brass leggings to the knee, brass wire gauntlets to the elbow," "innumerable necklaces of glass beads on her neck," with "a sway of fringed draperies" and "bared arms" (*Darkness,* 61).

Were she only physically beautiful, wonderfully accessorized, and merely Kurtz's trophy female, her dismissal as "some kind of mistress" (*Darkness,* 340), yet as Kurtz's mistress, and a sort of collaborator who is sleeping with the enemy, might be justified. Her physical beauty, however, only reinforces the commanding presence she attains regardless of her being an easy gunshot away from being destroyed. Moreover, the obvious vulnerability of her position—with only herself to confront "The Nellie" and its superior man- and firepower—also reinforces the resilience and humanity she represents despite such overpowering odds. The potential "fury" of her language, the fear she engenders, the demonstrable expressions of her strong will as Kurtz's equal in their relationship, the absolutely compelling way she moves, the "formidable silence" she sustains, her unabashed display of emotion and grief over her loss, and the strategic realism of her decision to withdraw and disappear combine with the power of her physical beauty to justify her as anything but negligible or repentant.

All the more, therefore, in this respect like Achebe, should her not speaking in the story be lamented. Yet if she did, there is no one else who could translate what she says, with the possible exception of the Africans onboard the ship, except Kurtz. *What does she say* is the question. To reprise and adapt the words of Benjamin about the translator, Kurtz's "own language" must "be powerfully affected by" hers. Hardly to be disparaged as a "dialect" (*Darkness,* 61), her language remaining unheard and untranslated is, after all, what dooms the expedition and the entire European colonial enterprise to, in Kurtz's famous last words, "The horror! The horror!" (*Darkness,* 69). It reflects an awareness of the Hobbesian state of nature in which life is "solitary, poore, nasty, brutish, and short" (*Leviathan,*186), imposed on Africa by European civilization and thus reflecting the "darkness" of its own "heart," too. How can it be much different until Africa speaks and is heard primarily in its own languages not only through translation, but through an increasing dialogue of native and non-native speakers, which includes African language literature, too? Nor is such a question merely rhetorical, since the historical record of communication toward mutual understanding, enlightenment, and benefit between European or American and African interests is not anywhere near as advanced as it should be since the time of *Heart of Darkness.*

When only "primal elements" prevail ("The Task," 81), they destroy "the foreign" as well as being self-destructive. Yet in Benjamin's terms, there can also be "primal elements of language," the effect of which are salutary, where work, image, and tone converge" with the foreign.

The dynamic of Conrad's story is the destruction that results through missing what the African woman has to say. "[F]rom right to left along the lighted shore…a wild and gorgeous apparition….in the hush…upon the whole sorrowful land, the immense wilderness" (*Darkness,* 60), opening her "bare… arms and" throwing "them up rigid above her head, as though in an incontrollable desire to touch the sky" (*Darkness,* 61), she is a moment before translation, which never happens.

What is the language of Conrad's "apparition," the "gorgeous woman" with "measured steps," who stands "still, and face[s]... us," an "unswerving steadiness" in "her glance," before she "turns[s]... away slowly...walk[s]... , following the bank...pass[ing]... into the bushes...her eyes gleam[ing]... back at us in the dusk of the thickets before she disappears...." What would she say? What would Kurtz translate? Could it be as beautiful as her instead of her "formidable silence" or the issues of most analyses of Conrad's story – political, social, historical, philosophical, and more: that prevail in most other kinds of critical discourse about Africa, including the literary, instead of translations of African language verbal performance, textual and oral? Could her voice instead be as real and autonomous as the imagination itself and make the world out of her language for whomever speaks or translates it? In a brave new world of African literary translation, might she even appear as a previously unrecognized kind of patron saint, or a kind of *nkisi n'kondi*, providing the power to move beyond antetranslation to translation?[19]

Again, there is no doubt that colonialism and neocolonialism as spelled out by Ngũgĩ and racism as demonstrated by Achebe have kept her from being heard. But has the power and ubiquity of their own profound and telling critical analyses in an overall understanding of African literature and languages overshadowed her justifiably withheld, imagined language and its literary translation so that it has not received the attention it so critically needs – with Ngũgĩ's and Achebe's critical analyses ironically still being the greatest testimonies to this need? Almost thirty and forty years ago, respectively, they thoroughly diagnosed the problem, but all too often their analyses are merely repeated, instead of working toward the solution: the widespread dissemination and translation of African language literature and orature. They remain, for the most part, in a state before translation—of antetranslation. It is, furthermore, a state of intellectual stagnation. If one book of African language fiction, nonfiction, or poetry was published and/or translated for every time such arguments, however indubitable, as Achebe's and Ngũgĩ's have been made and agreed to – time and time again – the problem of antetranslation might be closer to being resolved. If a half, if a quarter, if 10% of all the creative writers and literary scholars who know each other and are native and non-native or barely speakers of African languages paired off and decided to work together to produce a co-translation of an African language literary text, as is perfectly normal in the translation of European language texts, antetranslation would finally give way to translation as the norm for African literature. Of course, the greatness and eloquence of African literature in European languages is inestimable, but how could African literature in African languages be any less and not much more? But all too many other, all too familiar critical agendas attract attention. Wind of change, Jesus or Allah, tradition or modernity, black or white, socialist or capitalist, rights, strong man or strong woman, war – the list goes on. IT, globalization, democracy, dictators, diasporas, nation building, transnationals, trade, tourism, justice, journalism, reparations, rainbows, guns, bread, aid, AIDS, ebola, immigration – the list can seem endless.

But they're all contexts. Furthermore, considering how little African language verbal art is translated yet how long the need for translation has been recognized, they can begin to sound like alibis or poor substitutes, at least from a literary perspective, for not getting back to the original texts and onwards to their translations. Yet the issue is not that they need be exclusive of any social, political, economic, or historical consideration, like the proverbial "well wrought urn" of the prevailing literary criticism when African literature first began to emerge for scholarly study.[20] The problem of antetranslation in African language literature is that its translation, relatively speaking, barely exists at all. It requires an individual to be in "the state in which his [or her] language ...[is] powerfully affected by the foreign....[p]articularly when translating from a language very remote from his [or her] own" and, in the process, "go[ing] back to the primal elements of language itself... penetrate[s] to the point where work, image, and tone converge" to "expand and deepen his [or her] language by means of the foreign language" ("The Task," 81). This is literally the position I am in, and who isn't who doesn't know the language of an African verbal performance, written or oral, and really wants to understand and enjoy it, short of learning the language for themselves? Moreover, what great literature, which deserves to be known, while appealing to its own native speakers, does not also owe its life to its translation, like—to take some of the most obvious Western examples—the Bible, Greek tragedy, classical poetry, to Dante and Shakespeare? The language of the African woman in Conrad's *Heart of Darkness*, Tigrinya, Tigre, Arabic, Gĩkũyũ, Swahili – it is not my language. For me, therefore, their poems, songs, fiction, and nonfiction are moments of antetranslation, before translation, which almost never happens, but must happen.

1   See note 14, page 10 above.

2   See note 2, page 53 above.

3   Ngũgĩ wa Thiong'o, *Mũrogi wa Kagogo* (Nairobi: East African Publishers, 2004), *Wizard of the Crow* (New York: Pantheon Books, 2006).

4   See note 23, page 12 above.

5   See note 21, page 107 above.

6   See note 16, page 106 above.

7   See pages 'The Story on *Who Needs a Story*' above.

8   See https://groups.google.com/forum/#!topic/zimla-revival/xQyez N4L5P4. Accessed 7 December 2016.

9   See note 18, page 126 above.

10   See "Literature, Power, Translation, and Eritrea" above.

> African literature exists primarily in African languages, which require translation.   To speak of the relationship of one continent's languages and literatures to another's and to the rest of the world, how could this not be the case? Still, Africa is the exception to such a common sense notion. Of all the continents, Africa has the least amount of translation from its languages and literatures…. (97)

11   Cf. page 100 above.

12   Cf. page 100 above.

13   See pages 96-97 above.

14   See Charles Cantalupo, "Translating African Language Poetry: Is there Enough?" *Modern Poetry in Translation* 3:16 (2011): 123-24

So what's the problem? More specifically, I mean why aren't more editors and publishers, readers and writers clamoring for more African language translation,and supporting it themselves with their own actions? What's stopping them? In addition to the lack of work that is published and, in what is published, the generally low level of literary critical value and scholarly discussion, here are twomore possible answers to the question.

1. An underdeveloped poetics for African language poetry translation. Whilemany African writers who work in African languages contend that poems in these languages have elaborate sound and metric patterns, their translations almost invariably appear in free verse, without availing themselves of elaborate sound and metric patterns in the target language – English, for instance – that might make the poems sound more substantial and enjoyable to the target audience. Take the example of Mazisi Kunene, 20th-century Zulu's greatest poet and its greatest translator. While he can write page after page about Zulu poetics, when he turns to the poetics of his translations into English he can only offer that he relies on "an internal rhythm."

2. The promotion of the work's political or anthropological value at the expense of its literary value. I think the failure of translating African language poetry is due to an over-emphasis on anthropological and folkloric values of authenticity – both in sound and sense – and on issues of racial and ethnic identity considered to be inseparable from social and political advocacy for personal and/or national liberation. The powerful and inspiring liberation narratives of writers like Ngũgĩ wa Thiong'o, Kofi Awoonor and Kofi Anyidoho, and Mazisi Kunene notwithstanding, they bear a burden of concerns that great literature need not necessarily have, although nearly all great African literature, frankly, has been stereotyped with this. I would argue that translators of African language poetry now must find a way for their poetics to triumph over the vitriol of politics as African poetry joins global forces in search of connectivity. Paeans to mother Africa, pan-African aspirations that seem further from actually happening than ever before, African essentialism and exceptionalism, cultural stereotypes that presuppose that African languages and

literatures are necessarily best understood by Africans and/ or the African diaspora, and praising Africa at the expense of Europe or the West by more or less simply reversing the trope of "dark continent" generally make bad poetry. The radical displacement of African languages historically by colonial languages and presently by global languages has precipitated the relative absence and impotence of African languages and their poetry – both themselves and in translation – in the world of international letters, but so has the relatively poor quantity and quality of translations of African language poetry, a widespread misunderstanding among translators of critical issues and goals of literary translation, and a similar misunderstanding of the critical standards of quality literary journals and the means of their cultural production.

15 Chinua Achebe, "An Image of Africa: Racism in Conrad's *Heart of Dark*ness" (1977), *The Massachusetts Review* (1977), 18: 782-94. *Heart of Darkness* (1899) by Joseph Conrad. Norton Critical Edition, ed. Paul B. Armstrong. Fourth edition (New York: W.W. Norton & Co., 2006), 343. Further references to this source are noted parenthetically in the text as *Darkness.*

16 Marcus Tullius Cicero, *"In Catilinam," Orations, In Catilinam I-IV; Pro Murena; Pro Sulla; Pro Flacco*, trans. C. Macdonald (Cambridge: Harvard University Press, 1977) 22.

17 John Keats, "Ode on a Grecian Urn" (1820). *Keats Poetical W*orks, ed. H. W. Garrod (London Oxford New York: Oxford University Press, 1970), 209.

18 Susan Jones, *Literature, Modernism, and Dance* (London: Oxford University Press, 2013), 152. Further references to this source are noted parenthetically in the text as "Dance."

19 *Nkisi n'kondi*, or power figure, refers to a form of wooden sculpture in Central Africa, particularly southern Congo and northern Angola, during the 19th and early 20th centuries. The figure is usually human, roughly three-quarter size, and terrifying. It is warlike. Moreover, the figure appears aggressive and ready to wage war. The materials of the *nkisi n'kondi* can also include wood, metal, glass, fabric, fiber, cowrie shells, bone, leather, gourds, and feathers. The figure or parts of it are also often covered with nails and other sharp pieces of metal that have been hammered into it. In addition, the figure is supposed to contain magical materials. Cf. http://ha208africanart.blogspot.

com/2009/09/mangaaka-power-figure-nkisi-nkondi.html.

> *Minkisi* [pl. *nkisi*] are the creation of a sculptor and an *nganga* (pl. *banganga*), a ritual specialist in Kongo society. An *nkisi* is essentially a container of spiritual forces that are directed to investigate the underlying cause of some chronic problem. As spiritual experts, *banganga* are approached by clients to address any of a multitude of crises that may emerge in the community, including illness, political instability, and social strife. *Minkisi* are essential to the *nganga*'s profession, creating a focal point from which to draw upon the spirit realm and its powers. Just as *minkisi* are directed toward specific ends, the banganga that own and control them may be specialized to address specific issues. For instance, only experienced *banganga* assume the responsibility of the most powerful *minkisi*, those concerned with political matters and the administration of justice.

> After a sculptor carves the figure at the core of the *nkisi*, it is the responsibility of the *nganga* to customize it by adding symbolic materials. Consequently, each *nkisi* is a unique creation, and can be controlled only by the *nganga* that conceived of its arrangement. The *nganga* begins by packing various "medicines" about the head and body of the figure. These are weighted with sacred power and spiritual implications, and are often tightly wrapped in knots and nets to give visual expression to the idea of contained forces. The diverse ingredients of the medicines may include special earths and stones, leaves and seeds, parts of animals, bird beaks and feathers, and are specifically combined to attract and direct forces to the desired goal. The figure's belly, or *mooyo* – which, not coincidentally, also translates as "life" or "soul" – is another spiritual focal point, packed with medicines and then sealed with resin.

> As the figure is used and reused, the addition of materials enhances its ability to direct forces while simultaneously augmenting its visual intricacy. As illustrated in this example, nails, bits of cloth, beads, bells, even miniature carvings have all been added to literally and figuratively load the figure with spiritual power. Many of the objects are tied to a cloth collar around the neck, a feature not commonly found on other *minkisi*. While prevalent teeth and wide, aggressive

eyes characterize many other *minkisi*; this example is further distinguished by the serenity of its facial expression, a sharp contrast to the rusted nails and complex assemblage of accoutrements that ornament the body of the figure below.

The kingdom of Kongo was at the height of its power in 1482, when Portuguese sailors first visited the coast of Central Africa. Founded between 1350 and 1400, the kingdom was a model of centralized government, with a divine king and a network of advisers, provincial governors, and village chiefs who ruled as many as three million people. Portuguese navigators brought with them Catholic missionaries, who converted the kings of Kongo during the sixteenth century. It has been suggested that the practice of piercing the *nkisi* with nails, spikes, or other elements was adopted from Christian images of martyred saints introduced in the area during this time. Figurative wood sculptures such as these are sometimes called "fetishes," a misleading word derived from the term *feitico*, which was used by the early Portuguese explorers to describe anything artificial or manmade.

20   Cf. Cleanth Brooks, *The Well Wrought Urn: Studies in the Structure of Poetry* (New York, Harcourt Brace, 1947).

Brooks...isolated literary criticism by limiting it to intensive analysis of the text itself, ignored history, discounted readers, failed to consider writings by women and minorities, and disabled any and all attempts to relate literary study to political, social, and cultural issues and debates" (*The Norton Anthology of Theory and Criticism*, edited by Vincent B. Leitch (New York: W. W. Norton & Company, 2001), 1350).

9

Two Moments in Kongo

...the coast of Central Africa in 1483, the year a navigator named Diogo Cão, on a pioneering mission for the Portuguese court, landed near the mouth of the Congo River to scout possibilities for trade.... The Portuguese had landed in territory occupied by Kongo peoples, who formed several separate states ruled by kings in urban courts similar to those of Europe. And the initial encounter was auspicious, viewed by both sides as a meeting of equals.... The rapport between Europe and the Kingdom of Kongo was brief. Portugal soon made its colonialist intentions clear. Other Western nations — France, Britain, the Netherlands — aggressively followed its lead. Kongo peoples lost their gainful position as gatekeepers to the wealth of the continent's interior..... Worse, the effects of the Atlantic slave trade were catastrophic. Africans had always participated as suppliers. But by the mid-17th century, Kongo territory roughly corresponding to modern Angola, Congo and the Congo Republic – had itself become a primary source of captives. By 1850, a third of its population had ended up in chains in the Americas.... [T]he Scramble for Africa was on full-bore, with Western nations barbarously slicing up and devouring a continent. That depredation has never stopped, even if some of its participants have changed.... [1]

149

Joining two moments four hundred years apart and not the flood
All in between, what appears? I had a dream of the first and
Thought it was false. I was wrong, at least for this one moment of
History, if not thereafter, as the second moment cries,
Lost on the other side's total trauma, tragic, and alive.

Still, it connects to beginnings, also fragments but meaning
More than "exterminate" can be scribbled on the big picture,[2]
If it includes that first moment in the estuary and
Finding the harbor inscribed with language meaning another
There and already as much refined as can be imagined.

Enter to music of recognition mutually shared,
Currencies equal in art and social justice based on faith
Red as the riverbed making black for life and white for death
Or the reverse to accept more than the hunter and hunted
Giving their names to the place as if it never could be more?

What would it look like? To barely last one moment self-described?
How otherworldly yet absolutely worldly the same time?
Spirals on ivory trumpets as if it lasts forever
End up in Medici courts,[3] and woven raffia reveals
Seemingly endless designs of glory showing the closest

Way to the most unfamiliar moving in all directions:
Undyed to dyed black with yellows, browns and reds in diamonds,
(Most of the images of this moment have to be abstract)
Rectangles, squares, rows, and columns in diagonal grids of
Verticals and horizontals interlaced and interlocked,
Knotted in nuance to alternate chromatic wefts and warps
Into a spectrum reflecting and absorbing a golden
Darkness and light, with the brocade, velvet, silk and satin to
Follow, at least for a moment, with the oliphant heralds,
Claws in phalanges on strings, and pelts of wildcats like
    leopards:

So much more could have continued, but it stops, whatever the

Doctrines and altars, Nzambi a Mpungu and Jesus,[4]
Each other's bodies their own on crosses...holy, *nkisi,*
Naturally baptizing vision and immersion on both sides,
Words into river and river into words, the difference....

Difference? What it creates? A moment, and one moment more
After four centuries: neither timelessly primordial;
Different moments connected by their valorization
Barely escaping oblivion from what comes in between.
Call it biology, nature's laws, inevitable, and
Genocide. Genocide. All the more important two moments
Can be recovered before and after witnessing the truth:
Genocide. Slavery – transatlantic making the New World:
Men from the coast for plantations; women for them to survive
And reproduce: two to one, more men since more of the men die,
Die, and die, in Kongo, too, for its abundance: ivory,
Rubber, and gold, and its wealth in people: most of all the prey
For better guns, minds, and bodies to have their white only way
As, for example, a Churchill or a Leopold would say,
Wiping out civilizations on a very good day,[5]

Opening into the second moment: "fetish of war" and
"Mother and Child" dragged away from their last stand and total
  loss[6] –
Nothing heroic, more minor, tragic, no God-like magic –
Like the carved ivories and the woven raffia also
Brutally scattered as *objet d'art* in Western museums.

Power appears in this second moment more than in the first.
Beauty, fertility, elegance, devotion, and female;
Fearfully male physicality and its omnipotence:
Two kinds of power as if one could have been a deception.
Both come to ruin, however, isn't that their history?
Furthermore, how could this knowledge of four hundred years not
  guide
Each of their different artists' hands aware of all that died:
Come out of slavery, slaughter and their land's devastation

After the tragedy has already happened? It's over.
No more to fight for, the images speak only for themselves,

Even if most of them are destroyed, with the few remaining
Kept under glass. They come after not to stop or change the end,
But to express shock at what has happened, and they stand alone.
What happens next they don't know, and they know only what they
    see –
Some greater power they represent is no question for me.

Nor do I think it is for their makers, knowing beauty and
What they can say in a mother and a child: the well-being –
Graceful, commanding, submissive, and renewing kaolin
Brushed near a darkening cheekbone; body, nude, ethereal;
Carrying light's cultivation and seduction to nurture
Sacrifice and the renewal of a selfless compassion –
No greater good and no greater power standing anywhere
Other than making the image of a man, when none exists,
Looking like he could fight off what has destroyed her and the child.
Take the big, heavy and hard bole of this sacred tree to make
With a hand-forged and a simple iron blade a *mangaaka*.[7]
Looking like what? If he fought? As if his all knowing stare of
Absolute violence and inspired aggression to awe with
Unbounded power could really be the last ditch defense and
Triumph with no one and nothing left to save except itself

After the tragedy of the Kongo? Still standing in shock,
Oozing with resin afresh before it hardens to express
Spirit's last gasp as a monumental otherwise lost art?
After the raffia and the ivory, what did I expect?
More than the four-foot high bodies witnessing the total death

Packed in their heads while their white eyes and black pupils see
    the rest?
More than the mouth open with filed teeth and delicately carved
Lips having just said their last words? More than oversize torsos,
Arms hanging off overbearing shoulders wide as hips thrust out,

Ready to spring at whatever comes next or what I might say?
More than the belly sucked in completely, never to let go?
More than the medicines once stuffed in them – leaves and seeds,
    stones, dirt,
Bird beaks, and feathers or other bits of animals wrapped in
Specially tied nets and knots or shreds of cloth with miniature
Carvings or beads or a fragment no one knows – but now long
    gone?

More than the cowries, ceramic, sisal, animal hair, hides,
And all the pigments these bodies couldn't bear to be without?
More than the pieces of metal pounded over and over
Into these bodies – nails, needles, hatchets, knives and broken guns,
Sharp rods, and bolts, and the countless spikes where people put
    their tongues?

1   Holland Carter, "A People Suffered; Their Art Tells the Story," *New York Times* (18 September 2015), C2. "Review: 'Kongo: Power and Majesty' at the Metropolitan Museum of Art," http://www.nytimes.com/2015/09/18/arts/design/review-kongo-power-and-majesty-at-the-metropolitan-museum-of-art.html. Accessed 27 December 2016.

2   *Darkness*, 50. In Conrad's story, Marlowe, the narrator, reports that "the International Society for the Suppression of Savage Customs had entrusted…[Kurtz] with the making of a report for its future guidance" (*Darkness*, 49). Marlow finds it and comments:

it was a beautiful piece of writing. The opening paragraph, however, in the light of later information, strikes me now as ominous. He began with the argument that we whites, from the point of development we had arrived at, 'must necessarily appear to them [savages] in the nature of supernatural beings – we approach them with the might of a deity,' and so on, and so on. 'By the simple exercise of our will we can exert a power for good practically unbounded,' etc., etc. From that point he soared and took me with him. The peroration was magnificent, though difficult to remember, you know. It gave me the notion of an exotic Immensity ruled by an august Benevolence. It made me tingle with enthusiasm. This was the unbounded power of eloquence – of words – of burning noble words. There were no practical hints to interrupt the magic current of phrases, unless a kind of note at the foot of the last page, scrawled evidently much later, in an unsteady hand, may be regarded as the exposition of a method. It was very simple, and at the end of that moving appeal to every altruistic sentiment it blazed at you, luminous and terrifying, like a flash of lightning in a serene sky: 'Exterminate all the brutes!'

3   See Peter Schjeldahl, *The New Yorker* (October 12, 2015), "Kongo: Power and Majesty. http://www.newyorker.com/magazine/2015/10/12/power-surge. Accessed 12 December 2016.

When the Portuguese explorer Diogo Cão arrived at the mouth of the Congo River, in 1483, and erected a stele invoking the authority of his king, he encountered a courtly civilization that lacked little in refinement except written language. Fantastically carved ivory horns and geometrically patterned raffia weavings from that time bespeak lofty traditions. Amicable trade relations soon brought examples north. Two elegant horns entered the collection of Cosimo I de' Medici, in Florence.

4   Nzambi a Mpungu is the name for supreme God or creator in the Kikongo language. Early Portuguese explorers in the region knew the name and used it in their Kikongo translations of Christian texts.

5   King Leopold II (1835-1909) of Belgium presided over the genocidal colonization of the Congo, eventually declaring the colony as his own personal domain. England's superior weaponry in the colonial conquest of Sudan led Winston Churchill (1874-1965) to make this comment after the battle of Omdurman, in which the entire Sudanese army was annihilated. "It was a good moment...to live...to win...to mow them down." See Sven Lindqvist, *Exterminate all the brutes* (New York: New Press, 1996), 46.

6   The term "fetish of war" can demystify, disempower, and belittle the *nkisi n'kondi,* particularly when applied in the confines of a museum display. In a similar context, "mother and child" is a Western term all too readily applied to the equally culturally central Kongo sculptures of mothers nursing and caring for their children. Both forms of sculpture amounted to supreme and tragic expressions of local cultures confronting their violent and near total annihilation: one as

a consummate expression of war and death; the other as peace, life, and love.

7   Another name for a power figure or *nkisi n'kondi*.

10
Three Interviews with Ngũgĩ wa Thiong'o

Moving the Center (1993)

The following interview in English took place on the afternoon of January 23, 1993, in the living room of Ngũgĩ's home near Newark, New Jersey. Lawrence F. Sykes, who photographed the interview, and I arrived there slightly early than planned. Ngũgĩ was not yet back from New York University, where he taught and where he had enrolled himself in an intensive language course in French for a film project on Ousmane Sembene, the acclaimed Senegalese filmmaker and author. While we waited for him to return, Ngũgĩ's wife, Njeeri wa Ndũng'ũ, welcomed us with friendly conversation, a bowl of the new crop of clementines, that she refilled often, and glasses of a tropical fruit juice that I did not think was available in this part of the world, although I was born and raised here. We were joined by four of Ngũgĩ's children: Lashambi, the proud recipient of a letter from Nelson Mandela, responding to her homemade greeting card on his release from prison; Ndũũcũ, a student at Oberlin College, who was just about to leave for the Spring semester; Wanjikũ, a student at NYU, who was helping her mother in the kitchen; and Njooki, a student at Chad School, who was also helping her mother. When Ngũgĩ arrived, he invited Larry and me into the living room, where we spoke until we could no longer resist the aroma of roast goat, which Njeeri had prepared for us for dinner.

CC: Congratulations on the publication of *Moving the Centre*.[1] Was it a coincidence that its publication date coincided with the holiday celebration of Martin Luther King's birthday?

NWT: It was pure coincidence. It was supposed to come out in November, 1992, but I kept on doing corrections, and this delayed its appearance. But it was a good coincidence. Particularly just before his death, Martin Luther King was talking about moving the democratic center from its prison in the establishment to creative locations among the people.

CC: Does *Moving the Centre* develop and extend any of the ideas of your last book of essays, *Decolonising the Mind*?[2]

Since its publication in 1986, it has achieved the status of a popular, required text for non Euro -American and multicultural literary study. Does *Moving the Centre* pick up where *Decolonising the Mind* left off?

NWT: Some of the essays in *Moving the Centre* were written after *Decolonising the Mind*, so obviously they do extend some of the ideas already contained in *Decolonising the Mind*. Some of the items were papers given at conferences, and often these conferences were responding to some of the issues in *Decolonising the Mind*.

Decolonising the Mind as a text has become so talked about that wherever I go, in conferences, in countries, in Africa and outside Africa, that I'm obliged to answer questions about *Decolonising the Mind*. These questions are reflected in some of the papers in *Moving the Centre*.

At the same time, *Moving the Centre* is a book that developed almost accidentally. The initial suggestion had come from my publishers, who said that since I would no longer be writing in the English language, and that I would be using Gĩkũyũ as my primary language in writing, they wanted to put together all of the articles and papers I had already given and which were not yet published. It started as a project to bring together anything which I had and which had not yet been published. Yet in the process of putting the various items together, we came to realize that a certain pattern was forming, and that certain essays and papers, whether given in 1982 or in 1991, could be grouped around certain themes. In other words, we found that actually running through all the papers and items were certain motifs that held the essays together...

CC: ...and this explains the book's being organized into four sections: "Freeing Culture from Eurocentrism," "Freeing Culture from Colonial Legacies," "Freeing Culture from Racism," and "Matigari, Dreams and Nightmares."

Moving the Centre contains an emotional essay, "Many Years Walk to Freedom: Welcome Home Mandela!" on his historic release from a South African prison, after he had served twenty-seven years of a lifetime sentence. In the book's preface, however, you note that, although the essay appeared first in English in the New York based African-American news magazine, *Emerge*, "the Gĩkũyũ original of the Mandela piece is still in ... [your] drawer ... among a good many others" (*Centre*, xiv). You also say, "In their different destinies, the two pieces illustrate the difficulties in the way of those writing theoretical, philosophical, political and journalistic prose in an African language, moreover in conditions of exile."

NWT: What happened was this. In March I was at Yale. There was an announcement that Mandela was to be released. Planning a special issue on this historic event, *Emerge* asked me to write an article for it. I said to myself: I can't write about Mandela's release in English. I have to do it in Gĩkũyũ language. I have to do it in an African language. What does his release mean to me as an African? As a Kenyan? As a human being for whom Mandela and the South African struggle has meant so much? So, I wrote the entire piece in Gĩkũyũ language. And it became very interesting. The flow in the article arises precisely from that. There's a sense of engagement in Gĩkũyũ language.

In the preface, I was just trying to point out some of the difficulties that people writing in African languages currently have or can face. For instance, there are very few journals in African languages. There are very few forums that wholly utilize African languages. Write an article in Gĩkũyũ language, as I do, and often it does not have an outlet, unless it is published either in translation, as in the case of the article on Mandela in *Emerge*, or with an English translation published side by side with the original Gĩkũyũ text, as happened in the case of the article on language in *Moving the Centre*, "Imperialism of Language: English a Language for the World?" It was also originally given for the BBC, but later published in both languages by the *Yale Journal of Criticism*. In fact, the Mandela article in Gĩkũyũ language has not yet been published.

CC: To be asked to write suddenly on Mandela was a kind of supreme moment of theory in practice in terms of your decision to write in Gĩkũyũ, a theme that is...

NWT: ...very close to home, so to speak, yes.

CC: In your new book's title essay, "Moving the Centre: Toward a Pluralism of Cultures," you evoke your days as a student at Makerere University College in Uganda. Writing "I can still recall the excitement of reading the world from a centre other than Europe" (*Centre*, 4), you remember in particular "one of the characters in George Lamming's novel, *In the Castle of My Skin*, [who) talks of his suddenly discovering his people, and therefore his world, after hearing Paul Robeson sing, 'Let my People Go.'"[3] You go on to say, "He was speaking of me and my encounter with the voices coming out of centres outside Europe." Do you still experience this "excitement of reading the world from a centre other than Europe," when you read contemporary literature?

NWT: Of course, not the same way. Obviously there are more voices coming from Kenya, from Africa, the Third World. The literature from Africa, from Asia, from South America, is increasingly becoming a part, an integral part, of the teaching of literature in different places. For me that "excitement" really came at a particular moment in history: at a particular moment in my growing up, discovering this new literature. It's a moment that is obviously difficult to repeat, for me. But it will be a moment that many other people from Africa, Asia, and South America may experience, especially if they have not been exposed to literature from a world that has molded them.

CC: Let's discuss America. In *Moving the Centre*, you cite DuBois' observation that racism is "the problem of the twentieth century" (*Centre*, 150). Have the riots in Los Angeles in 1992, and/or Bill Clinton's election as President of the United States altered any of your views on racism?

NWT: I believe that what I say about racism as an ideology in the third section of *Moving the Centre* is still pertinent today.

Racism has been so much a part of the Western world, so much a part, and an integral part, of the 20th century, that it's something that has to be continually fought against consciously and deliberately. Obviously, there is a difference in a sense. Racism is recognized more and more as a social evil that has to be addressed, and that's very important. But, as I said, it's been so much part of structures of domination and subjugation that it cannot be really eliminated until those structures of economic, political, and cultural domination have been altered sufficiently to be the real base for group and social equality.

CC: American universities and academics have been attacked for advocating what has become known pejoratively as "pc" and "political correctness." Yet their efforts, at least in theory, and occasional excesses of puritan zeal notwithstanding, are primarily to become more sensitive to and, more importantly, inclusive of the many different kinds of people who attend universities today. Nevertheless, they are attacked precisely for being engaged in "moving the centre," to use the phrase with which you title your new book, within our nation and between nations to "the real creative center among ... people" of equal status, regardless of any conditions of gender, economics, race, religion, sexuality, and physical ability. Repeatedly and eloquently in *Moving the Centre* you advocate "opening out the mainstream to take in other streams" (*Centre*, 8), "moving towards a pluralism of cultures, literatures and languages" (*Centre*, 10), "understanding all the voices coming from what is essentially a plurality of centres all over the world" (*Centre*, 11). Your political agenda is international, yet it is distinctly applicable to American universities and the nation itself, too.

NWT: Yes, obviously it's a healthy trend. A trend that redresses imbalances obviously is important, and it should be encouraged. But it has to go beyond just the universities. It has to be at the very structure of economic and political power, where the problem is. In eliminating racism, as well as sexism, we're talking about empowerment: a people's lack of empowerment. The basic question is a question of economic, political, and cultural empowerment of peoples: of creating conditions that allow for that kind of empowerment. With that corrected, there's a question of people's attitudes, individual as well as group, which will ultimately change. But the fact that a trend consciously addresses the problem is a very, very positive thing. It's the real correct thing to do.

CC: In *Moving the Centre*, I find many of your political tenets more gently expressed than in *Decolonising the Mind*. For example, in the introduction to the latter you identify the United States as the leader of international imperialism, simply presenting "the struggling peoples of the earth and all those calling for peace, democracy, and socialism with the ultimatum: accept theft or death" (*Decolonising*, 3). Strong words. Do they fully and accurately describe the situation in the 1990s? How can the situation change for the better? How would you advise a new administration in Washington to begin constructive change of US policy in Africa?

NWT: To come back to an earlier comment: both in *Decolonising the Mind* and *Moving the Centre*, one is writing about moving the centre in essentially two ways. In the 20th century, what you see between nations is definitely structured on inequality. There's no doubt in my mind if you look at the world as it is today, the West, as whole, still bleeds the Third World, the countries of Africa, Asia, and South America. This is clear. Even if you take it at the level of the burden of debt, the financial burden. Many economists now say that the Third World countries are net exporters of the capital that they so badly need – through debt servicing, through their repayment of debt. Third World countries need capital but, in fact, they end up exporting capital to the West. Because they borrow money from the International Monetary Fund or World Bank,[4] or from the West generally, many of these countries are now completely burdened by the interest they have to pay on the loans. So, they end up giving more to the West: the very capital the Third World countries actually need for their own development. There is still a structural imbalance between the West and the rest of us, so to speak. This imbalance is basically economic, but it is also political, and it has cultural implications. So, moving the centre, in an international situation, is really a moment toward correcting this structural imbalance.

Within nations themselves, within Africa, or in America, or in the West, there is also social structural imbalance between the few in all these countries who control the resources and the majority of the people in each of these areas. I talk about moving the centre *within* nations, yes, and *between* nations. This thesis runs throughout *Decolonising the Mind*. It's also there in *Moving the Centre*. In the past, whenever countries in African have tried to opt for a different path of social development and to break with the colonizing or neo-colonizing structures of relationships, as in the years of the Cold War, there was hostility from the West. So, we se see some of the worst dictatorships being supported by the West. I'm talking about countries like, say, Zaire, with Mobutu, Kenya with Moi, Malawi with Banda, Central African Republic, in the days of Bokassa, say, and countries like Cameroon, with Biya, or Barre in Somalia.[5] The support of dictatorships, which repress their people internally, prevents the only possibility these countries have of getting out of this vicious encirclement. The ability to get out relies entirely on the energies of the people. But the energies of the people cannot be relied upon if they are repressed. So, my own feeling is that it's really in the interest of everybody in the world to encourage and support democratic trends in Africa, even when those democratic trends result in social and economic programs that do not necessarily meet the approval down to the details and fit the capital market economies of the West. I think if political change emerges democratically in these countries, this should be allowed to develop. Obviously the state in many African countries has to play a more active role in economic and social development, whether people like it or not. There's really no other way. The question is, what kind of state, controlled by whom? Are they just states under dictatorships, or are they democratic states that will respond to the people?

CC: Without government repression and its insistence on doing things only in its own way, the energy of a people on their own will emerge no matter what form it takes.

NWT: Yes, exactly. You need to release the energies of the people. You must create what one African thinker, Babu,[6] has called enthusiasm for production! But with the dictatorships in Africa, often supported by the West, there has developed a kind of cynicism: a collective disbelief and this is very dangerous for development. We need new people based democratic movements that will generate incentive for change and renewal.

CC: Have you just described what has happened in Somalia? Has such cynicism and collective disbelief destroyed Somalia from within? And allowed the traditional colonial powers, in lieu of any established local government, to return for the allegedly humanitarian reason of solely assuring the distribution of food?

NWT: Look at postcolonial Africa, whether Somalia or Kenya or Zaire – concrete examples. Moi, of Kenya, during the colonial days, was working with British colonial settlers to prevent independence for Kenya. In other words, at the height of the Mau Mau armed struggle against the British in Kenya,[7] he was a British appointee in the colonial legislature.[8] Yet now, in post-independent Kenya, he is the one who is wielding power, and until recently with the full support of the West, the British in particular. Mobutu of Zaire, during the colonial days, was part of the Belgian colonial army, suppressing the Zairian people. Yet post-independence, he becomes a leader. Take Uganda. Before Museveni, there was Idi Amin.[9] Idi Amin used to be, again, part of the colonial army, fighting against African nationalism. Yet in fact when he came to power, through a military coup d'état, he was immediately received by the then French president

Pompidou.[10] He was received by the queen of England.[11] He was given a state, red carpet welcome in the West. Bokassa of Central Africa – he's no longer there now – used to be a friend of the French president. Barre, of Somalia, was part of the Italian colonial army. All of these leaders had power supported by the West. They were a part of the Cold War era because they said, 'okay, we are anti-communist,' or 'we are anti-Marxist,' and, of course, it was supported.[12] Look at these leaders very, very carefully. They never see their inspiration as coming from the people, because they know very well that their being in power is not dependent on Somalian people, on Kenyan people, on Zairian people. They don't owe a single loyalty to those people, because such leaders don't feel – and essentially it's true – their power is derived from the people. So, they don't fear that they will lose their power to rule, as long as they have the monopoly of the gun and of support of Western governments. They don't feel accountable to the people. If democracy is not allowed to flourish freely in Africa, we shall continue to have a proliferation of the same problems.

CC: Lets shift from government and democracy to writers. In "The Writer in the Neo-Colonial State," you state a writer's alternatives: "silence or self-censorship... Or he can become a state functionary... Or he may risk jail or exile, in which case he is driven from the very sources of inspiration. Write and risk damnation, avoid damnation and cease to be a writer. That is the lot of the writer in a neo-colonial state" (*Centre*, 71). Do you yourself feel these restraints? Do you know writers who feel these restraints? In some ways, you have overcome them, or you've been forced to overcome them. Is democracy going to affect that? If democracy is allowed to flourish, surely the role of the writer will get better, too.

NWT: Obviously, I hope for more democratic space to give writers more room to articulate their visions, to be themselves as writers. In Africa, particularly the Africa of the Cold War, the political climate was very hostile to writers. Indeed, it resulted in horrible actions: writers have been killed in Africa, writers have been forced into exile, and other writers who remain at home have been forced to side either with the government, as has happened to some writers in Kenya, or else to practice self-censorship. Others, of course, continue writing and articulating their visions, but they risk all of those other things: death, exile, or jail.

CC: What about women writers in particular? They too must challenge and break through social conventions, yet there is the imposition of sexual stereotypes and the politics of gender. For a man to challenge social conventions and break free of hopeless alternatives is sometimes easier than for a woman.

NWT: Yes, it's true. But remember, there are prominent African women writers, and politically they face the same problems: speak out and face jail, exile, death, censorship and all that. There is also, of course, the habit, the problem of gender discrimination, or of structural discrimination, and women writers have to articulate all of these burdens of gender, race, and class.

CC: What happens if the democracy movement in African nations is suppressed and suppressed to a point of extinction? Is this possible? You write in the introduction to *Moving the Centre*,

> Cultures under total domination from others can be crippled, deformed, or else die.... Hence the insistence in these essays on the suffocating and ultimately destructive character of both colonial and neo-colonial structures. A new world order that is no more than global dominance and neo-colonial relations policed by a handful of Western nations, whether through the United Nations Security Council or not, is a disaster for the peoples of the world and their cultures.
>
> *Centre*, xvi

168

This sounds elegiac, although this feeling is mitigated at the end of your book. Do you think you have seen a culture deformed, dying and finally left for dead?

NWT: I was giving two alternatives. Cultures that are completely dominated can die. Equally well, countries that are in complete isolation from others can fade. In fact, cultures in the past have developed through a healthy balance of give and take. For instance, African cultures during the colonial era suffered structural damage because of colonial domination. In the era of slavery, there was even greater damage, because this meant the removal of human beings, who are the basis of the development of culture. There was structural damage to a people's capacity to evolve their own languages and their culture. There is a necessity of cultural give and take on the basis of economic and political equality between groups. Otherwise, as in the case of colonial or neo-colonial imbalances, the cultures of those who are the victims of imbalance are likely to be deformed. In a situation of economic and political equality between groups, cultures can develop on the basis of give and take. Countries will borrow from each other naturally those elements that are healthy to each country.

CC: You make a similar point about African languages and their borrowings. *In Moving the Centre*, you confidently assert,

African languages will borrow from one another; they will borrow from their classical heritages; they will borrow from the world-from the Caribbean, from Afro America, from Latin America, from the Asian-and from the European worlds. In this, the new writing in African languages will do the opposite of the Europhone practice. Instead of being appropriated by the world, the new writing will appropriate the world and one hopes on terms of equal exchange, at the very least, borrow on its own terms and needs.

Centre, 23

Your theory sounds as if it has an enormous, healthy appetite. In the same passage, you also cite Bakhtin's observation that "Latin literary language in all its generic diversity was created in the light of Greek literary language" (*Centre*, 22),[13] and you go on to ask "the rhetorical question...is it possible to conceive of the development of Greek literature and culture without Egyptian and other Mediterranean cultures?" In your view, African languages play as rich a role in the future as they have in the ancient past.

NWT: Look at the United Nations, in terms of imbalance. In my mind, it is an organization that should be strengthened. It should be the hope of the world. New and rising nations can be politically and economically strengthened by the empowerment of a United Nations. But it has to be democratized itself! The Security Council, the executive body of the United Nations, is dominated by basically Western, white, imperial nations. In other words, they can veto anything, even against the will of a majority from Africa, Asia. Look at the languages of the United Nations organization. They're nearly all Western, European languages. We want a strong United Nations organization, but we want it also to reflect genuinely the multiplicity of world cultures and peoples, and not for this organization to become an instrument of U.S. foreign policy, or an instrument of the foreign policy of Western powers.

CC: I was talking with the poet Michael Harper, and he recalled that James Joyce once said that a writer's language is his homeland.[14] Do you feel that way? Do you feel that way about English and/or Gĩkũyũ, or just Gĩkũyũ?

NWT: That language is one's homeland? Well...

CC: Is that enough emotionally, or just intellectually?

NWT: To have a language is to have a world, in more sense than one at the personal level – obviously a writer carries language in him, and he has his connection with whatever is the language of his choice. When he's writing a novel or a poem, he'll have dialogue with the voices or the characters in the language of his choice. But languages simply are not a matter of personal acquisition. They are also a matter of social communities. When languages of a group are suppressed – through whatever means, economic, military, or whatever – the language of the individual is affected. If I had a language as a writer, but that language had no community of speakers anywhere in the world, then I do not think that that language would really be my world. In other words, I am able to possess language as my world precisely because it is the language of the community.

CC: Maybe Joyce worked towards a language of no one's world. Maybe it was a solace yet a lonely world in the end, a world like *Finnegan's Wake*, which few could understand?

NWT: James Joyce comes from Ireland. Ireland has the longest colonial history: vis a vis England, vis a vis the West, and I think he may have been avoiding the implications of that: not facing up to that reality, that Irish reality. If there was no community of English speakers anywhere in the world, then that language for Joyce would not have been meaningful and enough. Language becomes meaningful at a personal level precisely because that language is part of a wider community.

CC: Do you ever feel alone or frustrated in your own strong advocacy for the cultural imperative of writing in Gĩkũyũ and African languages in general?

NWT: No, I don't worry. Throughout history languages have had to struggle, to fight. There is now a need for more literature in African languages, and eventually they will emerge out of their marginalization. In Africa, and in the West, there are now increasingly more and more debates about this very issue of languages. It really is important. I don't feel that I am very lonely and, of course, I'm not the only person who's advocating or who has ever articulated this. I'm only one of a whole series of people who have been saying, 'Look. This is important. It is crucial that people's languages are recognized. It is important that there is literature and philosophy, and so on, in these languages.' The problem is that there are often not enough financial resources given for the development of those languages.

CC: You have some remarkable stories, recalled in both *Decolonising the Mind* and *Moving the Centre*,

> of instances of children being punished if they were caught speaking their African languages. We were often caned or made to carry plaques inscribed with the words 'I am stupid' or 'I am an ass.' In some cases, our mouths were stuffed with pieces of paper picked from the wastepaper basket, which were then passed from mouth to mouth to that of the latest offender. Humiliation in relation to our languages was the key.
>
> *Centre*, 33

In another autobiographical passage from *Moving the Centre*, you recall your youthful, "whole heated affection" for Robert Louis Stevenson's *Treasure Island*, Charles Dickens' *Oliver Twist*, and the popular series of adventure stories based on a fictional 20th-century hero of the British empire, James Bigglesworth, nicknamed "Biggles."[15] Was the English language a kind of "first love" who betrayed you?

NWT: There's nothing wrong with the English language. There's nothing wrong with French. There's nothing wrong with any language in the world. It's very important that what has been produced in these languages – in Chinese, in Japanese, in Finnish, in Swedish, in whatever – is a part of human heritage. They're all very important. Equally well, what's produced in African languages – in Swahili, in Gĩkũyũ, in Yoruba – is also a part of human heritage. Suppressing the languages of three fourths of humankind, we are suppressing three fourths of human heritage. For persons growing up in Africa, fully in the world of their languages, in the literature of their languages, there's nothing wrong with them acquiring other languages as well, and enjoying fully whatever has been produced in those other languages. There's even nothing wrong in African languages appropriating whatever is best that has been produced in and through other people's languages. There would be nothing wrong with ancient languages appropriating the best that has been developed in African languages in a healthy give and take. When economic structural imbalance is corrected, these borrowings from each other would be a natural, organic, healthy development without competition, if you like. Acceptance or rejection would be a part of a healthy dialogue...

CC: ...which is a point you make repeatedly in *Moving the Centre*. I'd like to turn from the issue of what language to choose to a specific word. "Struggle" is a word that recurs often in your essays. In the preface to *Moving the Centre*, you cite Hegel's principle,[16] "Without struggle there is no progression" (*Centre*, xiv), and you go on to state that "Culture develops within the process of a people wrestling with their natural and social environment. They struggle with nature. They struggle with one another.... What is... often officially paraded as authentic African culture today is virtually a repeat of the colonial tradition: tourist art, dances, acrobatic contortions emptied of the content of struggle" (*Centre*, 27). When did you discover that "struggle," "the content of struggle," is a major theme in your writing? In your youth? At Makerere?

NWT: It was gradual. "Struggle" is a part of nature and part of our history and cultures. As a central concept in my aesthetic or cultural vision, "struggle" has been developing, I think, starting from my essays on writers and politics. One can see this theme become more and more dominant in my cultural theory and aesthetic theory. "Struggle" is central to nature, to human art, and to my history.

CC: In *Moving the Centre*, you say that *Devil on the Cross* was "an attempt to reconnect myself to the community from which I had been brutally cut by the neo-colonial regime in Kenya" (*Centre*, 106). You observe the same about yourself, though more generally, in another passage: "Writing

173

has always been my way of reconnecting myself to the landscape of my birth and upbringing" (*Centre*, 156). Described in this way, writing sounds like a kind of religious act, if we consider that the word "religion" is derived from the Latin "*re*," meaning "back" or "again," and "*ligare*", meaning "to bind" or "connect." For writing to be an act of reconnecting to a kind of happiness, solace, truth – yet to be primarily about struggle seems paradoxical.

NWT: There is a connection between the organic development of a language and the organic development of a culture. Each form of development is not one-sided and both are developed through struggle. As biological creatures that are human beings, we live in two conditions. We develop under conditions of internal development within our own biological structures. But we also live in conditions of an external environment, say, the air we breathe, and so on. Our external life is an integral part of ourselves. None of us can live without breathing in air, for instance. Yet at the same time, air is out there, external to us. It's give and take or die. By emphasizing the ideal of organic development, I mean that whatever comes from outside, say, the air we breathe, must not deform internal development. Taking in air supports our internal organs, yet if there is too much, like a blast of air, it can hurt one as much as a lack of air. This is a kind of healthy struggle and a system that must not be deformed by either external circumstances or by such internal imbalance so as to completely deform the possibilities of development.

CC: This almost sounds mystical.

NWT: Not quite. If you examine nature, that's how people develop; that's how even trees develop. When there are floods, for instance, or hurricanes, there is a kind of overdose from the external environment, so that trees break, and so on. But the same air, under normal circumstances – the air that trees and human beings breathe – helps their own development.

CC: Let's discuss *Moving the Centre*'s last essay, "Matigari, and the Dreams of One East Africa." It derives from a trip you made to Tanzania in 1987. Could your return to Kenya be on the horizon?

NWT: Not as long as Moi is in power. Anything can change, obviously, although it's been very disappointing that the Moi dictatorship continues in Kenya. There have been, of course, some healthy advances, and we hope that this will continue to develop. But I still would find it very difficult at present to go back under the Moi regime because what is really happening is that, although there have been some advances, some very important advances – I don't want to deny that – I do not think that the cultural, political climate has really changed. As long as Moi and his regime are there, the same distortions that created a community of Kenyan exiles will continue.

CC: Another "structure of domination and subjugation," to use your words from before.

NWT: This is a clear-cut dictatorship, and it continues. The Moi regime is one of the problems, and as long as Moi is there, we shall continue to have those problems. What we want in Kenya, in Africa, is not simply democratization in terms of having political parties. We're talking about a democratic culture. We're talking about the right to organize: not just political organizations, but cultural organizations, social organizations. We're talking about the right of people to move freely within their own countries. We're talking about whether they be workers, or peasants, their being able to organize freely. This is what some of us mean by a democratic culture in the country, which is not like life in a country like Kenya where, for instance, even now people cannot meet without a legal license. The right to move freely, the right to organize freely, the right to assemble freely, are the basis of creativity. The moment that that is affected, obviously, it also affects individual creativity.

CC: In the preface to *Moving the Centre*, irrespective of any particular economic or political power, you evoke as the greatest power "the real creative centre among the working people in conditions of gender, racial and religious equality..."(*Centre*, xvii)

NWT: ...of the people, wherever they are. And that we can actually do, to get real, genuine national and international creativity.

CC: If that was the case, would East Africa – East Africa in its entirety – become one country?

NWT: My own hope, quite frankly, is that. When I travel, say, from Kenya to Tanzania, or Uganda, or Somalia, or Sudan, I see their problems as so similar that I feel that these countries would be better off uniting. I don't have any mystical notions about nations. Nations definitely do grow, do change. There's nothing that says that nations cannot change and that they cannot combine. So my belief, my hope, is that African nations will come together, and that people will come together under one form of umbrella unity.

CC: "Matigari, and the Dreams of One East Africa" offers an embodiment in East Africa itself – its "kaleidoscope of colours, cultures, and contours of history" (*Centre,* 161) – of the book's recurring theme: the "plurality of centres" (*Centre,* 10) and the "pluralism of cultures, literatures and languages."

NWT: A united East Africa would, of course, have its own individual characteristics: again, all those particularities are very, very important. But there really is no reason why Tanzania, Kenya, Uganda, Somalia, Ethiopia, Sudan cannot be one political region.

CC: Does this last essay signal a new stage of development in your work? When you say that there's no reason why these countries can't be one, and, in the same essay, that an "awareness of the land as the central actor in our lives distinguishes East African literature" (*Centre*, 163), you sound less ideological than you sometimes do in your more recent work.

NWT: You mean the last essay wasn't as polemical?

CC: It was very beautiful, emotionally and visually.

NWT: More reflective.

CC: The political theory is perfectly embodied in vignettes of eating, fishing at night, or dress, and this is a style that is different from, though not necessarily unconnected to, most of the writing in *Decolonising the Mind*.

NWT: I occasionally use that style. Come to think of it, it's also partly there in *Decolonising the Mind. Decolonising the Mind* has a lot of personal recollection: childhood days, capturing this type of moment, but it is put in a wider, polemical, intellectual context. My essay on East Africa is a development of that. *Detained* uses it an awful lot – this personal life.

CC: Yes, but with not as much natural beauty, an "awareness of the land," as you say, and its domestic scenes.

NWT: It's in my novels a lot. Certainly in *A Grain of Wheat*, the landscape is beautiful; I am very conscious of the landscape. Some of the more interesting pieces in *Petals of Blood*, especially at the end, are actually pure description: of changing seasons, the season of harvest, the season of planting, the season of things growing.[17] There's quite a lot of that. In my last two novels, *Devil on the Cross* and *Matigari*,[18] the actual landscape is not so dominant. But even that's not true in *Matigari*: when Matigari is moving across the land, the hills and valleys, and when he dies – or rather, when he meets his fate, whatever it is – in the river, and when he's being hunted. In visual terms, you can see him as part of the landscape. Many times you don't see him as a figure but as almost part of the landscape.

CC: Do you have any new books that you're working on, any new novels?

NWT: Not at the present, you know, but there's always something, obviously.

CC: Would you ever think of putting on some of your plays again, in connection with the Performance Studies position you now have at New York University? Including students, the great wealth of musicians in New York, its large and diverse artistic community?

NWT: I've only been at NYU since June of last year. I'll have to see how things work out. I'll see how I fit in New York, before I know exactly what to do.

CC: It was just an idea. I think it would be great.

1   Ngũgĩ wa Thiong'o, *Moving the Centre: the Struggle for Cultural Freedoms* (London: James Currey; Nairobi: East African Publishers; Portsmouth: Heinemann, 1993). Further references to this source are noted parenthetically in the text as *Centre.*

2   See note 2, page xv above.

3   George Lamming (1927-) is a novelist, essayist, and poet from Barbados. *In the Castle of My Skin* (1953) is considered his nation's first and greatest novel as well as a masterpiece of pan-African literature. Paul Robeson (1898-1976) was an American singer, actor, cultural and political advocate, author, and icon of the American civil rights movement.

4   Created at an international conference in Bretton Woods, New Hampshire, in 1944, the International Monetary Fund and the World Bank are both based in Washington. Their respective missions are international and to engage with difficult economic conditions mostly in Third World countries but also in countries in Europe and around with world. Generally, the IMF focuses on economic structures and monetary exchange, and the World Bank focuses on poverty.

5   Mobutu Sese Seko (1930-97), Daniel arap Moi (1924-), Hastings Banda (1898-1997), Jean Bédel Bokassa (1921-96), Paul Biya (1933-), and Siad Barre (1919-95) are widely considered to be dictators of their nations, respectively Zaire (aka Democratic Republic of the Congo), Kenya, Malawi, Central African Republic, Cameroon, and Somalia.

6   A. M. Babu (1924-96) was a Tanzanian economist and writer who was a leader in his nation's struggle for independence from England.

7   The Mau Mau armed struggle in Kenya from 1952-1960 was a pri-

mary and major factor in Kenya's gaining independence form England in 1963.

8   Moi served as both a legislator and a minister in Kenya's government under British colonial rule.

9   Yoweri Museveni (1944-) became president of Uganda in 1986. Idi Amin (1925-2003) was president of Uganda from 1971-1979. His regime became infamous for the corruption and violence he inflicted on Uganda's people, as well as on non-Ugandans living in the country, including the widespread denial of the most basic human rights, mass murder, and ethnic cleansing.

10   Georges Pompidou (1911-74) was president of France of France from 1969-74

11   As president of Uganda, Idi Amin made state visits to English in 1971 and 1972, where he was welcomed and dined with Queen Elizabeth II in London.

12   "The Cold War" refers to the hostile relationship, although not open and direct warfare, between the Soviet Union and its Eastern bloc of countries – under the rule of Communism – and the United States-led Western and democratic nations from roughly 1945 to 1990, when the Soviet Union and its alliances collapsed.

13   Mikhail Bakhtin (1895-1975) was a Russian Marxist literary scholar, theorist, and critic who wrote extensively about language itself.

14   Michael Harper (1938-2016) was an American poet and professor whose writing highlighted African American history and jazz. James Joyce (1882-1941) was an Irish writer and Modernist whose works – including *Dubliners* (1914), *Ulysses* (1922), and *Finnegan's Wake* (1939) – established him as a major 20th-century author.

15   A Scottish novelist, poet, essayist, and travel writer, Robert Louis Stevenson (1850-94) published the adventure story, *Treasure Island*, in 1883. Its popularity has been perennial and universal. Charles Dickens (1812-70) wrote fifteen major works of fiction and is, perhaps, the most popular and widely read of all English novelists. James Bigglesworth, nicknamed "Biggles," was the main character of a popular series of adventure books for young readers by W. E. Johns (1893-1968).

16   Georg Friedrich Hegel (1770-1831) was a German philosopher and historian who wrote about a wide range of issues, including phenomenology and the nature of knowledge itself.

Non-Native Speaker

17   Ngũgĩ wa Thiong'o, *A Grain of Wheat* (London: Heinemann, 1967);
      Petals of Blood (London: Heinemann, 1977).

18   Ngũgĩ wa Thiong'o, *Matigari* (London: Heinemann, 1987; Trenton
      & Asmara: Africa World Press, 1998).

Penpoints, Gunpoints, and Dreams (1999)

No African writer has as many major, lasting creative achievements in such a wide range of genre as Ngũgĩ wa Thiong'o. His books include novels, plays, short stories, essays and scholarship, criticism, and children's literature. His fiction, nonfiction, and drama, from the early 1960's to the present, are frequently reprinted. He is the founder and editor of the groundbreaking, Gĩkũyũ-language journal, *Mũtiiri*. Political exile from Kenya, Ngũgĩ – as he is known worldwide – is currently the Erich Remarque Professor of Languages at New York University, with a dual professorship in Comparative Literature and Performance Studies.

Baudelaire writes, "*De la vaporisation et de la concentration du moi. Tout est la*" ("The dispersion and the reconstitution of the self. That's the whole story").[1] It's not. This is a primary message of African literature and art today. Ngũgĩ wa Thiong'o is one of its primary exemplars.

This interview focuses on Ngũgĩ wa Thiong'o's book of essays, *Penpoints, Gunpoints, and Dreams: Towards a Critical Theory of the Arts and the State in Africa*.[2] Based on the four lectures he was invited to give at Oxford University in 1996, as a part of the Clarendon Lectures in English Literature series, and subtitled "Towards a Critical Theory of the Arts and the State in Africa," the book moves freely and universally, from Plato to Okot p'Bitek,[3] pre-ancient Egypt to postmodern New York; the Macaulay,[4] colonial minute to Marx to Mau Mau: from the war between art and the state to "the beautyful ones...not yet born." In the book's preface, while Ngũgĩ gratefully recalls a pleasurable and productive stay at Somerville College, he also notes, somewhat tongue-in-cheek, perhaps, a feeling of rebuke from "a huge portrait of Queen Elizabeth I...[on] the wall of the dining-room of Jesus College for my unfavorable reference...to her edict of 1601 in which she had called for the expulsion of black people from her realm" (*Penpoints*, viii). At Somerville, the college of Margaret Thatcher when she was a student at Oxford,[5] Ngũgĩ feels "another rebuke for [his] claims...that the capitalist fundamentalism of which she and Reagan were the leading apostles was wreaking social havoc in the world and generating other forms of fundamentalism in opposition or alliance." His apartment abuts "Margaret Thatcher Court."

The interview takes place on a mild and gray Veteran's Day afternoon in 1999. A landscape of missing ceiling panels, hills and valleys of paper, mail clutter, catalogues, piles of folders that have never been vertically filed, books, empty bags, quite far-back issues of African literary journals, and many half filled boxes of copies of *Mũtiiri*, Ngũgĩ's NYU office looks out on a rare undeveloped patch of downtown Broadway. Noticing that Ngũgĩ has lost his voice due to a cold, I sympathize. He replies that characters in his new novel lose their voices, too.

NWT: My voice is back.

CC: Good. Many of your first publications appeared in the Makerere University English department's literary magazine, *Penpoints*. You call your new book of essays *Penpoints, Gunpoints, and Dreams*. What are some of the connections between the two? Is the repetition deliberate?

NWT: Yes, there is a connection. "Penpoints" is a good name: penpoints – the power of the pen. I was interested in the power of the pen. The echo is there.

CC: The subtitle of your new book is "Towards a Critical Theory of the Arts and the State in Africa." Much of your previous nonfiction – *Decolonising the Mind* and *Moving the Centre*, for example – might be described in similar terms. What provoked you to continue in this vein? What new critical and political issues for you in the last five years make these new essays further departures "towards" formulating an aesthetic as well as taking a political stance?

NWT: Two things. Although I'm calling it "Towards a Critical Theory of the Arts and the State in Africa," a better or more appropriate subtitle might have been "A Performance Theory of the Arts and the State in Africa." The question of performance is more pronounced here than in any of my previous works. That is quite important to me. Second, in this text I'm much more interested in the nature of art and the nature of the state, and their relationship: something that I have not explored in my previous works. I've touched on the subject here and there but without a coherent framework. Art's war with the state is basic to the nature of art and the nature of the state, any state. There is always the possibility of conflict between the state and art.

CC: The concept of "performance" has become a uniting theme in your work. You write of it "in the narrow sense of representation of an action as in theater and in the broader sense of any action that assumes an audience during the actualization. The concept of performance is opening out new possibilities in the analysis of human behavior, including literature. The exercise of power, for instance, involves variations on the performance theme" (*Penpoints*, 5). In fact, you are a professor of Performance Studies. What drew you to this new scholarly discipline? How did your life and writing prepare you, perhaps without your knowing, for this new field? There is a sense in your writing that you are learning from it at least as much as you are contributing to it with your work.

NWT: Of course, I've been in theater all my life. I've worked in community theater in Kenya: in the Kamirithũ Community Educational and Cultural Centre.[6] And this, of course, brought me into conflict with the state in Kenya. My work in theater has been a preparation for this. I have also gained from using the term as a conceptual tool. So much in society depends on "performance." It provides new insights into certain behaviors. It is central to so many things. For example, you can't have religion without performance: performance, weekly, daily. Think of all those festivals. Think of performance in a wide sense. Performance enables people to negotiate their way through the various realms of being. Performance is a means for people to realize their unknown, even if it's only in the imagination. Performance is a very important concept. I have learned from it, but also

I have been involved in it.

CC: Is an emphasis on "performance" a way of advancing post-colonial critical discourse? As you discuss it, the concept of "performance" would seem to broaden and, perhaps, revitalize postcolonial studies.

NWT: Yes, and not only the postcolonial but many disciplines. The concept of performance can also be used to look at some of the older disciplines and reinterpreting some of the older texts. For example, Elizabeth Claire's work on performance and dance in Jane Austen has let us see what we hadn't before in the 18th and 19th centuries.[7] Performance is a concept that enables many things to be looked at differently. In classical writings, too, like Plato, for instance, the context of the dialogues is a performance in the dramatic sense. If you look at Plato's *Republic*, the dialogues exist within the larger context of their dramatization and, furthermore, the contexts of dramatic and religious festivals. There is a kind of performativity all around. The concept, however, must not become too wide or so broad that "anything goes." I take, for example, two features like representation and the assumption of an audience to be very important. In other words, a farmer planting crops ordinarily for the production of whatever he wants to eat or sell could be called a performance. But if I'm demonstrating as a farmer that I plant crops so that people can come and see how this is done, that would be a performance that is assuming that there is an audience. Even though this is an act I am actually doing, I am representing another action. The audience is very important.

CC: Another large, perhaps parallel theme in this book is orature. You write that "Orature...is not seen as a branch of literature but as a total aesthetic system, with performance and integration of art forms as two of its defining qualities. It is more basic and more primary than the other systems of the literary, the theatrical, and the cinematic because all the other systems take one or more of their main features from orature" (*Penpoints*, 117). You consider orature, "a unifying force" (*Penpoints*, 119), including "the four aesthetic systems of the written, the oral, the theatrical and the cinematic" (*Penpoints*, 118). You argue that "The centrality of orature to all the other systems calls for a reconfiguration and regrouping of disciplines" in which "their hierarchical ordering...is denied" and there is an end of "the historical rifts separating theorist, critics, and practitioners."[8] What are some of the critical, historical and geographical factors that have led you to such a conclusion? How has it influenced and changed your own writing and thinking?

NWT: If you look at orature in all societies, classical or contemporary, it refuses to draw very firm boundaries between disciplines, genres or forms. If you take a story, an oral narrative for instance, it will contain dance or music. The work might also involve audience participation, a chorus, or even the audience as a chorus. Often there are songs themselves or songs that involve dance variations. In some cases the word for the song and dance is the same. A song, a proverb, whatever: it suggests other forms. As important, performance is central to the study and realization of orature, as well as narratives, proverbs, whatever you do. Performance is central, unifying. There is a performance to space, to architecture, to sculpture. The assumption in classical orature is that the boundary between the natural world and the supernatural is fluid. In terms of aesthetics, the integrative aspect of orature is a very important element. Many disciplines and activities come under the umbrella of orature. The theater is a halfway house in which the realization of the drama is for it to become orature. The realization on stage of a musical composition embraces the concept of orature. While it integrates the many different possibilities of performance, orature also allows for the differences, for example, among narrative, song or drama.

CC: Orature and performance work together. Is performance a means to embracing orature?

NWT: Performance is central. They are not synonymous. Performance is what distinguishes orature from literature, even in the most obvious way: when you are reading a novel, you don't need a performance.

CC: You're completing a new novel. Are there ways in which your thinking about orature and performance has affected the novel?

NWT: Yes, but we won't go into too much detail about it because writing is a complicated process. Performance is central to the new novel. It is a state of performance. The characters are engaged in the constant performance of their own being for the narrative. You never quite know who they are. Often they reinvent themselves through performance. Even I, as their author, do not know where or how the whole novel is going to end except in the constant performance of their own being.

CC: Is this a reinvention both in public and private?

NWT: Yes. The characters in this new novel constantly reinvent themselves. I don't know if they are making progress because I've only done the first two drafts. My wife, Njeeri, is now reading it. She's at the house and maybe you should call there.

CC: For sure – I'll call later. In the meantime, you may recall that William Blake called the Bible "the great code of art."[9] In the introduction to *Penpoints, Gunpoints, and Dreams*, you assert, "The goal of human society is the reign of art on earth" (*Penpoints*, 6). Taken out of context, this could almost sound like a kind of *fin de siècle* aestheticism for the 20th century much like what happened at the end of the 19th century in the West. The slightest familiarity with your work, however, reveals anything but the aesthete. What do you mean by "the reign of art?"

NWT: I associate my concept of art with creativity, movement, change, and renewal. I'm thinking of a much more ethical society than what we have now. This "reign of art" would subsume or transcend the coercive nature of the state: a more ethical, more human society that is constantly renewing itself; art embodies this. I remember, historically speaking, a time when there was no state because I grew up in a society where literally there wasn't a state, at least in its centralized form. Art precedes the formation of the state. The state embodies a static concept of conservation, holding back. Of course, when the state is also controlled by a class, it is an instrument for much more for holding back of society. Creativity, art embodies the principle of what our hands do anyway: change. Creativity is really the essence of what is God and what is human. God is changing: we change the environment, we change when we plant, when human beings sow. When human beings plant one seed, this will produce more seeds out of one. We take what we raise and transform it for the better. We see many transformations, like the advance of science and technology, although their benefits these days do not necessarily go to enhancing the lives of the majority of the people.

CC: This brings us back to the war between art and the state. A bomb hits the garden.

NWT: The central logic of both art and the state is for each to work itself free: which creates opposition. In reality, however, it is not always absolute. There is sometimes an attempt at mutual corruption. The state will corrupt art. Art will try to influence the state. Some artists try to align themselves with the state.

CC: Yet you describe the "war...between art and the state" (*Penpoints*, 38) as "really a struggle between the power of performance in the arts and the performance of power by the state – in short, enactments of power." You assert that "The performance space of the artist stands for openness; that of the state, for confinement. Art breaks down barriers between people; the state erects them" (68). What of an alliance or, at least, a correspondence between art and the state? Historically, maybe we have seen moments when this has been possible, but has it ever lasted? Are there any benefits when art and the state work together?

NWT: The moment you open out democratic space, this is important for art: you also open the space for creativity. Historically there are moments of great, revolutionary change when you can see art and the state anticipating and almost together working out a new world. Art anticipates a new world. Revolutionary forces in society are always anticipating that world. But once a state, even a revolutionary state, comes to power, the very nature of the state is to hold back. A permanently revolutionary state is almost an impossibility. Even a revolutionary state has to pass laws. It has to constitute what it considers to be stability of some kind. Its aim is to repeat itself.

CC: You write, "There is no state that can be in permanent revolution. Art, on the other hand, is revolutionary by its very nature as art" (*Penpoints*, 13); and "Art has more questions than it has answers.... The state, on the other hand, has plenty of answers and hardly any questions. The more absolutist the state, the less it is likely to ask questions of itself or entertain questioning by others" (*Penpoints*, 15).

NWT: Even a novelist at his poorest does not want to reproduce his previous work. I think of art in terms of permanent revolution. Permanent, constant revolution is not inherent in the nature of the state and its operations. Constant revolutionizing, reinventing itself is inherent in the nature of art. The artist considers reinventing himself all the time. The state has to conserve. Therefore, the possibility of conflict is always there.

CC: You write, "Where...there is no democracy for the rest of the population, there cannot be democracy for the writer" (*Penpoints*, 129). What is the role of African-language writers in contributing to economic, political, and cultural empowerment, strengthening civil society and current, emerging democratic traditions and governance, and reforming the language of African political discourse?

NWT: All over the world art is constantly attempting to return language to the people. Any moment of exceptional literary achievement in a national tradition signals a writer's return of language at its fullest to people in their daily life. In the context of Africa, writers need to return to the languages actually spoken by the people to enlarge the space of people's understanding to include more experiences. A writer makes a language for its speakers to comprehend their universe better than ever before. African languages can play a big role in Africa's democratization, its spiritual awakening and enhancement. But that spirit is repeatedly crushed because English and French continue to dominate a continent where most people speak African languages.

CC: *Penpoints, Gunpoints and Dreams* contains an extensive re-interpretation of the allegory of the cave from Plato's *Republic*. Roughly speaking, you argue that the dominance of European languages in the critical discourse of the majority of African intellectuals sets them, so to speak, forever outside the cave: the space of which they neither re-enter nor open. You also offer Ayi Kwei Armah's novel, *The Beautyful Ones Are Not Yet Born*,[10] as a kind of alternative to Plato's story. For example, replacing Plato's ideal, incorruptible, true philosophers with Armah's *"beautyful* ones" who are to lead the African state of the future, you write,

> Such intellectuals, whenever they are born, will grow their roots in African languages and cultures. They will also learn the best they can from all world languages and cultures. They will view themselves as scouts in foreign linguistic territories and guides in their own linguistic space. In other words, they will take whatever is most advanced in those languages and cultures and translate those ideas into their own languages. They will have no complexes about borrowing from others to enrich their own.... They will see their role as that of doing for African languages and cultures what all writers

and intellectuals of other countries and histories have done for theirs.

Penpoints, 100

What led you to Plato?

NWT: "The Beautyful Ones...Not Yet Born" is a very beautiful phrase. The image of the cave is very distinct. It's an image with a logic that goes against Plato's philosophy itself. The assumption of the allegory of the cave that philosophers who see the light must come back – that an elite should come back to the people in a cave – goes against Plato's advocacy in the same book of an hierarchical society with categories like philosopher kings, the warriors, and guardians of the state as opposed to its more lowly workers. Such an elite in fact does not return to the people. My work in performance has led me to re-examine more and more, or go back to and revisit classical Greece. I've found that it was a very oral society. To think of that society being literate in terms of writing is a 20th-century projection. In reality, we see a very oral society. Socrates, for instance, is working within theories of orature, conversing in the market place. Dialogues take place as he's coming from there or going to a festival. They take place in and around the house, by the fireside. He's not a writer. In a sense, this society exemplifies a kind of orature and Socrates is actually a philosopher within the oral tradition. Plato's dialogues assume a kind orality. Even bad translations cannot kill or hide this. It is everywhere.

CC: In *Decolonising the Mind* (1986), you identified the conflict between African and Europhone languages as

a deliberate dissociation of the language of conceptualization, of thinking, of formal education, of mental development, from the language of daily interaction in the home and in the community. It is like separating the mind from the body so that they are occupying two unrelated linguistic spheres in the same person. On a

larger social scale it is like producing a society of bodi-
less heads and headless bodies.

Decolonising, 28

In your new work, you write

[A]n intellectual is a worker in ideas using words as
the means of production. It means that for Africa the
thinking part of the population, the one with the pool
of skills and know-how in economics, agriculture, science, engineering is divorced from the agency of social
change: the working majority. At the level of economics, science, and technology Africa will keep on talking
about transfer of technology from the West. There are
countless resolutions about this in regional, continental,
and international conferences. Yet the African intellectual elite...refuse to transfer even the little they have already acquired in the language of the majority below....
knowledge researched by sons and daughters of Africa, and actually paid for by the entire working majority who need it most, is stored in European-language
granaries. There can be no real economic growth and
development where a whole people are denied access to
the latest developments in science, technology, health,
medicine, business, finance, and other skills of survival
because all these are stored in foreign languages. Ignorance of progress in ideas is a guarantee against rapid
economic growth.

Penpoints, 90

Do you see any signs that the African mind and body need
not be split by language in the future? As you yourself write,
"If some of the best and most articulate of the interpreters
of African total being insist on interpreting in languages not
understood by the subject of their interpretation, where lies
the hope of African deliverance?" (*Penpoints*, 94)

NWT: In Greek mythology, Zeus employs Prometheus to make men out of mud and water but, in pity for their state, he steals fire from Olympus and gives it to them. The image of fire is very strong for me. It is central to knowledge... light, technology, heat. Fire changes things. Fire is almost everything. I'm not surprised that many people used to worship the sun. They were not all that wrong in seeing the sun as God, the source of everything. The question is whether Prometheus leaves the fire to the gods or gives it to humans. Does he give them the fire or does he say that they can only use this fire when they come up the mountain. The whole idea is that he brings the fire to them. But where is the fire when we African intellectuals refuse to dialogue in African languages, the language of the vast majority of our people?

CC: Citing Marx's observation "that an idea grasped by the masses becomes a material force," you suggest that "language is obviously the best, the cheapest, and the most effective way of disseminating such ideas" (*Penpoints*, 97). Does this imply that the discouragement and outright suppression of education and writing in African languages, even now in a postcolonial era, is a deliberate means of social and political oppression of, perhaps, the worst sort?

NWT: If and when African intellectuals are progressive, for example, through an emphasis on democracy, there can still be a fundamental contradiction about their ideas if, as in the biblical parable, their light is hidden under the bushel basket of European languages that the majority of the people do not understand. In this sense, African intellectuals continue, ironically, a tradition of their own enslavement. They are like people who work for a feudal lord. Their happiness, even though they are honest, depends on working in his house. Their sense of being connects to their constant narration of what goes on around the feudal lord, his comings and goings.

CC: American slave plantations also had their house hands and field hands.

NWT: We are operating with European languages where there are African languages whose space we could be opening out.

CC: Are you suggesting that writers and scholars make a deliberate choice of language and that there is no sitting on the fence" concerning this issue amidst the struggle of African people for greater cultural, political and economic empowerment within a democratic space?

NWT: Yes. After much wavering, I came to this conclusion in my book, *Decolonising the Mind*. But in *Penpoints* ...[and] *Gunpoints* I take a firmer position. I look at language and a whole history of interpretation over five hundred years. I trace the issue of plantation slavery and how language is used as a way within the plantation of keeping practical communication bound exclusively to itself. Not only are various African languages suppressed as a means of communication among the slaves. Colonial plantations themselves enforce their own language as a means of enclosure, be they English, French or Spanish. They never meet unless through conquest or re-conquest. The colonizing power in Africa of Europe similarly keeps people bound to its languages. Yet the struggle of African people in the "New World" also takes the form of creating new languages. These people's conditions of life also mean a struggle to construct the world in their own terms. Thus we find Creole languages, patois, and much more. Africa should learn from that tremendous struggle to recompose a new world: to create new languages that owe their being to African languages. Colonizing principles are very clear about the role of language. The widespread practice of linguistic engineering would create a vast army of Africans whose interpretations in the languages of their colonizers would reinforce their power over their subjects.

CC: Linguistic engineering: this sounds a little like ethnic cleansing. To recognize the hyper-conscious and deliberate imposition of colonial languages and not merely their absorption is a horror.

NWT: Ironically, in not working more through African languages we are continuing, even when we are conscious of it, a neocolonial system that still binds African people. At an economic level, Africa produces raw materials that are processed in Europe and returned to Africa. At the level of culture, we see the same pattern. We draw our own resources in African languages and this is processed in English or French and then brought back as a finished product in French or English for African consumption. And still it does not reach a level of consumption as great as if it had remained in African languages, in the same way that gold that is mined in Africa and brought back from Europe is too expensive and inaccessible to all but the few. In the same way, we draw upon the linguistic resources and life of Africa, even in political struggles, and they are processed in English or French. But when they are brought back in this form they are lost and inaccessible to the vast majority of the population who only speak African languages.

CC: You call "the ascendance of capitalist fundamentalism and the Darwinian ethical systems which it is generating ... the mother of all fundamentalisms, religious and nationalistic" (*Penpoints*, 130). You insist, "there should be no ambiguity about the necessity to abolish the economic and social conditions which bring about the need for charity and begging within any nation and between nations, and language should sensitize human beings to that necessity" (*Penpoints*, 131). "Art," you claim, "should join all the other social forces in society to extend the performance space for human creativity and self-organizations and so strengthen civil society" (*Penpoints*, 131-32). You even predict that "just as it was the case in some pre-capitalist societies, it is possible that ...[in] a post-capitalist society, production will be geared not towards social domination of others but towards meeting human needs, culture and creativity" (*Penpoints*, 131). Is a "reign of art" (*Penpoints*, 6) precisely in African languages a key to democratic empowerment and success in such a struggle?

NWT: The empowerment of African languages is clearly part of this process. If we look at the period in our history when questions of privatization and profit become the barometer for progress in society instead of class solidarity, what do we find? Consider Yugoslavia now with its ethnic massacres and when there was more emphasis on class solidarity. The moment we come to a post-cold war de-emphasis of class begins a new period of ethnic fundamentalism. It corresponds to a puritanism of capitalism. This fundamentalism of finance capital occurs within the same period of all sorts of other fundamentalisms, sometimes even in alliance with it, as in Christian-right fundamentalism; or in opposition to it. How do we fight against this force of fundamentalism, whatever form it takes, which seems to threaten people who often do not understand what is threatening them, as class solidarity has been de-emphasized in recent thinking in favor of national wars, ethnic and religious boundaries or whatever seems to present some kind of assurance and stability more readily known? Art connects. It says that human beings are connected. Art says, "Look. We are connected. It's like ecology. Human beings are connected: trees to animals to other human beings." Art tends to say, "We live in one universe, you know?" Art seems to emphasize spirituality, the spiritual expression of human life.

CC: The role of art is to break through fundamentalisms?

NWT: Yes. To break boundaries and borders that separate.

---

1   Charles Baudelaire, *Journaux Intime* (1887; Paris: G. Crès, 1920), 45; Charles Baudelaire, *Intimate Journals*, translated by Christopher Isherwood (1887; New York: Howard Fertig, 1977), 53.

2   See note 8, page 9 above.

3   Okot p'Bitek (1931-82), a Ugandan poet, is the author of *Song of Lawino*, a long poem and a major, pioneering work of African language writing in Acholi, which he also translated into English.

4   Thomas Babington Macaulay (1800-59) was a British historian, politician, and essayist, and educator. His "Minute on Indian Education" (1835) asserted that only the English language and English culture, not native language(s) or indigenous culture(s), would foster the development of Britain's colonial possessions.

5   Margaret Thatcher (1925-2013) was the prime minister of the United Kingdom from 1979 to 1990. As a Conservative and the first woman to hold the office, she instituted major political and social changes.

6   In 1977, Ngũgĩ wa Thiong'o's play *Ngaahika Ndeenda*, or *I Will Marry When I Want*, was performed at the Kamirithũ Community Educational and Cultural Centre. The play was innovative in a number of ways, including its performance in Gikũyũ, use of non-community members instead of professional actors, creative collaboration between author and cast members, use of song, and political content. Ever since, *I Will Marry When I Want* has had a major influence on Kenyan and African drama. Soon after its first series of performances, however, the play was shut down by the Kenyan government. Subsequently, the theater was destroyed, Ngũgĩ lost his teaching position at the University of Nairobi, and he was "detained," that is, imprisoned in Kamĩtĩ Maximum for nearly the whole year of 1978.

7   Elizabeth Claire (1973-) is an American scholar, writer, and performer whose work focuses on gender, history, and dance.

8   Cf. Akintunde Akinyeme, *Orature and Yoruba Riddles* (New York: Palgrave Macmillan, 2015).

>   Orature is that vast field of knowledge in which cultural information and messages are transmitted verbally from one generation to the next. It is a complex corpus of oral arts created to recall, honor, and preserve the past. On occasion, the term *orature* is used interchangeably with oral tradition, oral literature, and folklore or storytelling elements – language and belief systems shared by a common group. It is a verbal legacy contributing significantly to cultural and national identity. In contemporary usage, orature is reflected in popular and group-oriented cultural expressions.

>   Orature is governed by certain characteristic features – including the situation or context in which it is produced, the audience, language, and structure of format. A primary fea-

ture of orature, which relates to the nature of performance, is community involvement (both in the creative and critiquing process). Each performance is for and about the audience. The main objective of the performer is to entertain, amuse, and impress the audience so as to earn praise, admiration, and, on occasion, material gifts. In creative performance, members of the audience neither listen silently nor wait for the invitation of the performer before joining in. Instead, the audience spontaneously interjects, queries, and comments (1-2).

9   William Blake (1757-1827) was an English poet and visual artist, including painting and printmaking, His writing ranged from intense, relatively short lyric poems to neo-biblical epic.

10   Ayi Kwei Armah (1939-) is a Ghanaian novelist, essayist, and poet. *The Beautyful Ones Art Not Yet Born* (1968), his first novel, is considered on of Africa's greatest.

African Literature – Says Who? The Last 50 Years with Ngũgĩ wa Thiong'o (2016)

The title, "African Literature – Says Who? The Last 50 Years with Ngũgĩ wa Thiong'o,"[1] contains an equation with a constant and a variable. Harkening back to an epic dawn of, even the darkest hour before, African independence, the literary works of Ngũgĩ Thiong'o over the last fifty years are a constant, and their value is as certain as any major contemporary writer's in the world can be.

African literature – what it is or is understood to be – is a variable. What "African literature" refers to or signifies can vary or change and seem uncertain, depending on who is conceiving it, almost as if African literature is as up for grabs as Africa itself. It's a wide-open field, and there is so much yet to know. To try to conceive of all of the literature in the languages of Africa is bewildering, bordering on all but impossible, as if trying to contemplate a verbal genome.

As a constant over the last fifty years, Ngũgĩ's literary milestones over such a long period of time amount to an epic catalogue. Although there are more, his landmark moments include:

- The "Conference of African Writers of English Expression" at Makerere University in 1962

- His three historical English novels published in the 1960s: *Weep Not, Child* (1964), *The River Between* (1965), and *A Grain of Wheat*, (1967). Their golden anniversaries are upon us.

- "On the Abolition of the English Department" at the University of Nairobi in 1968

- The Kamirithũ Community Education and Culture Centre's productions of his plays, *The Trial of Dedan Kimathi* and *I Will Marry When I Want*, to use the English translations of their Gĩkũyũ titles, in 1976

- His Gĩkũyũ novels from 1982 to 1986 – again translating their titles, *Petals of Blood, Devil on the Cross*, and *Matigari*

- His most famous and groundbreaking book of essays, *Decolonising the Mind* in 1986 and its historic "farewell to English"

- His *magnum opus, Mũrogi wa Kagogo* or *Wizard of the Crow* in 2006

- His critical works *Moving the Centre* in 1993, *Penpoints, Gunpoints, and Dreams* in 1998, *Something New and Torn* in 2009, and *Globalectics* in 2012

- Two books childhood memoirs, *Dreams in a Time of War* (2010) and *In the House of the Interpreter* (2012)

Might not Ngũgĩ's memoir of African literatures and languages have been already written, at least partially, throughout these books? Hopefully the following can make this memoir a little more evident.

CC: To cite a passage from your book of essays, *Something Torn and New* (2009): I always remember how, upon learning how to read in English, my classmates and I would carry the English-language Bible to church. The service was entirely in Gĩkũyũ. Everybody else had the Gĩkũyũ-language Bible. The preacher read passages from the Gĩkũyũ-language Bible. But we who had been to school would follow him through our English text. The Gĩkũyũ voice had to come to us in English sounds.... This was to become the practice in African writing as well...."[2] What do you mean by the "Gĩkũyũ voice" that came to you "in English sounds." How does this dynamic become a paradigm of "the practice in African writing as well?" What are the differences between that "voice" in English sounds and the "voice" in Gĩkũyũ itself?

NWT: The voice is that which my mother gave me. The conquering sound is that of the colonial. After the conquest my voice came to me swaddled in English sounds. Or rather the voice that my mother gave me was buried under the English sounds. It could only be heard through English.

Let me tell you more about the voice that my mother gave me. First it was oral. All languages are oral. The literary always mimics the oral. At night and around the fireside, this voice reached me in the form of stories. We were told that stories went away in daytime. Where did they go? We didn't know. Fortunately, they always came back in the night, after all the chores of the day. My mother did not know how to read or write. But she had a dream of education – an education for me. Even though she didn't know how to read or write, she supervised my homework. She always wanted to know how well I had done. If I told her I had a 100% in something, she would ask, "Is it the best? The best you could have done?" The question became a constant refrain, an aspiration. And thus I learned to write and read. In Gĩkũyũ language.

And then the magic. The stories came back in daytime. I could now tell stories to myself regardless of the time of day. It was thanks to my mother. I read the stories in the Gĩkũyũ translation of the Bible, the Old Testament. Today when I hear the song, "Amazing Grace,"[3] and the line "I once was blind, but now I see," I remember that time when I learned how to read through my mother's efforts. How did I repay her? Consider my first novel, *Weep Not, Child*.[4] It was my own life, but it was not written in my mother's voice. I wrote it in another language. This is the contradiction I was trying to capture in the passage from *Something Torn and New* that you quoted. Instead of accepting that we had a good language and that through it we could read along with the people around us, we acted special – feigned foreign.

This encapsulates the central contradiction in much of the writing from the continent. I call it Europhone African literature. This is the literature written by Africans but in European tongues. Some of what I have written – *Weep Not, Child*, *The River Between*, *A Grain of Wheat*, *Petals of Blood*, and even my memoirs and my literary and critical theory – are part of the Europhone tradition.

In reality there is another literature, another tradition that is deep and long and found throughout Africa in African languages: in Ge'ez, Amharic, Hausa, Kiswahili, Luganda, IsiZulu and isiXhosa, Shona, Yoruba, and in many other African languages. But its voice has been muffled: its identity stolen. We all are aware of and talk about "identity theft." But what about *literary identity theft*? Europhone African literature has stolen the identity of African literature; it wears the mask of African literature. It is a good example of *literary identity theft*, a phenomenon that is now global, a maturation of the colonial.

CC: Identity theft, in literature. Maybe the world is catching up to you, Ngũgĩ. Way back in an interview from the early 1980s that was revised and republished in 1996, you state:

> I have come to the view that literature written by Africans in foreign languages like French, English, Spanish, Danish...etc. falls into a category of its own. It is a misnomer to call it African literature. It can only be called Afro-European literature in general and more particularly Afro-Saxon literature when the literature is written by Africans in the English language, or Afro-French literature that is written by Africans in the French language. According to the new view, African literature is that literature written by Africans in African languages like Yoruba, Igbo, Hausa, Swahili, Gĩkũyũ, etc.—languages that are indigenous to Africa.[5]

This viewpoint prevails in your work ever since. In 1986, you call "the tradition of African literature in English, French, and Portuguese," in Europhone and colonial languages, "a minority tradition. It has no right usurping the term 'African literature.' In years to come it will be in footnotes when people talk about African Literature" (*Speaks*, 235). Your comment about "footnotes" reminds me of the current status of elaborate poems written in Latin during the European Renaissance or Early Modern Era. Almost no one reads them, even in graduate school, that is, even among the few who read Latin. Are you forecasting a time when reading African authors who only write in English, French or other colonial languages will look as obtuse as someone only reading authors who write in Latin during the European Renaissance? Then again, I ask myself, what would be known about it *without* European vernacular, Renaissance writers like Petrarch, Dante, Chaucer, Shakespeare, Donne, Rabelais, Montaigne, Cervantes, and more, if only their Latin-composing contemporaries were read?

From a different perspective, nevertheless, you have given African literature in European languages high praise. From a technical standpoint, you have applauded the intertextuality of Europhone African literature, even claiming to have used this yourself in *A Grain of Wheat*. You have also called for the translation of European African literature into African languages. You have also written, for example, in your most recent book of essays, *In the Name of the Mother*:

> African literature in European languages is the nearest thing we have to Pan-African common literary inheritance.... They have...enabled a dialogue between Africans of the continent and the diaspora. In short, they belong to the continent as much as to the nations of their origin. You have only to see the reverence with which African writers are held in every part of the continent to realize the validity of the claim. I can testify to that. I have been stopped in the streets of Zimbabwe, Ghana, Nigeria, by people who have never seen me before to say what my books have meant to them.[6]

You further add, "Take any major African writers, say Ama Ata Aidoo[7] or...Wole Soyinka.[8] If you travel anywhere in Africa, be it Zimbabwe, South African, Kenya or wherever, people...do not say, 'This is a Ghanaian writer' or 'That is a Nigerian writer.' They rather see them as African writers wherever they go." Isn't this a conundrum? Isn't such recognition the result of their works primarily being known in European languages that themselves are pan-African, in many cases even more than African languages themselves?

Critics and readers have been defensive, dismissive, and intimated by your distinctions between African language literature and Europhone literature. Why shouldn't they be?

NWT: When I talk about *literary identity theft*, it's not to demean the actual quality of the work produced in European languages. In fact, the quality of the work that has been produced by members of my generation who, for example, learned English many years after already speaking African languages, is amazing. Later generations may be different, too, in that there are some African writers who write in English because English in reality is their mother tongue, meaning that their parents brought them up as English-speaking children. This doesn't take away from the genius of what is produced.

The question of *literary identity theft* is not peculiar to Africa. Let's talk about the well-known Irish writer, James Joyce.[9] He could speak many languages – Greek, Latin, Italian, even some Japanese. Living in Italy for some time, he wrote for Italian newspapers in Italian. He published in Italian. He was aware of the problem. The English translation of one of his Italian articles is called "Ireland at the Bar." It tells the story of an Irish man who is arrested and accused of murder but who only speaks Gaelic and no English. The trial is in English, but everything he answers and tries to explain is translated as "No, your honor." As a result, he is found guilty and hanged. Joyce could see the problematic relation between Gaelic or Irish and English, but he wanted to be seen more as a European than Irish. It was as if Ireland was not part of Europe. Joyce chose to write in English. He is a part of this tradition of Europhone literature or, in this case, Anglophone. In *Finnegan's Wake*, Joyce tries to smuggle Gaelic words and expressions into the narrative. This does a lot for English, but it does nothing for Gaelic.

Let's compare Joyce with a contemporary Irish writer, Nuala Ní Dhomhnaill.[10] She has degrees in English, speaks and reads Turkish, French, and German. She is almost a replica of Joyce, but she chooses to write in Irish. She is always asked the question: why do you write in Irish? If so much of what is written in English is called Irish literature, she responds, what do I call the literature actually written in Irish by the Irish? In one of her most brilliant essays, "Why I Choose to Write in English,"[11] Nuala Ní Dhomhnaill says she will not sit idly by and let the identity of Irish literature be stolen.

Advances in technology have made stolen identities possible. It is a serious crime that can affect nations and peoples. Even at personal survival level! Stealing your identity, someone can access your bank account. You go to your bank and ask for your money, and you are told, "You've already taken it." You will say, "No, no, that's not me." *Literary identity theft* is as serious as what has been called stolen identity.

CC: James Joyce came up in our first interview in 1993.[12] I talked about language as his homeland, and you were skeptical. Languages were as much a matter of social communities, I recall you saying, as personal acquisition of the languages one uses in a novel or a poem. You insisted on the connection between the suppression of a language by economic or military means and the effect on the individual. You wondered how you could have a language that did not have community of speakers. I answered that maybe Joyce worked towards a language of no one's world, which could be a kind of lonely solace – and a Modernist monument – like *Finnegan's Wake*. But you weren't hearing that. Instead you brought up Ireland's long colonial history in relation to England and the West in general: a reality – an Irish reality – that you thought Joyce might not have fully considered. Joyce, of course, lived in a kind of exile and never returned either to Ireland or the Irish language. You have had the experience of exile, too.

NWT: I'm not a Joycean scholar, but his was a chosen exile – he wanted to be European, although I don't fully understand what that means since Ireland is an integral part of Europe.

But the Europe he identified with, for example, Italy, was the Europe of the empire: the Europe that colonized Africa; the Europe that colonized Ireland. Which Europe did he want to be a part of? I'm not talking about the quality or the genius of his work but the implications of his linguistic choice. He ran away from his Irish self, but one can also argue that his English works contain a longing for the Irish he chose to runaway from.

CC: Back to identity theft. When someone steals something, you want it back. You gave a talk a few days ago called, "Decolonising the mind – are we there yet?" When the Against All Odds conference was held in 2000 in Eritrea, you said that one of its most significant outcomes was the "Asmara Declaration on African Languages and Literatures" because it settled once and for all the African language question.[13]   When I heard the title of your talk, I wanted to ask you about the ascendancy of African languages – "Are we there yet?" Yet we find that more often than not the struggle of African languages is emphasized. For example, 90% of all the books in African languages have been published since 2000. To take another example: there was a moment during a conference I attended last summer at Kenyatta University. A young woman, one of the plenary speakers, stood up and asked a group of nearly two hundred young African language scholars, "Have any of you ever been colonized?" They roared in response, "No!" I had never heard that kind of response. I also found that there is so much African language literature and scholarship that is going on that we in the United States and Europe are not aware of. In this respect, the study of African languages and literatures is not the same in both places and is almost like a different discipline. Perhaps this is natural and should be expected. It is less of a struggle there and more plentiful. Your now longstanding Gĩkũyũ journal, *Mũtiiri*, is online, there are all kinds of African language apps for cell phones, and hip-hop thrives in African languages. There is a lot now that wasn't going on in 2000. If more people knew that African identity in this respect is being taken back, I wonder if there would be as much alarm that it has been stolen? There is more than one front in the struggle, and there are different levels of success.

NWT: I always like to add that as a writer I have absolutely nothing against English. I like all languages. They are marvelous. I'm now learning Español on YouTube. I try to learn French. It is very beautiful. I am learning several greetings in Chinese and other languages. When I went to Wales, I wanted someone to teach me some Welch so that I could at least read the road signs. I value all languages. What I reject – what has become more and more an anathema to me – is a hierarchy of languages: as if some languages inherently have more than other languages. This is imperial nonsense. All languages are capable of expressing the highest beauty. Instead of in a hierarchy, languages should relate to one another in a network of give and take. In that sense, there isn't such a thing as a big or small language. A network and a hierarchy exhibit a different kind of relationship. Hierarchy is a question of power. Network is a question of give and take.

The irony is that, in Africa, there has always been a tradition of writing in African languages. The translation of Thomas Mofolo's *Chaka* (1925)[14] originally written in Sotho had an impact on the work of Sédar Senghor.[15] Kiswahili language in terms of poetry and recently in the novel has a highly developed literary history, but its very identity as an African literature is buried under this other identity of European literature. Europhonity becomes Africanity, and what about the Africanity of Kiswahili and Yoruba and isiZulu?

The term Europhone African literature is not necessarily a negative. It is a correct description of a global phenomenon, a cultural aftermath of imperialism. There is Asian Europhone literature. Pacific Europhone literature, too. This Europhone tradition has its own identity. What is wrong and offensive is when it takes on the identity of the other, in what I have called *literary identity theft*. It doggedly refuses to recognize and accept its literary self as Europhone. It demands that literature in African languages beg for recognition, beg back its own name. "Europhonity" is, of course, a reality. In Africa there is Anglophone, Europhone, Francophone, Lusophone, Spanophone. Departments of literature all over the world can really help by calling writing by Africans in European languages by its correct name: Europhone African literature, which is part of worldwide Europhone literature.

CC: You mention hierarchies. For all the advances, progress, health, and robustness of African language study and literature, it is still against some staggering odds. As I was preparing for this interview, I Googled "African literature," and the "Goodreads" list of popular African literature books lists your latest novel, *Wizard of the Crow*, at #81. There are no other African language books or translations in the first one hundred and fifty. More specifically Googling "African literature books," I find in the first fifty that there are only two that were first published in African languages: Nawal El Saadawi's *Women at Point Zero* (1975) and,[16] perhaps surprisingly, Okot p'Bitek's *Song of Lawino* (1966).[17] The self-proclaimed list of "Africa's 100 Best Books of the 20th Century" is little better. Amazon's list of "African bestsellers" – the first 100: you don't even want to go there. I work in translating African language poetry, and websites that might be supposed to have a sampling of such work are disappointing. The UK Poetry Translation Centre has work in only three African languages, and the Poetry Society has next to nothing. The USA's Poetry Foundation also has nothing. Even the SOAS website only has .2% African languages. *Wasafiri* and *Callaloo*, British and American journals that are supposed to have a strong connection to African cultures, have next to nothing, too.[18] I could go on, but discretion here might be the better part of valor. Under the Soviet regime of Stalin in the 1930s, 1500 writers were executed: 750 of them were Ukrainian. They have been called an "executed Renaissance."[19] You have spoken of the history of African language writers, the odds against them, and we devoted the conference in Asmara to them. Surely there has been an executed Renaissance in African literature.

NWT: The key and cause for hope is that despite hundreds of years of imperial and neo-colonial repression, African languages have refused to die. The conference we had in Eritrea, where we produced the "Asmara Declaration in African Languages and Literatures:" even for me, an advocate of literature in African languages – I was totally amazed by the number of writers in African languages. I didn't know where they all came from. You did all the groundwork, so you knew! They came from Ghana, Ivory Coast, North Africa, South Africa, East Africa. We were all there, in Eritrea – writers who primarily wrote in African languages. I could make that claim, too. I was editing the journal *Mũtiiri* in Gĩkũyũ and was now writing all my novels in Gĩkũyũ. It was a beautiful thing to see. But to get the resources, even within Africa, or to get the gathering going again, there is a problem. These days the resources that go to African literary prizes to promote African literature are given on the condition that it is not written in an African language: a prize to encourage African writers but they cannot write in their African languages if they want to submit their work. Governments in Africa and financial institutions like the World Bank have policies that are aligned to ensure that European languages remain the dominant languages of education, intellectual production, and literary production.

CC: This makes me wonder how we got the World Bank to give us funding for the conference. We weren't very threatening, perhaps. Yet we made sure the conference hall had the equipment to translate the plenary sessions into six African languages. We produced your play, *I Will Marry When I Want* (1977) translated into Tigrinya. We couldn't find a Gĩkũyũ speaker to translate the original into Tigrinya, but we used the English translation. It gave us a ride from

Gĩkũyũ to Tigrinya like a taxi.

NWT: It's not that I am against what is available in English or French in any shape or form. I'm a great believer in translations. I have translated Moliere[20] into Gĩkũyũ. Since I started emphasizing African language literature as an organizing principle in teaching literature from Africa, I have come to appreciate Shakespeare much more than I used to because I can now see and properly appreciate what he was able to accomplish, and I can link his work to Africa much more meaningfully, comparatively, rather slavishly so. I have been able to appreciate more the rise of European languages because English, French, German, and Spanish went through what African languages are going through. There was a time when people who used English to translate or write about the Bible or medical terms were being told, even by other English intellectuals, "You can't do that." English was thought of as rude and crude. You can find the same resistance in French. Descartes found it necessary to explain why he was writing some of his philosophic discourse in French rather than Latin.[21] In 1536 William Tyndale was executed for translating the Bible into English.[22] Dante is very interesting for me.[23] When he started writing in his Tuscan language instead of Latin, some of his fellow writers advised him that he wouldn't get anywhere; he would lose literary immortality. He should write in Latin. What did Dante do? He wrote a reply in Latin in which he compares his Tuscan vernacular to a female sheep (ewe) whose udder is full of milk. "You can write in Latin, but I want to milk this richness," he said. But he wrote it in perfect Latin to show, "I can write in Latin if I want to, but I'm choosing to write in Tuscan." I love that. I love translations. They are a very good way to make languages communicate with each other so that their richness is in mutual conversation. And as cited above, there was a time when it was a crime to translate the Bible into English.

CC: Knowledge of literature depends on translation. No one can know literature without translation. For all who read Dante, comparatively few read him in Italian. For all who read and know the Bible – in its myriad of translations – its readers in actual biblical languages, like Hebrew, or later translations, long-standing translations like the Septuagint Koine Greek or the Vulgate in Latin, are miniscule. I'm very interested in talking about why there aren't more African language translations. Until there are, the question of what is African literature must remain wide open. Your analysis thirty years ago in *Decolonising the Mind* (1986) of African languages' lack of standing or status in comparison with other languages in the world primarily as a result of their political, social, and economic repression is now a critical given and rarely if ever contended. Still, as a non-native speaker, I have to plead for more translations of African language literature. Gĩkũyũ, Swahili, Tigrinya – they are not my languages. And until their poems, plays, and novels are translated, I won't know them. I need them, they have to be translated, and they have to be translated beautifully. Otherwise, I can't know them the way I know and love translations from so many of the world's great literatures in languages that I also don't and won't know. This day has to come, but when? There is plenty of focus on the problems of Africa, but the translation of African language literature is a huge problem, too. We know all too well the litany of other problems: globalization, dictators, democracy, fundamentalism, economies, immigration, Ebola, war, rights, reparations – the list can become endless. It seems endlessly repeated, too. And no one can or should deny such problems. But if there was one African language literary translation for the hundreds of times when we hear about these other problems and respond, "Yes, that's true. Yes, that's true. Yes, that's true," the problem of the dire lack of African language literary translations would be much closer to being solved. The unending recital of Africa's political and social problems can even begin to seem like excuses or alibis for not going ahead and translating the African literary texts. We have so many contexts for African language literature but all too few texts. What is going to change this? African language translation must succeed like the translations of other languages, ancient or modern. They must be translated and they must be read, and inevitably they will be called great. What is holding us back?

NWT: African countries have to change their own policies about African languages first. There must be an enabling linguistic environment. Apart from Tanzania, there are very few countries, maybe one or two others, where investments are put into African languages. Let me share a personal experience. It was overwhelming for me.

In 2014, I was offered an honorary doctorate , my ninth honorary doctorate, by the University of Dar es Salaam, right next door to Kenya. I thought, "In what language am I going to accept that doctorate?" This was a big challenge for me. My friends in Tanzania said that since I was there, I had to give public lecture. I asked myself, "Am I going to give a lecture in English, to a Kiswahili speaking nation? No." I didn't tell them because I wasn't sure I could do what I intended. To be frank, I wrote a speech in English on language and metaphysical empires, but I had Abdilatif Abdalla, a native speaker of Kiswahili and one of the leading Swahili poets in the world, translate it.[24] Five minutes before I was about to be introduced to around a thousand people who turned out for my talk, I told my hosts that I was going to speak in Kiswahili. I sensed their surprise. They had assumed I was going to speak in English. Professor Penina Mhando was going to introduce me,[25] and for my sake she was going to speak in English. When she got to the platform she said, "Ngũgĩ is going to speak in Kiswahili. I cannot introduce him in English." Then she did an amazing thing. She read the entire introduction, which she had written in English, in an instant translation in Kiswahili without any hesitation. Beautiful. Then, the best part for me, I gave my paper in Kiswahili. I can read Kiswahili, by the way, and I can answer in Kiswahili, but I cannot write a sustained academic paper in Kiswahili. After my delivery, there was another hour of question and answer, and I told myself, no matter what, come rain or whatever, I must respond to every question and comment in Kiswahili – which I did. People were engrossed. It became the talk of radio and television. And later, when my time came to receive the degree, I gave my acceptance speech in Kiswahili. The entire degree-awarding ceremony was conducted in Kiswahili. All the names and titles of degrees – literature, engineering, chemistry, physics, medicine etc. – were all in Kiswahili. I am now 77 years old. In all these years I have never once been in a situation where an entire academic discourse from beginning to end was conducted – without any apologies – in an African language. I felt teary afterwards...because it confirmed what I believed: it can be done. When later I went to get my tenth doctorate, in Germany, I accepted it in Kiswahili.

CC: In *Globalectics,* you quote Goethe: "National literature is now a rather unmeaning term; the epoch of world literature is at hand, and everyone must strive to hasten its approach" (*Globalectics,* 35). Two hundred years ago Goethe didn't know he was describing Kiswahili. How can we make more language experiences like what you describe at the University of Dar es Salaam happen? It happened, but there is still incredulity about it happening. As you say, it was the first time in your life. How do we change that?

NWT: It has to happen in theory and also in practice if the relationship between languages and cultures is not a hierarchy but a network. The structure of hierarchy can transform the politics of translation to enforce the hierarchy. Networking with translation is the answer. Translation has played a great role in human civilization, and in my own intellectual life. My knowledge of Russian literature, and early Greek theater, is through English translation. I read the Bible translated into Gĩkũyũ. Translation formed me as a reader and as a writer. Translation within a network creates a basis of conversation among literatures and cultures of the world. When I talk of "globalectic" imagination, I am expanding on the Blakean statement: to see the world in a grain of sand; to see eternity in an hour.[26] The reading and organization of the teaching of literature can be done globalectically. Globalectics encourages conversation among languages, literatures, and cultures. At Nairobi University in 1961, when we started to reorganize literature, we were not abandoning English and English literature but only trying to organize literature differently: starting with African literature, Europhone for that matter, at the center. We brought in Caribbean literature, African American literature, Asian literature, Latin American literature, and then we brought in European literature. If we were in Europe, European literature would be the center, and this would organize African literature, Asian literature, and Latin American literature in relation to it. If we were in America, we would have to put American literature – Euro, Afro, Asian, Native American etc. – at the center. But within American literature, I would place African-American and Native American at the center.

Why would I put African American literature at the center of the study of American literature and culture? Because the only really new in American literature is African American literature, right? I want to repeat. What is really at the heart of modern American literature and culture is African American literature. I can prove it, if you give me two minutes. Can I prove it?

CC: Yes! Even three minutes.

NWT: America belongs to Native Americans. All the others communities are newcomers to the continent. European people went there by choice. African people did not go there by choice. For European peoples who went there as colonists and slave owners, their linguistic connection with Europe was never cut off. In fact, the connection to European cultures continued – sometimes in resistance to it, sometimes emulating it, but always within its framework. Native Americans always had their languages. Many bad things were done to Native Americans, but they still had their languages. Its only African people who had their systematic connection with Africa denied. The languages of Africa were banned on slave labor plantations. Many who were caught speaking their languages were hanged. Even the drum, the talking drum, was banned. So the African had to create new languages out of the imposed language of the master and the memories of the rhythms of the banned African languages. New languages merged. Call them what you want: Ebonics, Creole. They are new languages, born out of the new environment that produced the spirituals, jazz, and today hip-hop. Deprived by law and the gun of their connection to Africa, they created new cultures and idioms out of their new environment. This is something new not because Africans were geniuses or better than other people, but the very nature of their situation forced them to invent new languages and cultural expressions of being. Compare their situation with that of the European in America! Europeans in America could still connect with cultures and literatures of the continent of their origins. In fact, we know that for many American writers, going to Europe was mandatory. T. S. Eliot even migrated to England. So, what is American, in terms of being built out of the American soil, is African American literature.

CC: I like that you have turned the discussion to an America that, as you write in *Globalectics*, "offers a significant example of the postcolonial as the site of globality. There is no community, language, or religion anywhere in the globe that has no presence in the United States.... U.S. literature as much its music and performance is not just European. It is also African, Asian, and Pacific" (*Globalectics*, 54). From its origins until today, the United States has been a nation of immigrants, "transnational" *avant la lettre*. America's indigenous and its slave populations, of course, burst such a formulation. Nevertheless, all of these constituencies have produced writers who have become, albeit through a variety of struggles, a distinct part of American literature. Over the last decade, many young writers with first generation family links to Africa, yet who live, write, and work – mostly teach – in the United States, where most of them were raised and educated, even born, have received high literary critical acclaim. They write in English, and they enrich American culture. Yet a lot of writers from Asia, India, and China, for example, who have similar first generational links, are now a part of the canon of contemporary American literature: Jhumpa Lahiri[27] and Ha Jin,[28] to take two famous instances. Should young African writers also be thought of more as American than African? When is he or she African and/or American?

NWT: Let's be clear. If I speak English and not Gĩkũyũ or Malayalam with my friend, Meena Alexander,[29] who speaks Malayalam, there is no point in pretending that we are speaking anything other than English. It's the same with literature. If she and I write in English, we are a part of English language literatures. We can say we are from Kenya or India but, in terms of the language that defines us, we are part of English language literatures. If we want to be part of African literatures, we write in African languages. If my friend learns and starts writing her novels in Kiswahili, she becomes a part of Kiswahili writing culture, and if I write in Malayalam, then I am part of Indian literature. Yesterday at City College I spoke with a woman, and her Kiswahili, including her gestures and intonation, was so good that I thought she must have been a Swahili who came to America to live. I learned that she was American, but when she spoke Kiswahili, she was more part of a Kiswahili culture and a Kiswahili language tradition than I am, although she was born in America and I in Kenya. When James Joyce writes in English, he is not writing Irish literature but contributes to the whole universe of English literature. John Millington Synge invented his own Irish.[30] He didn't write in Gaelic. He wrote how he thought Irish spoke English. In the end he was part of English literature. Whatever we say, when we African writers write in English, we are part of English literature. There is an encyclopedia of British literature that puts Achebe at the head of a list of English writers.

1 "African Literature – Says Who? The Last 50 Years with Ngũgĩ i wa Thiong'o" is based on an interview that took place as a part of the Warscapes Public Lecture Series in the New School's Humanities Action Lab, New York City, April 24, 2015. A video of the event can be seen at http://www.warscapes.com/videos/african-literaturesays-who-last-50-years-ng-g-wa-thiongo. Accessed 28 December 2016.

2 Ngũgĩ wa Thiong'o, *Something Torn and New: An African Renaissance* (New York: Basic Civitas Books, 2009), 51-52.

3 "Amazing Grace" (1779) is one of the most popular Christian hymns in the world. The lyrics are by the Anglican priest and poet, John Newton (1725-1807).

4 Ngũgĩ wa Thiong'o, *Weep Not, Child* (London: Heinemann, 1964).

5 See *Ngũgĩ wa Thiong'o Speaks: Interviews with the Kenyan Writer*, ed. Reinhard Sander & Bernth Lindfors (Trenton, NJ and Asmara, Eritrea: Africa World Press, 2006), 152. Further references to this source are noted parenthetically in the text as *Speaks*.

6 Ngũgĩ wa Thiong'o, *In the Name of the Mother: Reflections on Writers and Empire* (Suffolk, GB and Rochester, NY: James Currey, 2013), 8-9.

7 Ama Ata Aidoo (1942-) is a Ghanaian writer whose work includes poetry, drama, fiction, and essays. She has also served as Ghana's Minister of Education.

8 Wole Soyinka (1934-) is a Nigerian writer whose work includes poetry, drama, fiction, and nonfiction, and who won the Nobel Prize in 1986.

9 See note 14, page 179 above.

10 Nuala Ní Dhomhnaill (1952-) is an Irish writer whose poetry is in the Irish language or Gaelic.

11 Nuala Ní Dhomhnaill, "Why I Choose to Write in English: The Corpse That Sits Up and Talks Back," *Selected Essays* (Dublin: New Island Books, 2005).

12   See pages 170-71 above.

13   Cf. note 2, page 53 above.

14   Thomas Mofolo (1876-1948) wrote *Chaka* (1925), a fictional account of the Zulu monarch, in Sotho, which stands among the first great pioneering works of African fiction in an African language. The novel has been translated into many languages, including English.

15   Léopold Sédar Senghor (1906-2001) was president of Senegal from 1960 to 1980. He was also a Senegalese poet and cultural theorist.

16   Nawal El Saadawi (1931-) is an Egyptian writer whose work includes fiction, essays, and memoirs. Feminist, activist, physician, and psychiatrist, she has also served as a Director General in Egypt's Ministry of Health. *Woman at Point Zero*, originally written in Arabic and published in 1973, is a first person account, based on a true story, of a female prisoner in Egypt's Qanatir Prison who is to be executed for murder.

17   See note 3, page 195 above.

18   See pages 96-97 above.

19   See note 13, page 106 above.

20   French playwright known most for his comedies, Moliere (1622-73) was the stage and pen name of Jean-Baptiste Poquelin.

21   French philosopher, mathematician, and scientist, René Descartes (1596-1661) was one of the most important writers in 17th-century Europe.

22   William Tyndale (1494-1536) was a British scholar and theologian whose pioneering translation of the Bible into English became a basis for the King James Bible. Cf. note 119 above.

23   Dante Alighieri (1265-1321) was among the first to champion writing in vernacular Italian (or its Tuscan variety) in his critical essays, lyrical poems and epic, *Commedia*. He also wrote in Latin.

24   One of modern Swahili's leading scholars and writers, Kenyan scholar, Abdalatif Abdalla (1946-) is also a professor and cultural activist.

25   Penina Muhando (1948-) is a Tanzanian playwright and professor whose scholarship focuses on the development of theater and literature in Swahili.

26   William Blake, "Auguries of Innocence," *The Complete Poetry and Prose of William Blake*, ed. David Erdman (Berkeley: University of California Press, 2008), 490.

27   Jhumpa Lahiri (1967-) is an American author and professor whose work includes novels, short stories, and nonfiction. She often focuses on Indians and Indian Americans.

28   Ha Jin (1956) is an American poet, novelist, and professor who grew up in Communist China, which is often the focus of his work.

29   Born in India and raised there as well as in Sudan, Meena Alexander (1951-) is a poet, memoirist, scholar, and professor.

30   John Millington Synge (1871-1909) was an important, early 20th-century Irish writer whose work – poetry, drama, and nonfiction, including travel writing – focused on traditional Irish culture. He wrote in English, but in his plays it was heaviiy modified by everyday Irish usage.

11

Return to Kenya

Almost three decades ago, my first time visiting Kenya –
Starting a poem, "I went back...."[1] It's ironic as ever,
Probably more, only then referring to having seen a
Wildebeest skull in the Serengeti[2] dust and my wanting
This on my living room wall in Pennsylvania – meaning
Breaking the game park lodge rules and walking out by myself to
Get it, whatever supposed danger. That's all the meaning?
What about stereotypes of my colonialism?
Neo or post? Neo-post? Post-neo? Please let me move on.
Now I'm back here again, having added what I'm not sure of
To what I'm also not sure of, since it, however silly,
Innocent, guilty or telling led me farther than I could
Ever expect or imagine, making my return likely
If unexpected (at least by me), oblivious still but
Less than I was and connecting not detaching now from then.

Though it seems buried or overwhelmed by what's come in between,
Not knowing Africa always has been Africa to me.
Not only in the beginning, it continues to answer:
Definite, holding the upper hand, the back- and foreground, too.
Frankly, the same would apply to trying to talk about love,
Beauty, the true, and whatever metaphysical battles
Animate histories, places, individuals, and how
They're understood in their language by my poetry like this:

221

Non-Native Speaker

This very form I began to pick up in California
Writing again about Kenya only two decades later:
Nearly ten years ago and not thinking I'd do it again;
First time adapting the ancient Greek heroic line,[3] also
Used in the Latin heroics, though the languages differ
Radically, just as my English differs radically, too, yet
Writing my poem in praise of language – this is ironic –
African-born not imported and for Africans to use
In their own ways, strong as any other language in the world.

African languages, me non-native speaker or silent?
Getting to here in a kind of poet's dream that led back to
Kenya my first time led first to Eritrea, not knowing:
Starting with how to pronounce it; where the accent falls and
How many syllables (two is best); then dozens more visits,
Told by my friends there it was my second home, and how to join
Writing the "Asmara Declaration" as my own, fifteen
Years ago now as I come to Kenya knowing a little
More than the first time but not forgetting *tabula rasa*
Gave me my start here and should continue, just the way I swore
Fealty to Western culture when the writers I'm with now
Overthrew English for African departments since it was
Africa where they were: like Taban lo Liyong[4] who can see
Homer through African folklore, finding the "Penelopey"[5]
To be salvation instead of our time's lust for "fast poems."
All these years later why not see how their word revolution –
Wholly unknown to me at the time and not even dreamed of –
Parallels what I had vowed and had to break, expanding now:
Coming back, feeling continuous with what I didn't know
Then and whatever I did? Let both sides, three sides and more sides,
At least in me, raise your weapons.

                             Tightly holding my notebook,
I take a cab from Nairobi airport out to the lush green
Lavington.[6] Who ever heard of Ngũgĩ? I'm in a lavish
House with electrical fence and armed guard who keeps his family
Back in the vegetable garden. Who's imprisoned for writing?

Government issued a warrant to arrest his new novel's
Hero? I'm sipping delicious, cool and plentiful *Vinho
Verde*[7] and feeling consoled by Anglophile colonial
Housing, the shape of the doorknobs perfect Canterbury, too.
Later I'm driving a new Izuzu – Nairobi game park,[8]
Galloping herds of giraffes! Lost in the library of the
U.S.A. embassy, I want one of my books to be there.
Not really caring for gin and biltong,[9] sleek and rich flight clubs,
Paneled mahogany, I'm announced, "a writer," but I don't
Want to aspire to or be a character in Hemingway,[10]
Markham[11] or Blixen[12] updated, their books pressed into my hands
Lovingly and recommending: "See real Kenya." I demure.
They seem so strong, self-asserting, individualistic:
Anything but what I'm feeling out near Tanzania's line.
Kilimanjaro[13] pours through the sky and windshield to my eyes.
Vulnerability is more like it – self-disappearing,
Gripping a wildebeest horn as if I'm losing my language:
Silenced, abandoned, and meaning nothing other than I'm there.
Why not aspire to a reed where hippos float like detached, dark
Clouds down a stream where a peaceful martial eagle and leopard
Perch in the cedar? I want a style to sharpen the bones of
Sunbirds and weavers – their nests hung in the air like ideas.
Where are the words like a wand of carved teak waved like a
    question
Answered by thrones of creation all around me in their song;
Paths through the night necklaced with impala eyes gleaming
    yellow,
Same as the stars on the wildebeest tsunami flooded plain?
Wanting a phrase for the lions culling weak ones from the herd,
I hear the cry of hyenas, and my ivory ring is gone.

Later way out on a beach along the Indian Ocean,
North of Lamu[14] in a breaking storm, the pounding in my ears
Echoing surf and my bloodstream, sky and waves black and hoary,
Blacker and brighter – exploding wind and rain. Where can I go?
Seeing a big bush and slipping through its branches and long thorns,
I'm looking into a stranger's eyes. Surprised, I feel no fear.

What do they see? What do I? Together hiding from the storm?
Crouched in the sand no one says a word and listens very hard.

Ngũgĩ: "the politics…cultures…and economy…control…."
Ngũgĩ: "decolonize" – most of all the "language" of the "mind."
"Self-definition" remakes "creative…language of the mind."[15]
Yet he is writing this, exiled in the town where I was born,
Orange, New Jersey, while I'm in Kenya riding out the storm,
Almost ten years since Achebe's 'You dehumanize me and
Africans…Africa…if my story is not my language.'[16]
Thirty years, forty years later who can disagree? History!

Merely repeating it still is not enough without asking,
What has been done? How much further have these languages come
    past
Milestones we know towards the *plus ultra*:   this non-native
    speaker's
Tongue so original – my name, Cantalupo, my language,
English, and meter I write in all are distant translations;
Vice versa, too, or at least in part, although who knows from what,
When? If we keep going back to…where, and forward to converge?
Let it be seamless – the seams we see, regardless, merely what
Someone has ripped or conceded someone else to rip apart:
Pure language under another's spell to liberate language
Through recreation of work imprisoned too long in itself.
This is where coming to Kenya thirty years ago has led:
Come from America, also now come from Asmara, too,
Bringing its African language declaration, one author –
Just as unlikely a Cantalupo signing for U.S.
Freedom from Britain and independence: Philadelphia,
1776[17] – but who cares? That's not the question.
I'm back in Kenya because the newer declaration is
Called "inspiration" and "needed more than ever" in the words
Of all the young for whom "raise your weapons" must be a
    given.
"Look around. Who has been colonized? And how far have we
    come?

Not where we were, we go forward, and the tide has finally turned.
No more professional mourners, we must write our own new song.
African languages – action, great books, resources, esteem,
Governance, all institutions in their advocacy, and
Dictators have no last word."

                    And I thought I came far from when
I was here last, now with Ngũgĩ asking me for reports on
What I see happening; daring to accept affirmation
Linking my name with Asmara and the declaration there
We wrote together; my new book, *Where War Was*,[18] to be published
In Tanzania, the place beyond what I could imagine
Almost three decades ago; and knowing I was returning –
Based on my having raised my own weapon, language then and
    now –
Once more to Kenya, invited for a joining of language,
Anything of mine to theirs and powerfully affected
Mutually? Still I had one bad moment worrying, "Why were
Only a few Europeans and Americans in the
Audience. I wasn't black…." But then the storm and the beach –
Looking for shelter, the bush, my looking in those eyes came back.

1   Charles Cantalupo, *Anima/l Wo/man and Other Spirits* (Peterborough: Spectacular Diseases, 1996), "Anima/l," 17.

2   A geographical region in both Kenya and Tanzania that is famous for its natural beauty, including the landscape and wild life.

3   See note 25, page 12 above.

4   Taban Li Liyong ((1939-) is Sudanese writer born in Uganda. His work includes poetry, fiction, and nonfiction. He is also a cultural activist and professor. With Ngũgĩ wa Thiong'o and Owuor-Anyumba at the University of Nairobi, he co-authored the historic *On the Abolition of the English Department* in 1968.

5   Or Penelope, the wife of Ulysses in Homer's *Iliad*, who waited twenty years in Ithaca for him to return from war with Troy.

6   Lavington is a high income, residential suburb outside of Nairobi.

7   *Vino verde* is a popular white wine from Portugal.

8   The Nairobi National Park is a game park less around 5 miles outside of Nairobi.

9   Biltong is dried, cured meat. It is also called jerky.

10   The famous American novelist and 1954 Nobel Prize winner, Ernest Hemingway (1899-1961), traveled in and wrote about Africa, including *The Green Hills of Africa* (1935) and "The Snows of Kilimanjaro" (1936).

11   Born in England, Beryl Markham (1902-86) lived in Kenya and wrote *West with the Night* (1942), a memoir that recounts her childhood there and her becoming an aviator and bush pilot.

12   Born in Denmark, Karen Blixen (1885-1962), aka Isak Dinesen, lived and wrote in Kenya. She based her memoir, *Out of Africa* (1937), on her seventeen years of living on a farm in Kenya, specifically a coffee plantation, and her relationships with the people who lived around her, both native and colonist.

13   Located in Tanzania but readily seen from its border with Kenya, the widely storied Mount Kilimanjaro is the highest mountain in Africa.

14   Lamu is an island in the Indian Ocean, close to the east coast of Kenya and famous for its Islamic and Swahili culture.

15   See page 134 above.

16   See page 155 above.

17   The Second Continental Congress declared its independence from Great Britain with the ratification of the Declaration of Independence in Philadelphia, July 4, 1776.

18   See note 36, page 108 above.

Index

A

A Grain of Wheat 180, 199
A History of Tigrinya Literature in Eritrea 11, 92, 106, 112, 125
Abdalla, Abdilatif 218
Achebe, Chinua xiii, 36, 92–95, 106, 130, 134–138, 141–142, 146, 224
Acoli 78
Adem, Mussa Mohammed 49, 51, 78
Aeneid x, 7, 69, 120
Afghanistan 70
Africa World Press iv, xxi, 9, 11, 27, 106, 125, 180, 217
African American 179
African Books Collective xix, 9, 57, 105, 126–127, 129
African language ix, xii–xiii, 7, 21–22, 35, 77–78, 81, 84–85, 91–92, 94, 96–99, 116–117, 121–122, 129–131, 133–134, 138, 141–143, 145, 195, 218, 224
African language literature ix, xiii, 91–92, 94, 96, 98, 117, 122, 131, 133–134, 141–143

African literature v, vii, xii–xv, xvii, xxi–xxii, 8, 77, 84, 91, 97–98, 101, 113, 115, 117, 126, 129, 142–143, 178, 181, 199, 217
Afrikaans 131
Against All Odds xii, xviii, xxi, 9, 34–36, 41–43, 46, 57, 83–86, 89, 91, 98, 101, 113, 115–118, 122, 125–127, 129–131
Against All Odds: African Languages and Literatures into the 21st Century 9, 57, 84, 126
AIDS 143
Akan 78, 89, 129
Alcalay, Ammiel 70–73, 75–76, 80–81
Alemseged Tesfai xix, 46, 57, 86, 94–95, 105–106, 113, 116, 120, 122, 126–127
"Alewuna, Alewana" 10, 13–14, 22, 101–103, 114
Alexander, Meena xv, 219
Alighieri, Dante 88, 218
Ama, Ata Aidoo 217
"Amazing Grace" 217
American viii, x–xi, xxi, 10–11,

20, 32, 36, 38–39, 42, 55, 70,
227 80, 83, 97, 102–103, 110,
117, 121, 127, 141, 178–179,
196, 219, 226
American literature viii, x, 110
Amharic 20, 27, 89, 131
Amin, Idi 179
Angola xiv, 146, 149
antetranslation v, x, xiii, xv,
xxi, 81, 127–128, 132–135,
142–144
anthology xi, 11, 31–32, 34, 37,
40–43, 68, 73, 77, 90, 96–97,
104, 107, 110, 126, 130
Anyidoho, Kofi 145
Arabic xi, xix, 9, 12, 21, 26,
32–35, 37, 40, 56, 68, 73, 81,
96, 112, 117, 129–130, 144,
218
Aramaic 21, 131
Arezzo 59, 63
Armah, Ayi Kwei 197
Arnold, Matthew 123, 128
art iv, xv, 9, 15–17, 22, 27, 31, 40,
44, 46–47, 60, 62–64, 73, 95,
113, 120–121, 129–130, 132,
137, 143, 153, 181, 197
Asian 169, 207, 214–215
Asmara xii, xviii–xxii, 7, 9–10,
12–13, 15, 27, 31–38, 40,
42–43, 53, 56–57, 60, 63,
81, 83–84, 86, 89–90, 93,
101, 104, 106, 108, 114–115,
117–118, 121, 125–127, 129,
131, 180, 217, 222, 224
"Asmara Declaration on African
Languages and Literatures"
xviii, 34, 53, 83, 115, 129
Athena 25, 28
Auden, W. H. 109–110, 125

audience xi, 13–14, 27, 40, 69, 75,
79, 114
Austen, Jane 88
author 6, 11
Awoonor, Kofi 145

B

Babel 19, 24
Babu, Abdulrahman Mohamed
166, 178
Babylon 69
Badme 115
Bakhtin, Mikhail 170, 179
Banda, Hastings 165, 178
Barre, Siad 165, 167, 178
Baudelaire, Charles 122, 181, 195
beauty 6–7, 44, 69, 73, 75, 94,
105, 113, 121, 132, 137,
140–141, 151–152, 177, 207,
221, 225
Beirut 33
Belew Kelew 40, 56, 83, 90,
110–111, 113, 119, 121
Benjamin, Walter 99–100, 103,
107, 131–134, 141
Beowulf 69, 120
Bethlehem xviii, 43, 60
Beyene Haile xii, 83, 95, 105, 107,
119–120, 130
Bible 95, 100, 107, 111, 122, 131,
144, 186, 200–201, 210–211,
213, 218
Bigelow, Kathryn 80
Biko, Steve 1, 8
Bilen 5, 9
Biya, Paul 165, 178
Blake, William 186, 197, 218–219
Bokassa, Jean-Bédel 165, 167, 178
Boston xviii, 12, 28
Bowker 7
British xi, 27, 32, 55, 69–70,

80–81, 101, 105, 107, 109, 113, 117, 166, 172, 179, 195, 208, 217–218
British Council 101
Bruno, Giordano 62, 64–65
Brussels 5
Bunyan, John 120, 127

C

Cairo xi, 1, 8
California ix, xxii, 8, 219, 222
Callaloo 96, 208
Cammarano, Michele 61–62, 64–65
capitalist 143, 181, 194
Caravaggio, Michelangelo Merisi da 61, 64
Caribbean 169, 214
Carroll, Lewis 71, 107
Carthage 61, 64, 97
Casaubon xi, 1, 8
Cervantes, Miguel de 203
Chaucer, Geoffrey 71, 88, 203
Chichewa 89
China 111, 216, 219
Chinese 5, 121, 172, 207
Christian 40, 127, 148, 154, 195, 217
Cicero 137, 146
Claire, Elizabeth 184, 196
Clarendon Lectures 181
Clinton, Bill 98, 107, 162
colonialism viii–ix, xiii–xiv, 20, 53, 97, 121, 131, 134–135, 139, 142, 221
colony xi, 106, 154
Conference of African Writers of English Expression 199
Congo xiv, 137, 146, 149, 154, 178

Conrad, Joseph xiii, 134–142, 144, 146, 153
copyright 6, 39
Creole 193, 215
Cristofori, Tomasso de 62
Cultural Affairs Bureau xix, xxi

D

Dactyl (dactylic) 10, 29
Danish 42, 202
Death and the King's Horseman vii, xv
Decolonising the Mind vii, xv, 84, 134, 159–160, 164–165, 172, 177, 182, 190, 193, 199, 206, 211
Dehai xviii, 114, 126
Dekemhare xix, xxii
democracy xxii, 11, 20, 25, 37, 52, 54, 63, 143, 164, 167–168, 188, 192, 211
Dergue 18, 28
Descartes, René 210, 218
Dessale Berekhet 33, 50, 106
development v, xi–xii, xx–xxi, 10–11, 14, 35, 39, 49, 54, 84–85, 98, 105, 109–110, 113–114, 116–123, 130, 153, 165–166, 169–170, 172–174, 176–177, 190–191, 196, 218
Devil on the Cross 93, 106, 173, 177, 199
diaspora 9, 14, 32, 53, 55, 107, 146, 203
Dickens, Charles 40, 172, 179
dictator 59
Dogali 62, 64–65
Donne, John 203
drama xv, 90, 111, 127, 129, 138,

181, 185, 196, 217, 219
Dreams in a Time of War 200
Dryden, John xv, 39, 107
Dubois, W. E. B. 162

E

East Africa 78, 174, 176–177, 209
East African Educational Publishers xv, 86
ebola 143, 211
Egypt 27, 29, 69, 111, 125, 181, 218
El Cid 69, 120
El Saadawi, Nawal xviii, 36, 53, 208, 218
Eliot, T. S. xiii, xv, 8, 88, 215
England 27, 38–39, 56, 69, 79–80, 88, 91, 95, 154, 167, 171, 178–179, 205, 215, 226
English viii–x, xii, xv, xviii, xx, 2, 4–5, 7–9, 11–12, 15, 18–21, 26, 32–33, 37, 39, 45, 48, 56, 59–60, 68, 71, 73, 75–76, 78, 84, 92, 94, 96–102, 105–106, 110, 112, 119, 121–122, 125, 127, 129–130, 135, 145, 159–161, 170–172, 179, 181–182, 189, 193–197, 199–200, 202, 204–207, 209–210, 212–214, 216–219, 222, 224–225
epic x, xv, 7, 12, 69–72, 75, 80, 104, 127, 197, 199, 218
Eritrea v, xi–xiii, xvii–xxii, 2–7, 9–11, 13–20, 25–27, 29, 31, 33–46, 48–49, 51, 53–57, 60, 62–64, 67–68, 73, 78–79, 81, 83–87, 90–95, 98–99, 101–106, 108–123, 125–127, 129–130, 144, 206, 209, 217, 222

Eritrean iv, vii, ix–xiii, xviii–xx, xxii, 4–6, 9–12, 15–16, 19, 21–22, 24, 26–27, 31–32, 34–37, 39–46, 48–49, 56, 63, 67–68, 73, 75–79, 81, 83, 85–87, 90–95, 98, 102–103, 105–106, 109–115, 117–125, 129–130
Eritrean Liberation Front (ELF) 67
Eritrean literature xii–xiii, 31, 40, 83, 87, 90, 92, 94, 98, 105, 109–114, 119–123
Eritrean People's Liberation Front (EPLF) 11, 67, 125
Eritrean poet x, 81
Eritrean poetry iv, ix, xi, xix–xx, 12, 26–27, 31–32, 40, 42, 48, 56, 67–68, 73, 76–77, 81, 86, 90–91, 103, 105, 112, 117, 130
Ethiopia 10, 14, 27–28, 35, 41–42, 60, 67, 85, 93–94, 101, 106, 108, 113, 115, 119, 125, 176
Euro-American xi, 1
Europe 2, 15, 40, 59, 94, 108, 139, 146, 149, 162, 178, 193–194, 204–206, 214–215, 218
European viii–x, xiii, 8, 11, 21, 29, 32, 63, 83, 90, 98, 106, 117, 129, 137, 141, 143, 169–170, 189, 191–193, 201–205, 207–210, 214–215
European language 143
European literature viii–ix, 202, 207, 214
Europhone 169, 190, 201–204, 207–208, 214
Ewe 129, 210
Exodus 69, 74, 120
Expo xxii, 13, 27, 114

F

Faitlovitch, Jacques 90, 106, 112
Fanon, Frantz 119–120, 126
Fellini, Frederico 60, 63
Ferlinghetti, Lawrence 11, 22, 28
Fessahazion Michael 37, 49, 51, 78
Fessehaye Yohannes 78
"*Fognatura*" 104
Ford Foundation 84, 89
Forum 55, 61, 107, 144
France 69, 79, 88, 149, 179
Francophone 208
French xi, 2, 5, 32, 96–99, 110, 117, 121–122, 129, 159, 166–167, 172, 189, 193–194, 202, 204, 207, 210, 218
From Asmara 2000 to Nairobi 2014: New Horizons and Trends in African Languages and Literatures xxii, 115, 126, 131
fundamentalism 181–182, 194–195, 211
Fussell, Paul 71–73, 81

G

Gaelic 204, 216–217
Galleria Nazionale d'Arte Moderna (GNAM) 64
Ge'ez 6, 20, 26, 38, 117, 121, 202
genome 34, 199
genre xi, xix, 21, 112, 124, 127, 181
Germany 15, 213
"Gerontion" xiii, xv
getamay v, x, xx, 10–11, 13, 22, 28, 37, 43, 73
Ghebreyesus Hailu xii, 11, 92, 94, 106

Ghirmai Negash xix, 5–6, 11, 31, 33, 37, 49–52, 56, 81, 92, 94, 106, 112, 125
Ghirmai Yohannes 44–49, 51–52, 56, 86, 92, 96
Gikuyu 8, 78, 84, 89, 93, 100, 122, 129–130, 144, 160–162, 170–172, 181, 199–202, 206, 209–211, 213, 216
Gilgamesh 69, 74, 120
Global Conversations ix, xxii, 8
Globalectics 127, 200, 213–215
globalization 6, 143, 211
Goethe, Johan Wolfgang von 122, 127, 213
Gramsci, Antonio 126
Greece 29, 69, 79, 88, 95, 111, 190
Greek ix–x, 4, 7, 11–12, 21–22, 25, 59, 97, 121–122, 131, 144, 170, 192, 204, 211, 213, 222
Greek Anthology 4, 11
Greek literature ix, 11, 170
gtmi 11, 22

H

Habesha 50, 93
Haddas Eritrea 33
Hardy, Thomas 69, 80
Haregu Keleta 67–68, 78–79
Harper, Michael 170, 179
Hausa 89, 202
Hdri Publishers xix–xx, 10, 12, 31–32, 56, 81, 86, 106, 125
Heart of Darkness xiii, 93, 134–135, 137–141, 144, 146
Hebrew 21, 121–122, 131, 211
heroics xv, 128, 222
hexameter x, xv, 7, 12
hip-hop 21, 206, 215
history iv, ix, xi–xii, 8–9, 11, 20, 24, 26–27, 38–40, 49, 53, 56, 61, 63, 67, 69, 71–72, 76,

79, 81, 84–88, 91–92, 94–95,
100, 103, 106, 110, 112–113,
116–117, 120–121, 125, 130,
133, 148, 150–151, 162, 171,
173, 176, 179, 193, 195–196,
205, 207, 209, 224

Hobbes, Thomas 2, 7, 9, 23, 87–88

Homer x, 7, 22, 74, 88, 95, 222,
225

Hopkins, Gerard Manley 71

Horace 55, 70–71, 73, 80, 88, 112

Horn xx, 7, 28, 67, 223

I

I Will Marry When I Want 196,
199, 209

Iliad x, 12, 22, 69, 81, 120, 225

immigration 127, 143, 211

In the House of the Interpreter 200

In the Name of the Mother 203,
217

India 111, 216, 219

indigenous vii, 77, 79, 92, 94–96,
117, 119, 121, 130, 137, 196,
202, 215

international viii, xi–xii, xviii, xx,
xxii, 8–9, 19–20, 23, 33, 36,
39–40, 42, 50, 55, 77, 84–85,
90, 101, 116–117, 122–123,
146, 153, 163–165, 176, 178,
191

Iraq 70, 79–80

Ireland 88, 171, 204–206

Irish xi, 32, 41, 45, 109, 117, 171,
179, 204–206, 216–217, 219

Isaias Afewerki 115

Isayas Tsegai 87, 105, 118

ISBN 6–7, 32, 39–40

IT (Information Technology) vii–
xi, xiii–xiv, xviii, 1–3, 5–9,
13–16, 18, 20–21, 23–24,

26–27, 31, 33–34, 36–48, 52–
53, 59–64, 67, 69–80, 83–95,
97–105, 110–111, 113–121,
123–124, 130–148, 150–154,
159–168, 170–175, 177–178,
181–188, 190–192, 194–196,
199–216, 219, 221–224, 226

Italian xi, 5, 22, 32, 40–42, 59,
61–65, 86, 92, 110, 112,
121–122, 129, 167, 204, 211,
218

Italy xi, 15, 27, 62–65, 88, 95,
204, 206

J

Jameson, Fredric 120, 127

Jericho xi, 1

Jesus 21, 49, 143, 151, 181

Jin, Ha 216, 219

joiner 4, 22, 43, 73

Joining Africa vii, ix, xvii, 7, 10,
12, 56, 115, 126

Jones, David 57, 71, 76, 80, 139,
146

Jones, Susan 57, 71, 76, 80, 139,
146

journalism 81, 143

Joyce, James 88, 170–171, 179,
204–205, 216

K

Kajerai, Mohammed Osman 49,
52, 78

Kassahun Checole xvii–xviii, 2, 9,
53, 89

Keats, John 137, 146

Kenya v, xiv, 8–9, 27, 83, 89,
98–99, 162, 165–166, 168,
173, 175–176, 178–179, 181,
183, 203, 212, 216, 221–226

Keren xix, xxii, 38

Key, Francis Scott Key 8, 38, 102, 113, 133, 172, 194, 209
Kikongo 138, 154
King, Martin Luther vii, xv, 27, 95, 100, 107, 139, 148, 154, 159, 218
Kipling, Rudyard 81, 120, 127
Kolmodin, Johannes 90, 106, 112
Kongo v, xiii, xv, 137, 147–149, 151–154
Koran 111
Korea 70
Kunene, Mazisi 145
Kurtz xiii, 135, 137–142, 153

L

La Chanson de Roland 69, 120
Lahiri, Jhumpa 219
Lamming, George 162, 178
Latin x, 2, 6–7, 12, 26, 59, 61, 63, 71, 73, 79, 97–98, 101, 104, 122, 169–170, 174, 202–204, 210–211, 214, 218, 222
Lebanon 6, 33
Lee, Spike 1, 8
Leviathan 9, 23, 28, 87, 141
Libya 92–93
Light the Lights 104
Lingala 138
literacy 39, 56
literary history xi–xii, 84–85, 92, 94–95, 100, 110, 112, 116, 130, 207
Littman, Eno 106
London xxi, 8, 39, 49, 55, 63, 80, 95, 101, 106–107, 146, 178–180, 217
Luganda 202
Lusophone 208

M

Macaulay, Thomas Babington 181, 195
Mahmoud-El-Sheik, Abdul Hakim 51
Mahmoud-El-Sheikh, Mohammed (Madani) 79
Makerere 8, 115, 162, 173, 182, 199
Malawi xviii, xxii, 89, 165, 178
Malayalam 216
Malcolm X 8
Mali 69, 79
Mandela, Nelson 159–162
Mandinka 78, 129
Mangaaka 137, 147, 152
Mars 1
Martial 62, 223
Marx, Karl 63, 181, 192
Marxist 27, 60, 67, 86, 95, 119, 126–127, 167, 179
Massawa xviii–xix, xxii, 62, 64, 93
massé 109, 112–113, 124
Matigari 160, 174, 176–177, 180, 199
Matisse, Henri 137
Mau Mau 166, 179, 181
Medici 60, 63, 150, 154
Mehmedinovic, Semezdin 71, 81
Meles Zenawi 115
melkes 109, 112–113, 124
Melville, Herman 71, 80
Memphis 59
Menelik 18, 28
meter x, 10, 12, 224
Mezghebe xii, 95, 105, 107, 113, 130
Mhando, Penina 212
Mieras 90, 106

Ministry of Education xix
Mkuki na Nyota Publishers xix, 86, 91
Mobutu, Sese Seko 165–166, 178
Mofolo, Thomas 207, 218
Moi, Daniel Arap 165–166, 175, 178–179, 181
Mongo 138
Montaigne, Michel de 88, 203
Moving the Centre 159–165, 168–169, 172–175, 178, 182, 200
Musa Aron 33
Museveni, Yoweri 115, 166, 179
Mussolini, Benito 59, 62
Mutiga, Jayne 121
Mutiiri 181–182, 206, 209
Mzamane, Mbubelo xviii, 53

N

Nairobi xv, xxii, 115, 121, 126, 131, 144, 178, 196, 199, 214, 222–223, 225–226
"Naqra" 37, 43, 49, 51
nation xii, xviii–xix, 2, 9–10, 13–14, 21–22, 27, 31, 35, 44, 60–61, 78, 85, 87–88, 92, 99, 111, 113, 116, 120, 122, 130, 143, 163, 178, 194, 212, 215
nation building 143
national v, xi–xii, xviii, xx, xxii, 7, 11, 20, 23–24, 38, 40, 63–64, 72, 85, 90–91, 95, 105, 109–111, 113, 116–124, 127, 133, 145, 176, 189, 195–196, 213, 226 nationalism 73, 86, 120, 166
native i, iii–v, vii–xiv, xvii, xix–xxi, 1–4, 6–8, 11, 63, 95, 122, 131, 141, 143–144, 196, 211–212, 214, 222, 224, 226

Native American 11, 214
Naydan, Michael 91, 106
Nazreth Amlessom 32
Nefa'e Ethman 90, 106, 112
neocolonial 194
neocolonialism 36, 97, 131, 134, 142
New Jersey xvii, xxii, 3, 20, 42, 159, 224
New York xv, xxi–xxii, 8, 10, 14, 19, 28, 31, 48, 50, 52, 55, 57, 80–81, 106–107, 115, 125–127, 144, 146, 148, 153–154, 159, 161, 178, 181, 195–196, 217
New York University (NYU) 10, 14, 115, 159, 178, 181
Newark xxii, 20, 42, 159
NGO 101
Ní Dhomhnaill, Nuala 204–205, 217
Nigeria 83, 203
nkisi n'kondi xiii, 137, 142, 146, 154–155
Nyerere, Julius 122

O

Olson, Charles 3, 10, 72, 102
"On the Abolition of the English Department" 199, 225
oral xix, 4–5, 15, 21, 34, 37, 39, 46–47, 49–50, 68, 83, 86, 90, 92, 98, 102, 109–110, 112, 142–143, 185, 190, 200
Orange xvii–xviii, 224
orature 90, 110, 112, 137, 142, 184–186, 190, 196
Orthodox 40, 118–119
Osman, Mohammed Said 51, 52
Owen, Wilfred 69–71, 80

Oxford University 57, 81, 107, 146, 181

P

p'Bitek, Okot 181, 195, 208
Palazzo Massimo alle Terme 63
Paris 195
Parsons, Claudia Moreno 69–71, 75, 79
Paulos Netabay 51, 78
Pennsylvania State University (Penn State) xx, xxii, 105, 115
Penpoints, Gunpoints, and Dreams v, xxi, 9, 181–183, 185–194, 200
People's Front for Democracy and Justice (PFDJ) 5, 11, 63
performance 4, 26, 39, 46–47, 53, 68, 114, 125, 142–143, 177, 181–187, 190, 194, 196–197, 215 performative 26, 34, 37, 135
Petals of Blood 177, 180, 199, 201
Petrarch 59, 61–63, 88, 203
Philadelphia 39, 224
Piazza Cinquecento 61
Picasso, Pablo 137
Plato 181, 184, 189–190
Pliny the Elder 59, 63–64
Poe, Edgar Allan 69, 80, 88, 95, 122
poetics 4, 7, 50, 72–73, 76, 133, 145
poetries xii
poetry iv, vii, ix–xii, xv, xix–xxii, 3–7, 10–23, 26–29, 31–32, 34–36, 39–45, 48–51, 53, 56, 59, 63, 67–70, 72–81, 86, 90–91, 95–98, 102–112, 114, 117, 123–125, 127, 130,
142, 144–146, 148, 207–208, 217–219, 221, 225
Poetry Foundation 11, 96, 208
Poetry Society 28, 96, 208
Poetry Translation Centre 96, 208
politics xv, 5–7, 9, 20, 23, 27–28, 43, 45, 88, 105, 112, 115, 120, 127, 134, 145, 168, 173, 213, 224
Pompidou, George 167, 179
popularity xi, 11, 15, 20, 22, 179
power figure xiii, 146, 155
precolonial xiii prose vii, x–xi, 7, 38, 68, 75, 77–78, 80, 127, 161, 219

Q

Queen Elizabeth 179, 181

R

Rabelais, François 88, 203
racism xiii, 134–135, 138–139, 142, 146, 160, 162–163
Rahel Asgedom 32, 79
rap 21
Red Sea Press xvii, xx, 9–11, 27, 39, 86, 108
Reesom Haile v, x, xvii, xx, 3, 10, 13–24, 26–27, 29, 31, 36, 42, 45, 48–50, 52–53, 76–77, 101–104, 114, 118–120, 123
Renaissance xv, 2, 6, 35–36, 55, 91, 98, 115, 127, 202–203, 209, 217
reparations 143, 211
Research and Documentation Center (RDC) xix, 10, 37
"Return to Kenya" v, xiv, 175, 221
Return to Rome v, xi, xx, 59
Ribka Sibhatu 78

Robeson, Paul 162, 178
Rockefeller Foundation 84
Roma 59–63
Roman literature 7
Rome v, xi, xx, 24, 53, 59–61,
    63–65, 69, 79, 88, 95, 108
Rosenberg, Isaac 69, 80
Rossini, Carlo Conti 90, 106, 112
Russia Russian 138, 179, 213

S

Saad, Ahmed Mohammed 78
Saba Kidane 50–52, 78
Sabur 7, 40–41
Saho 9, 129
Said, Abdulhay 33
Saleh, Adem 32
Sassoon, Siegfried 69, 80
Sembene, Ousmane 159
Semitic 20
Senegal 83, 218
Senghor, Sédar 207, 218
Septuagint 122, 211
Shakespeare, William 19, 27–29,
    48, 56, 88, 95, 104, 122, 144,
    203, 210
Sheikh, Ahmed Omar 78
Shona 129, 202
short story xi, 67–68, 75, 77–78
Sidney, Philip xv, 45–46, 57
slave 87, 149, 192, 214–215
Socrates 190
Solomon Drar 49, 78
Solomon Tsehaye xix, 38, 50, 78,
    95, 106, 112, 125
Somalia 165–167, 176, 178
Something Torn and New 200–
    201, 217
Sotho 89, 207, 218
South Africa xxi, 15, 20, 83, 130,
    209

Soviet Union 35, 179
Soyinka, Wole vii–viii, xv, 203,
    217
Spain 69, 79
Spanish 193, 202, 210
Spanophone 208
Spivak, Gayatri 127
Stalin, Joseph 91, 208
state of nature 88, 141
stele xii, 40, 56, 83, 90, 110–114,
    119, 124, 154
Stevenson, Robert Louis 172, 179
Stone, Oliver 23, 80
Sundiata 69, 120
Swahili 78, 89, 122, 131, 144, 172,
    202, 211–212, 216, 218, 226
Swift, Jonathan 38, 55, 136
Sykes, Lawrence (Larry) xviii, 2,
    9, 159
Synge, John Millington 216, 219

T

Tanzania 108, 130, 175–176, 212,
    223, 225–226
Teaching English as a Foreign
    Language (TEFL) viii
tegedelti 34, 79, 85
Thatcher, Margaret 181–182, 196
"The Girl Who Carried a Gun"
    67– 68, 77, 79
The Conscript xii, 11, 92–95, 106,
    113, 130
The Guardian 113, 125
The River Between 199, 201
The Trial of Dedan Kimathi 199
Things Fall Apart 92–95, 106, 130
Tigre xi, xix, 5–6, 9, 12, 20, 26,
    32–35, 49–52, 56, 68, 73–74,
    81, 90, 106, 111–112, 117,
    125, 129–130, 144
Tigrean 28

Tigrinya xi–xii, xix, 3–6, 9–12, 14–17, 19–22, 26–27, 32–35, 37, 40, 45–46, 48–53, 56, 62, 67–68, 73–74, 79, 81, 85, 89, 92–93, 96, 101–102, 106, 109–110, 112, 114, 117, 122, 125, 129–130, 144, 209–211

tourism 20, 143

translation v, viii–ix, xi–xiii, xx–xxii, 3, 5–6, 8, 11, 21–22, 29, 31–36, 40, 43, 45, 48–49, 51, 54, 67–68, 77–79, 81, 83, 86, 90–92, 94–104, 107, 109, 111, 118, 122–123, 127, 130–135, 137, 141–146, 161, 201, 203–204, 207–213, 218

translator v, x–xi, xix–xx, 4, 11, 22, 26, 33, 67, 73, 99–100, 107, 121, 127, 131–134, 141, 145

transnational 91, 120, 215

Tsegaye Gabre-Medhin 36

Turkish 19, 204

"Two Moments in Kongo" v, xiii, 149

Tyndale, William 210, 218

U

Ukraine 91, 106, 208

"Under the Sycamores" 50, 125

UNICEF 41, 52, 115

UNISA 130

United Nations (UN) 168, 170

United States xxii, 14, 35–36, 38, 40–41, 78, 88, 91, 108, 162, 164, 179, 206, 215–216

University of Asmara xxii, 31–33, 36, 115

Urhobo 129

ut pictura poesis 36

V

verse vii, ix–xi, xiii–xv, 3, 10–12, 38, 45, 57, 71, 127, 145

verse essay vii, ix–xi, xiii–xv

Vietnam 68, 70, 80

Virgil x, 7, 74, 88, 95

Vulgate 122, 211

W

wa Thiong'o, Ngũgĩ iv–v, vii, xii, xiv–xv, xviii, xxi–xxii, 8–9, 17, 27, 36, 40, 53, 84, 89, 93, 99, 106–107, 116–117, 126–127, 130, 134, 144–145, 157, 178, 180–181, 196, 199, 217, 225

Wales 207

war xi, xviii–xx, 6, 10, 16–17, 20, 24, 26–27, 31, 35–38, 40–41, 49–52, 63, 67–81, 85–86, 89, 91, 101, 104–105, 108, 110–112, 116–117, 119, 125, 143, 146, 151, 154–155, 165, 167, 179, 181, 183, 187, 195, 200, 211, 225

War and Peace in Contemporary Eritrean Poetry xix–xx, 73, 81, 86, 91, 105

Wasafiri 96, 208

We Have Our Voice x, 10, 15, 20, 31

"We Have" x, 10, 13–15, 20, 22–23, 31, 43, 69, 75, 89, 98, 102–103, 114, 186–187, 203, 211

We Invented the Wheel x, 10, 20, 27, 31, 36

Weep Not, Child 199, 201, 217

Weil, Simone 72–73, 81

Weldedingel 49, 112–113, 119–120, 125
West xxi, 53, 64, 77–79, 146, 164–167, 171, 186, 191, 205, 226
West Africa 78
Western viii, x, xxi, 12, 29, 38–39, 68, 77–78, 104, 108, 118, 120, 144, 149, 151, 154, 163, 167–168, 170, 179, 222
Where War Was xix–xx, 108, 225
Whitman, Walt 71, 80
Who Needs a Story? Contemporary Eritrean Poetry in Tigrinya, Tigre, and Arabic xix, 68, 73, 117, 130.
"Who Needs a Story?" 44-46
Who Needs a Story 5, 32-37, 39-45, 48, 104, 117-18, 130
wind of change 86, 105, 143
Winfrey, Oprah 115
Wizard of the Crow 55, 130, 144, 200, 208
Wolof 89
Wordsworth, William 71, 80, 88
World Bank xxi, 84, 117–118, 164, 178, 209
world literature xii, 91, 95, 122, 127, 213
World War I 70, 80
World War II 27, 63, 70

X

Xhosa 89

Y

Yeats, William Butler 45, 57, 88, 109, 125
Yoruba 78, 89, 97, 129, 172, 196, 202, 207

Z

Zeineb Yassin 50, 111, 125
Zemhret Yohannes xviii, 3, 10, 31,
    42–43, 53, 68, 102
Zimbabwe Book Fair 130
Zulu 19, 129, 131, 145, 218